P9-CSH-089

ACADEMIC DUTY

ACADEMIC
❦ DUTY ❦

Donald Kennedy

HARVARD UNIVERSITY PRESS
Cambridge, Massachusetts
London, England

Copyright © 1997 by the President and Fellows of Harvard College
·All rights reserved
Printed in the United States of America
Fifth printing, 1999

First Harvard University Press paperback edition, 1999

Library of Congress Cataloging-in-Publication Data

Kennedy, Donald, 1931–
  Academic duty / Donald Kennedy.
    p. cm.
  Includes bibliographical references and index.
  ISBN 0-674-00222-9 (cloth)
  ISBN 0-674-00223-7 (pbk.)
  1. Education, Higher—Aims and objectives—United States.
  2. Academic freedom—United States. 3. College teachers—United
  States. 4. College teaching—United States.   I. Title
LA227.4.K465 1997
378.73—dc21
97-13210

CONTENTS

PREFACE

In 1993, after I had left the presidency of Stanford University and rejoined the faculty, I decided to offer a seminar for doctoral students who were planning academic careers. Over the two years during which the seminar was offered, the students in it responded to (and in many cases raised) and debated a range of issues pertaining to higher education and to their own places in it. Their energy, commitment, and intellect were inspiring, and gave me confidence in the future of higher education. At the same time, their lack of familiarity with the organization of the university and with the kinds of personal and professional challenges they were likely to face was troubling. I found myself writing a series of essays on some of these: teaching and how success at teaching can be evaluated; ethical problems in reviewing the work of others; research and how it is supported; outside commitments; and even research misconduct.

Working with the students on these issues persuaded me that a broader audience of prospective academics might benefit from what we were trying to do together. That conviction was deepened by an experience during the second year in which the seminar was offered. The students decided to prepare a questionnaire for advanced doctoral candidates about their experiences and their perceived readiness for their own academic duties. The early results, from about seventy Stanford students (a sample since expanded greatly at other institutions), showed that accompanying a high level of confidence about their futures as research scholars was a disturbing uncertainty and confusion about teaching, institutional governance, and other dimensions of an academic career.

During that period, public concern about higher education was growing, in part because of well-publicized issues such as racial conflict, intercollegiate athletic scandals, and research misconduct, but also because of deeper misgivings about cost and quality. If the future professoriate is uncertain about the purposes and organization of the university, how can one expect that the public patrons of higher education will be more knowledgeable? And if they don't understand the university and its duty, how can they support it?

So what began as a set of notes for a class of academic aspirants metamorphosed into a book about universities. It therefore reflects some of the concerns I had about my first audience, and in response I have tried to engage future faculty members with a vision of academic duty that includes the responsibilities to put students first and to restore the values of institutional commitment and loyalty. To these was added a larger and more difficult task: to convey to a broader public some of the complexity of the modern university and the difficulty of the challenges it faces.

Although I have tried to deal candidly with some shortcomings in contemporary higher education, I hope I communicate no discouragement with the enterprise. On the contrary, I think the modern American university is a real triumph; it is, with all its shortcomings, like Churchill's democracy. The avalanche of recent alma-mater trashing in popular literature has offered little by way of serious diagnosis, and nothing at all of cure. A more positive and far more thoughtful effort, Henry Rosovsky's *The University: An Owner's Manual,* treats the way in which universities are run. My own aim is to write primarily at, about, and for members of the faculty: their central role in the institution's mission, the way they relate to its legal owners and managers, and their responsibility to students.

The theme I have chosen—academic duty—is the counterpart of academic freedom, a concept endlessly raised for discussion in the university. Little is said about duty, partly because faculty work is relatively uncodified; in a sense, universities are societies without rules. They nevertheless perform rather well, but much of what goes on behind the walls is deeply mysterious to those outside. The missing information amounts to a lesion in accountability, which I think has much to do with the rising chorus of national discontent with higher education. The best remedy is sympathetic understanding, and I hope the reader will have more of that at the end of this book than at the beginning.

To the future professoriate, I will say only that you are entering a life full of the most interesting challenges—and the most important mission that can be found in a modern society. The university is above all else about opportunity: the opportunity to give others the personal and intellectual platform they need to advance the culture, to preserve life, and to guarantee a sustainable human future. Could anything possibly matter more than that?

1

ACADEMIC FREEDOM, ACADEMIC DUTY

THE PHRASE "academic freedom" is heard so often around colleges and universities that it has come to resemble a mantra. Though the term has only been in use since the early twentieth century, it seems as if it has always been with us. As easily understood as it is important, academic freedom refers to the insulation of professors and their institutions from political interference. It asserts the claim that in the academy more than in other domains of American life, heterodox notions and unconventional behavior deserve special protection.

At various points in the twentieth century, that kind of protection has proved essential. During the outbreak of anti-Communist sentiment in the early 1950s, committees of the Congress, especially those chaired by William Jenner in the House and Joseph McCarthy in the Senate, put great pressure on universities to fire faculty for past membership in organizations thought to be "un-American," that is, sympathetic to Communist aims. Presidents and governing boards met that pressure with varying courage, but the tradition of academic freedom lent strength to the capacity of universities to resist it. Thus to academic men and women that tradition protects a treasured space for intellectual experiment—treasured in part because it is safe.

In practice such freedom extends further, permitting unusually creative people to lead unusually creative lives. Indeed, academic freedom connotes loose structure and minimal interference. There are no time clocks and few regulations about the direction of effort or even about the locations at which it is to take place. So distinct is the academy from other workplaces that we have developed an informal vocabulary to describe its separation: we call it the ivory tower, and we call everything else the real world.

Academic freedom has a counterpart, academic duty, that is much more seldom used. Democratic societies such as ours regard these two as opposite sides of the same coin. John Gardner put it well when he said, of the symmetry between individual freedom and communitarian obligation, "Liberty and duty, freedom and responsibility: that's the deal."

That, indeed, is the deal. Why, then, when we talk so freely about academic freedom, does academic duty sound so much less idiomatic? The difference lies at the heart of an important paradox. On the one hand, higher education in America has never been stronger or more successful. It serves more people, and better, than it ever has. It sets an international standard that brings students here from all over. It supports the strongest university-based research system in the world. And it is thought by many to be an innovation incubator essential to national economic progress. Yet public criticism of higher education has become increasingly more strident. The assault comes from various sources, Left as well as Right. It sounds a variety of themes: the failure of science and policy studies to provide answers we desperately need (why isn't AIDS a thing of the past, and why is K-12 education in bad shape?); inadequacies in the quality of undergraduate instruction (why can't Susie's calculus teacher speak English as well as Susie can?); failure to respond adequately to economic stringency (corporations everywhere are downsizing; why isn't productivity in higher education improving?). The attacks are being felt, and morale in the academy is as low as those inside it can remember.

The evidence suggests a kind of dissonance between the purposes our society foresees for the university and the way the university sees itself. For although the freedoms necessary for teaching and scholarly work are understood and reasonably well accepted, the counterbalancing obligations are vague and even obscure. Put baldly, there is confusion about what is owed: by the university to society, by faculty to students, by administrators to both. Academic freedom is a widely shared value; academic duty, which ought to count for as much, is mysterious.

It is no less a mystery within the walls of the ivory tower. Little is said about duty to new faculty members; little is to be found in the academic literature about the nature of faculty responsibilities. It is part of the tradition of freedom, perhaps, that in higher education there are no job descriptions, no annual performance evaluations. But one result is that expectations of the professoriate are murky, and public understanding murkier still.

As a result, people outside the academy have few criteria by which to judge it, leading quite naturally to the suspicion that there is simply too much freedom and too little direction. Perhaps as a consequence, *accountability* is a word increasingly linked with higher education: the public wants to know more about how the store is being minded and is less satisfied with reassuring statements about product quality.

Despite the doubts that are surfacing today, more Americans are receiving college educations than ever before. Universities and colleges, and their faculties and even their leaders, continue to enjoy solid respect in comparison with other institutions and other professions. More people are paying more to educate their children (or, increasingly, themselves!). The value of postsecondary education, measured in incremental lifetime earnings, rose during the 1980s to create the largest gap in history between those who are college-educated and those who are not.

Higher education today is challenged to fulfill a new and staggering burden. Always expected to make young people more skilled, more cultured, and more thoughtful, it now is seen as the motive power for regional economic improvement and even for international competitiveness. It is looked to for research underlying everything from better health care to military preparedness. And we are disappointed if it does not provide us with cultural inspiration and, on weekends, athletic entertainment.

Higher education, in short, is woven into our lives. We depend on it for all sorts of things, and we want to believe in it. When it fails us, we become disappointed; and when it costs too much, we become angry. What is this extraordinary institution that matters so much, and how did it come to be all these different things?

The American system of higher education is full of paradoxes. For some, "college" is a place of memory: it is where one grew up, learned about life, fell in love, and, perhaps, first thought great thoughts. For others it is a locus for economic aspiration, where one first confronts the hard task of preparing for a profession. For still others it is a center for national intellectual life, a place where our culture develops new shoots. And of course in many of us these different portraits are all mixed together, with other, more subtle elements added. Our perceptions of what institutions of higher education are thus depend on our personal experience as well as on a more detached vision of how society should work and what we want our children to have.

We have so many different ideas about higher education because the institutions themselves are heterogeneous. There are more than three thousand four-year institutions of higher education in this country. Some grant every possible kind of degree: professional doctorates in law and medicine, higher academic degrees such as the familiar Ph.D. and the less familiar Doctor of Musical Arts, and bachelor's degrees in everything from art history to zoology. Small, highly experimental colleges with a few hundred students exist side-by-side with huge state institutions of more than fifty thousand students. There are evangelical colleges, Catholic colleges, and aggressively nondenominational colleges. Some are "land-grant" institutions—state universities established following the Morrill Act in 1862, and responsible among many other things for agricultural research and extension; some are city colleges supported municipally. Some are strictly technical, others are committed to arts and letters, still others are so comprehensive that they leave out almost nothing. Some, by virtue of location and tradition, serve few minority students; others, like the Historically Black Colleges and Universities, are explicitly intended to serve such students.

No license is required to found and run a college. To be taken seriously, however, an institution of higher education must be accredited. Having accreditation means that an institution is operating within the established criteria of a voluntary accrediting association, and that compliance is checked through regular visits by committees of academics from other institutions.

Fully accredited institutions have formed consortia to pursue collective purposes. A suggestion of their extraordinary heterogeneity can be gotten from the names of these associations, most of which were located in a large building at One Dupont Circle in Washington, a location convenient for occasional visits to congressional or administration figures who need advice about American colleges and universities. The most prestigious is the Association of American Universities (AAU), a group of about sixty research universities whose members grant nearly three-quarters of all U.S. professional doctoral degrees. Private institutions like Harvard, Stanford, and MIT belong; so do the great state universities like Michigan, California, and Illinois. The American Council on Education (ACE), a much larger organization, is an umbrella for institutions of all kinds, as is the American Association for Higher Education. NASULGC, one of the world's more unfortunate acronyms, stands for the National Association of State Universities and Land Grant Colleges. It includes the top land-grant state institutions that would also be AAU members, and others (Oregon State and Kansas State, for example) that would not. The Association of State Colleges and Universities takes in the comprehensive public institutions that are generally non–Ph.D.-granting: the California State University system, and Bowling Green and Kent State in Ohio, would be examples. The National Association of Independent Colleges and Universities serves the private sector, from AAU members down to very small liberal arts colleges. Community colleges have a vigorous association as well.

Given this vast array of institutions, it is small wonder that the public has so many different perceptions of higher education. It is difficult for people to wrap a simple, unified set of values around CalTech, Montana State, the City University of New York, and Mount Saint Mary's. The ambivalence with which Americans have always viewed higher education also helps to explain these varied perceptions: on the one hand, higher education is seen as a valued avenue for upward social mobility, but on the other hand it appears elitist, "stuck-up." In the romance of higher education, Frank Merriwell and Horatio Alger accomplish a kind of fusion. Yet there is an ingrained, populist suspicion of too much learning. Its early reflections are found in the cartoon images of the absent-minded professor and the haughty student who cannot converse with ordinary people. This suspicion is part of contemporary folklore: of the college baseball player thrown into the major leagues, Casey Stengel says, "Say he's educated, and he can't throw strikes. Then you don't leave him in there too long." Even those of us who are devoted to environmental biology can recognize a hint of this theme in Louis Agassiz's famous aphorism "Study Nature, Not Books."

That higher learning is, in our national tradition, at once admired and suspect helps to explain the contemporary paradox that higher education is more successful than it has ever been yet at the same time subject to extraordinarily intense critical scrutiny. The successes are easily summarized. Universities in the United States attract students from all over the world for graduate and professional study, and American parents are now preparing their sons and daughters for the college admissions race with such formidable zeal that a cottage industry of consultants and tutoring services has grown up to help them. But the criticisms are complex and multiple, and their nature and severity need close examination if we are to understand this apparent failure of academic duty.

Tuitions are too high; racial tension is leading to segregation; faculty aren't paying attention to undergraduates; universities and colleges are loosely managed, soft on sexual harassment, and unable to deal with what appears to be an epidemic of research misconduct; athletic scandals and campus drinking are out of hand; political correctness is an epidemic. And that's just the short list.

The American health care system in the late 1970s was described by one observer as "doing better but feeling worse." The same could be said of higher education today. During the 1980s, for example, media accounts of racial incidents on college campuses were so common and so prominent that many Americans without direct experience assumed that constant tension among African-American, Hispanic, and white students was the rule rather than the exception. I remember being asked by visitors to the Stanford campus during this period whether all our minority students lived by choice in separate dormitories (only a tiny fraction chose ethnic "theme" houses, and these by rule were less than 50 percent minority). Often I was asked whether "they" ever talked with nonminority students. When I informed the visitors that the frequency of interracial dating approximated what one would expect on the basis of random collision, they were astonished. Television and the newspapers had led them to believe that the campus must be about to explode in a race riot. At its height, the media frenzy over race on campus caused the Harvard sociologist Orlando Patterson to suggest that it might actually be a good time to shoot the messenger!

Academic misconduct is regularly billed as a common problem in university research. Sexual harassment charges, especially if they involve a faculty member, receive front-page scrutiny; that is, unless they are shown to be without foundation, in which case the exoneration appears on page seventeen. The media have promoted "political correctness" on campus into a national mantra. One analysis of media coverage shows that attention to such topics has migrated among different media venues, with extensive recycling of such past stories as the famous revision of the Stanford "Western Culture" curriculum, discussed below.[1]

Even relatively narrow, rather technical matters often invite unexpected reactions from the press. In 1994 the Academic Senate at Stanford had an extended debate about certain provisions of the grading system. For some years the university, like a number of other institutions, had allowed students to retake courses they had failed and substitute the second grade on their transcripts. In the view of some, this practice encouraged students to take courses outside their areas of confidence, to take some risks in the interest of breadth. Others felt that it permitted students to "game" the evaluation process. For some reason the policy became a symbol of grade inflation, even though in fact it contributed little to that phenomenon. The Senate decided in the end to abolish the rule and return to the earlier practice of letting every grade stand in the record. To the astonishment of the Stanford participants, who thought the matter worth arguing about but hardly earth-shaking, the action made national news. The *New York Times* greeted it with an editorial notable for its harsh and hectoring tone. At last, readers were told, the coddling of students was being stopped, and the outside world would be able to make sound judgments about their relative worth.

The *New York Times*'s position reveals one aspect of the public mistrust of higher education. Whereas those within the system generally believe that their mission is to produce graduates who can think well and work effectively, and who are able to understand, analyze, and reflect upon their culture and upon the natural world, much of the world outside sees higher education as a credentialing device: a way of estimating, for employment or other purposes, the comparative worth of individuals. Of course there are times at which these goals are not in conflict. But when they are, those who deliver education and those who are its patrons and eventual consumers suddenly find themselves at cross purposes.

This collision of values is related to the more celebrated clash over what students should learn about great works and great ideas—in particular, whether non-Western works should be added to the traditional canon of "great books." In the 1980s a long and complicated book by the late Allan Bloom entitled *The Closing of the American Mind* ushered in a powerful conservative case against the introduction of non-Western works. Supported by the public enthusiasm of Bloom's Chicago colleague Saul Bellow, the book was widely reviewed and purchased, though perhaps less widely read. It bemoaned the lack of a program of general education based on the great works of Western culture, and occupied the intellectual right wing of a debate that soon became both more widespread and more political. The combustible material for its spread was provided by another, earlier decision by the Stanford faculty.

That decision, made in 1987, mandated several changes in a required course for freshmen. The course itself had been through at least two previous incarnations—a trip that in itself tells us something about the history of higher education. Once called "Western Civilization," it was basically a course in European history and culture. During tumult of the late 1960s it was discarded, only to return a decade later with the title "Western Culture." No longer a single course, it featured several tracks: a Great Works course, a history course, a course with a science and technology emphasis, and so on. The tracks were coordinated in that all had to draw from a common reading list, which was organized rather like an old-fashioned Chinese restaurant menu. The A list contained fifteen works; the B list was much longer. The faculty responsible for a particular track had to use all the books on A and could pick from among the B list of entries. The idea, only partly successful, was to give the entire class a common core of the most significant readings, and thus stimulate conversation among students from the various tracks during dinner in the dormitories. (The kindest thing that can be said about this notion is that it is wistful; even the best and the brightest have limited appetites for thoughtful discussion during the ten-minute calorie race in the dining hall.)

The changes proposed and debated during the academic year 1987–88 were actually rather modest. They included a new title for the course ("Culture, Ideas, and Values"), an added track, new methods for focusing on issues of ethnicity and gender, and a reduction from fifteen to eight in the number of readings on the A list. The removed readings appeared on the B list, and that change occurred in response to pleading on the part of the teaching faculty that fifteen readings common to all tracks simply placed too many constraints on the design of their courses.

The process was entirely typical of what goes on—and should go on—in academic institutions. Two faculty committees studied the problem and made recommendations to the Senate. In five lengthy sessions, the entire Senate debated the proposals and made compromises. The ultimate resolution passed resoundingly and was enthusiastically supported by the teaching faculty in the program.

But to the surprise of many at Stanford, the debate created a national media firestorm well before the final action of the faculty. The *Wall Street Journal,* of course, published acidic editorials. The secretary of education, William Bennett, joined the fray; he charged Stanford with having succumbed to coercion, on the grounds that minority students had protested the old program and demonstrated in support of the changes. A charge that has found its way into the academic muckraking literature asserts that at a critical point in the decision the Reverend Jesse Jackson led a group of demonstrators shouting, "Hey, hey, ho, ho . . . Western Culture's got to go."[2]

Newsweek headlined its story on the Western Culture debate "Goodnight, Socrates." Nearly every major metropolitan newspaper in the United States commented on the subject, and on the op-ed page George Will, Charles Krauthammer, and others were weighing in against the changes while Ellen Goodman, Amy Schwartz, and others countered in favor of them.

From the president's office, I found the campus debate an inspiring example of how academic change is—and should be—debated and eventually adopted. Surely there can be no more vital question for us than the one at stake here: what should be the common intellectual property of educated men and women? By contrast, the public discussion seemed superficial and often misleading.

Curricular change became an object of intense external concern because of a deep relationship between knowledge and values. Many of the objections to the new course, which were expressed with special vigor by the neoconservative pundits who gave it so much attention, had to do with the fear that Western beliefs and values, and not just a reading list, were being pruned. "Cultural relativism," a phrase used by many of the critics, reflected a fear that if we give too much attention to the non-Western elements that have helped shape contemporary American culture, we will be suggesting that the values represented by them have equal status. Perhaps the most extreme form of this view came from Bernard Lewis, an emeritus professor at Princeton. In the *Wall Street Journal* he wrote: "If Western Culture does indeed go, a number of other things would go with it and others would come in their place."[3] Among the "other things" he listed slavery, the harem, and the loss of political freedom.

People want guidance in developing their own knowledge. In the early part of the twentieth century leading academic centers, including Harvard and the University of Chicago, gained much attention for publishing anthologies of Great Works for public consumption. The same zeal for packaged knowledge supported a generation of door-to-door salesmen, who readily persuaded earnest parents to impoverish themselves so that their children could have the latest encyclopedia. Now the desire to Know What One Needs to Know is even more intense. We live in the information explosion, and to know that essential knowledge has finite boundaries is deeply reassuring. And so, when elements of a canon appear to be discarded, a certain insecurity sets in. We have seen it before: with Darwin's publication of the *Origin of Species* the unity of natural philosophy was suddenly made obsolete. The reaction from the academy and the educated public, as John Dewey has pointed out, was harsher than that from the pulpit. The need for knowledge boundaries is even more powerful now. When the head of the National Endowment for the Humanities (NEH) publishes a list of Things to Know it is seized upon eagerly. And when a leading university opens the door to new kinds of knowledge in a required freshman course, it makes news—discomfiting news.

Indeed, change itself is often a source of public disaffection. Most often, it is not change in the curriculum or in educational programs that generates the concern. Rather, the concern results from the perception that the very role of the university, or the way it is being governed, or the way in which it relates to other social institutions, has been changed in some fundamental way.

Beginning in the 1970s the public view of all these relationships underwent a dramatic revision. The traditional image of the university has been that of ivory tower—a place removed from the hubbub of marketplace life in which great thoughts, even unthinkable thoughts, can be developed and argued without serious interference. Part of the price for this immunity was the very disengagement of the university from the world of commerce: the former was seen as high-minded, austere, almost seminary-like in its eschewal of profit and glory. That image was able to survive even the postwar transition into high-powered science and technology—so long as the practitioners asked little beyond support for their work and reputation within the craft.

But then several things happened. As government resources became more limited, higher education became a more aggressive claimant for its share of discretionary domestic expenditures. In the search for more research funds and more student aid, America's colleges and universities became more proficient lobbyists, and as a result lost some of the luster of being special. At the time that the 1986 tax law revisions were being debated in Congress, private institutions in particular fought for several provisions, including especially favorable tax treatment for the donation of appreciated assets and the right to issue tax-exempt bonds to support the construction of new facilities. These were not exactly unreasonable requests; indeed, both provisions had been part of national tax policy for some time. The surprise was not that the universities lost on both, but that—as they were told by young congressional staff members who were their own alumni—they were viewed as "just another interest group, like Big Oil."

That view may have been reinforced by another phenomenon: the increasing need of colleges and universities for money. There is something inexorable about the growth of higher education budgets. The economist Howard Bowen once described the simple formula for academic financing: "raise all you can, and spend all you raise." There is much truth in that. Universities are hooked on excellence; when there are more resources, better faculty are hired and better buildings are built. And when savings are realized, they are much more likely to be put into program improvements than employed as revenue relief.

That is not merely lack of fiscal discipline or observance of custom. There is an implacable law of the economics of knowledge, first stated as far as I know by the German physicist Max Planck: each incremental unit of new knowledge costs more than the last. It's not hard to explain. We tend to answer the easier questions first; the answers to those then suggest harder questions. Furthermore, we develop new tools in the course of our investigations and then apply them to subsequent work. For a constant increment of gain at the frontier we thus find ourselves allocating more and more resources. So it is that scholarship, by its very nature, builds on itself. That appetite for growth is demonstrated by the rate of increase in the volume of scientific literature in the twentieth century, which has averaged between 6 and 7 percent per year.[4] The cost implications for the universities, not only in the research function but for teaching as well, are enormous.

Such explanations, I discovered, never worked very well with alumni— or with parents, who were making tuition payments for their children that were nearly tenfold, in nominal dollars, what they had been a quarter of a century earlier. To be sure, tuitions in our colleges and universities have risen somewhat faster than disposable income. The central problem, though, is that growth in disposable income has stagnated, and families feel squeezed. Their housing costs have skyrocketed while their real incomes have declined, and the tuition check is often the largest single check they write. It is small wonder that it makes them angry. And they are often joined by those who view rising state taxes for education, or the persistent fund-raising appeal from their alma mater or a neighboring college, as further evidence of institutional greed.

At the same time there has been a growing interplay between universities and for-profit companies. In public iconography, shabby gentility is just as characteristic of the professoriate as absent-mindedness. It is all part of how academics are forgiven for being so smart. That quiet little social contract between ivory tower and general public is broken if the professor (or the institution) suddenly looks rich and clever. And that has been one effect of the recent set of alliances between academic research and the world of commerce. In the context of public attitudes toward higher education, the problem is much simpler than conflict of interest or anything that subtle. It is mainly one of too much money. When professors of molecular biology appear to be enriched by off-campus ventures, public attitudes toward them and toward their institutions change. When the university makes a multimillion dollar deal with a drug company to support research, and the company subsequently obtains rights to the resulting intellectual property, hard questions are raised. To some, it even seems improper that universities can patent faculty inventions themselves and receive a royalty return from them. The sense is that faculty members are paid enough salary, given the freedom they enjoy, and that universities ought not to be profiting from their research. This is not exactly a thoughtful or fair-minded view; after all, other professionals can earn outside income without reaping criticism, and if universities don't receive some return on their intellectual output more pressure will be placed on tuition. Nevertheless, the view is firmly implanted: academics and profitability don't mix.

From these multiple causes public dissatisfaction grew. To the Allan Bloom opus was added a veritable flood of confessional literature from disaffected academics, as well as critiques from the outside. A few titles are enough to tell the story: *Illiberal Education; Killing the Spirit; Profscam; Impostors in the Temple.* Government bodies and commissions, alarmed by all the fuss, were declaring that the public's confidence in universities had reached new lows. Derek Bok, nearing the end of a long and distinguished tenure as president of Harvard, said in his annual report to the Board of Overseers in 1989: "Critics in this country have attacked [the universities] more savagely during the past ten years than at any time in my memory."

The perception that universities are no longer loved, of course, makes them more politically vulnerable. During the 1980s, serious government efforts to control research in the university and to limit the rights of faculty investigators appeared for the first time. That decade also saw other federal initiatives to limit traditional institutional prerogatives or attack institutional processes. For example, new legislation intended to control drugs mandated that colleges and universities certify that they were actively enforcing laws and regulations regarding drug and alcohol use. Everyone agrees that drug and alcohol abuse are bad things, but the effect of the federal intervention was to turn the university's role into that of cop on the beat.

In 1991 the Department of Justice initiated a civil investigative demand against fifty-six colleges and universities, on the theory that they may have exchanged information about tuition, faculty salaries, and student financial aid awards in violation of the antitrust laws. The volume of paper required to respond to the accusations was enormous, and the time invested in giving depositions and preparing paperwork was equally significant. The matter was eventually decided, on terms generally favorable to the universities, but of course the institutions never recovered the money they spent in responding—overall, certainly in excess of twenty million dollars.

One cannot know for certain whether public disapproval of universities made them more vulnerable to such assaults. But in one recent instance, the intervention was so blatantly political that it can hardly have been made without an assessment that the institution lacked the popular support needed for effective resistance. In 1995, California's Governor Wilson, in the early stages of a campaign for the presidency, announced his support for proposals to eliminate affirmative action as a criterion in making state appointments. He then began a very public effort to persuade the regents of the University of California to vote to eliminate affirmative action considerations in the admission of students as well as in hiring. It is usual for the regents to take with utmost seriousness any recommendation made by the faculty, the chancellors of the nine campuses, and the president of the system. All of these strongly favored the retention of the university's right to set its own admissions policies—a power normally delegated fully by governing boards. Governor Wilson's importunings succeeded, however (nearly all the regents were appointees of Wilson or of his Republican predecessors), and the decision was made to end affirmative action. This incident established a high watermark for political intervention in higher education—for the recent era, at least—and it could hardly have happened if the university had been seen as a more politically robust target.

Despite all the adverse publicity and the political encroachments, it may be that the public view of the university is, as Mark Twain once said of the music of Wagner, not as bad as it sounds. The evidence, fragmentary though it is, suggests that the popular disdain so many of us in academia now fear is actually not very well developed, on comparative measures, and that what we are witnessing in public attitudes toward higher education may be but one facet of a much larger phenomenon.

An analysis of changes in public attitudes toward higher education, using data from annual surveys conducted by the National Opinion Research Center, shows that over the two decades between 1972 and 1992, Americans expressed the greatest confidence in the leaders of medicine, science, and education; the levels were substantially higher, for example, than for the Congress, labor, the press, or the executive branch of the federal government.[5] There was little change in the rankings during that period; indeed, the leaders of science and education actually scored higher in public confidence in 1991 than they had at the beginning of the 1980s.

That, however, is small comfort. Despite the strands of truth in the contemporary critique of our colleges and universities, it seems strange and unfair to those who live and work in them that the public view is so negative when the record of accomplishment seems so strong. Nostalgic critics may yearn for the comfort, friendly scale, and social homogeneity of the institutions they attended in an earlier day. For them, the kindly and attentive professor, the Great Books course, and the presence of like-minded and approachable fellow students all seem missing from the intense, hurly-burly atmosphere of the modern university, with its aura of "political correctness." By contrast, those who hope for a more egalitarian, progressive society may see contemporary institutions of higher education as instruments of elitism, and as devices for putting research efforts into the service of "business as usual."

Both kinds of critics are apt to preface their complaints with a statement that colleges and universities are important; they go on to concede that change is inevitable, though of course they disagree about the direction it should take. Such a conversation among thoughtful, well-intentioned graduates of the very institutions they are discussing exposes the degree to which the participants fail to understand how colleges and universities actually *work*—how they are structured, organized, and financed, what their faculties do, and who is responsible for securing their future. Academic institutions and their faculties remain mysterious to the many millions of Americans who have attended colleges and universities. Most of them care for their alma mater and have a deep interest in the character and direction of the broader enterprise of higher education. When they were students, there was neither opportunity nor incentive to study their institutions. The resulting misunderstandings are damaging: it is much easier to distrust an institution whose operations and purposes are obscure.

The failure of understanding extends further, onto even more dangerous ground. The very heart of the institution's academic duty to society is the work of its faculty. They make many of the important decisions about institutional process, and of course they are largely responsible for the university's day-to-day work: teaching undergraduate students, preparing graduate students for professional careers, conducting and publishing research, and serving the university's external communities in a variety of ways. Through the fulfillment of their academic duties, they fulfill the institution's duty to society. In that sense it can truthfully be asserted that they *are* the institution. Yet, surprisingly, many prospective professors, despite having spent anywhere from eight to fifteen years in university preparing themselves for the academic profession, are quite ignorant about the organization and the functioning of the places in which they hope to work. Their beliefs and behaviors are largely formed "on the job."

As one who has spent thirty-five years on the faculty of a lively research university—including seven as department chair, one as provost, and a dozen as president—I can attest that the university is on the front lines of a running conflict. Sometimes the conflict is between different values that coexist, often without harmony, inside the university. More often it is between institutional values and a changing society. The latter struggle represents a powerful challenge to the university, which desperately needs both its independence from the society around it and the support and understanding of that society.

I gained a new appreciation of this dual need from an extraordinarily trying personal episode that had a significant impact on the public perception of my own university, and perhaps others. In brief, a congressional investigation and a national television program accused Stanford of having improperly charged government "overhead" against expenditures that should not have drawn such charges. The investigation and the media attention that accompanied it focused heavily on expenses (flowers, furniture repair, entertainment) incurred at the president's residence. A few of the charges to the indirect cost accounts were clearly errors on our part, and embarrassing ones at that. Others were within the government's rules, but looked improper. Still others were quite legitimate, but were vulnerable to distortion by congressional staffers and those in the media to whom they regularly leaked material. Stanford as an institution, and I personally, became the subjects of intense and highly critical public attention.

The episode was painful but in one way salutary. The contested expenditures amounted to a small portion of the university's total government reimbursement for the period in question, and in a subsequent settlement the university and its officers were absolved of all wrongdoing. But it made me reflect more deeply on the sensitivity of the relationship between universities and the public that supports them, and on the need to pursue more actively the challenges of explaining the institution and its public accountability.

There is always much to explain. During most of my time as president, from 1980 to 1992, Stanford led the nation in the level of its annual federal research support and was the first choice of more National Science Foundation (NSF) fellowship winners than any other institution. Its graduate programs in biomedicine, the physical sciences, engineering, and in several departments in the social sciences and humanities had gained widespread recognition. It attracted wonderfully well qualified undergraduate applicants, and enjoyed both financial and spiritual support from alumni.

Yet despite the abundant evidence of its success, the university during that time regularly faced various kinds of internal conflicts. Some were well-publicized; for example, charges by a female faculty member that the Medical School was a place in which sexual harassment was tacitly condoned, and an accusation of research misconduct by one faculty member against another. A larger number of conflicts were resolved quietly in the interest of protecting the privacy of complainants and defendants. These included several other charges of sexual harassment involving various combinations of faculty, students, and staff, but too frequently faculty members were those being complained about. There were disputes among faculty members, or between faculty members and students, about the proprietorship of ideas, as well as conflict-of-interest problems with respect to outside commercial activities. As I learned more about these, I worried that somehow the university was failing to protect the academic community from itself. But as I discussed these problems with faculty members and university officers elsewhere, I learned that far from being especially vulnerable, we at Stanford were part of a more widespread phenomenon.

Indeed, problems of the kind that troubled us are probably endemic to the culture of the research university. The careful attention of the media to any fracture lines in the ivory tower may suggest that scientific fraud, racial disharmony, commercial greed, or unacceptable sexual conduct are more common than they were, say, two decades ago. The evidence available on this point is disappointingly (though perhaps necessarily) anecdotal, but I think it supports the view that these problems are neither new nor even significantly more abundant than in the recent past. What *is* new is the openness with which they are raised, discussed, and published in the newspapers. And that, of course, is why I believe that these issues need to be talked about with a wider audience as well as with future members of the professoriate.

The contemporary style of dealing publicly with problems in the academy is probably a healthy sign. Surely it makes it less likely that the plagiarist, the bigot, or the coercive seducer will be privately reprimanded for such conduct or—worse still—that it will be readily forgiven and forgotten. On the other hand, it may lead to a perception that these behaviors are more common than they really are. We know that people tend to overestimate the frequency of well-publicized, spectacular events compared with more commonplace ones; this is a well-understood phenomenon in the literature of risk assessment and leads to the truism that when statistics plays folklore, folklore always wins in a rout.

But whether or not problems of sexual harassment, academic misconduct, exploitation of students, or conflict of interest are more common than in the past, or less common than most people suppose, they are more common than they ought to be. Their occurrence is destructive to the health of academic communities, as well as to their public credibility. Furthermore, it enhances the public impression that the university cares only for intellectual development and eschews responsibility for other, more personal dimensions of the lives of its students—even of those destined to make their careers in the academy.

Some of the blots on faculty behavior have an explanation, if not an excuse. The pressures on academic practitioners, especially young ones, are increasing. Research support is much harder to get than in the past, and even those projects that do win out in the competitive grants process are likely to be underfunded. Studies indicate that, as compared with the beginning of the 1980s, faculty members must obtain 50 percent more grants to achieve the same dollar value of support. With competition increasing for the individually initiated research grants that are the basic fuel for academic research, the quality requirement for each application and for interim reports has been raised.

Committee burdens, too, have become weightier. This is partly because universities are bigger and more complicated places: large research programs, many of them government-sponsored, have led to staff growth and more complex systems of management. Faculty members now devote significant time to decision making about everything from parking to health benefits. The rapid growth in government regulation has ushered in a whole new set of demands on faculty time. There are now federally mandated panels on the treatment of human subjects and of experimental animals, as well as on radiation safety and laboratory procedures. Most of these result from government regulations that did not exist twenty years ago.

Tenured faculty positions are now harder to obtain. Faculties grew rapidly in the palmy days of government support, from the mid-1950s to the late 1960s. Faculty growth slowed as the support reached a plateau, and as the baby-boom generation left college. The large cohort of professors appointed in the high-growth era is still unretired, and the number of new positions is accordingly small.

Even in those institutions in which internal promotion to tenure is a real prospect it is more difficult to move up. In the 1960s, nearly half of Stanford's assistant professors in the natural sciences, engineering, and the "hard" social sciences could expect to earn tenure. Today the proportion is between one-third and one-quarter. The result is increased pressure to do and to publish more research—just at a time when other demands on faculty time have increased dramatically. It is perhaps no wonder at all that faculty members generally, and scientists in particular, are unhappy. One has only to read Leon Lederman's report on morale in the scientific community in 1991 or sample the letters column of *Science* or the *Chronicle of Higher Education* to feel the breadth and intensity of this malaise.[6]

Of course discouragement and pressure do not excuse research misconduct, or the failure to give one's students credit for their work and ideas, or the shirking of other dimensions of academic duty. But they may help to explain the kind of attention these failures are getting; any atmosphere in which morale is low and time short is a fertile place for the amplification of differences. Universities, in short, are less forgiving environments than they used to be. In such environments prevention is especially preferable to cure.

Prevention in this context surely means education and preparation. Future teacher-scholars, like other professionals in the making, need to become acquainted with the kinds of challenges they are likely to face. Without some thoughtful consideration of what their own responsibilities are to be, and an examination of the ethical issues teachers and scholars regularly confront, is it reasonable to expect that they will get it right the first time? Surely that places too much faith in instinct, or in the general kind of moral guidance that is part of the average upbringing.

The terms *responsibility* and *ethics* are often used interchangeably in speaking of the professions, and it is tempting to elide them here and let it go at that. But there is a distinction between two different kinds of obligation, one worth making at the outset. Responsibility suggests the duty one owes to the institution—and, first and foremost, to one's students. It means meeting one's classes well-prepared and maintaining one's standards of scholarship. It means giving a student the time he or she needs to work out a problem. It means retaining some detachment and objectivity about highly partisan issues in which it might be possible to exert an unfair influence over students. In essence, it means delivering full support to a set of institutional objectives. A colleague of mine who is superbly dutiful in this way learned about responsibility to students as a boarding-school teacher, early in his career. He recalls that in that other academic setting the central element of academic duty was something called "coverage." If another teacher was ill or unexpectedly absent, a faculty volunteer covered that teacher's class or residential monitoring task; it was understood that every obligation to students had to be met, and extra effort was part of the culture. Looking at the university's faculty through this lens, my friend says of his less dutiful colleagues: "They never got taught about coverage."

There is something about this version of professional responsibility, perhaps its implication that faculty members are responsible for more than just the intellectual development of their students, that is threatening to many members of the professoriate. Yet it may well be a vital part of the misunderstanding between the university and its public about what constitutes academic duty. The university and its faculty, with their contemporary focus on knowledge production, seem inclined to limit their responsibility to a domain that is strictly academic. But the public almost surely expects more. The disjunction appeared in dramatic form in the spring of 1995 at Harvard, where the murder of a student by a roommate who had a record that suggested some emotional disturbance, produced a rush of journalistic reappraisal: had it been Harvard's duty to intervene more actively when it was suggested that the student had an emotional problem? The facts are in some dispute, but the nature of the reaction tells us much about the divergence of views about academic duty.

Professional responsibility includes, but is not limited to, "professional ethics." In the latter category, there are abundant challenges for the professoriate. Temptations to favor students because of a romantic attachment, or to appropriate credit to which one is not entitled, or to employ institutional resources for personal purposes exemplify the kinds of ethical dilemmas that not infrequently confront teacher-scholars. Failures to meet them responsibly give rise to much of the grist for the mill of public hostility toward academic institutions.

The careful attention now given to the development of professional responsibility or the teaching of ethics in other domains of graduate training only calls out a remarkable disparity. Hardly a medical school in the country is without an "ethicist," and many have groups that bring a mixture of disciplines to bear on such ethical challenges as informed consent, no-code orders, confidentiality, and conflicts of interest. Law schools all offer courses in professional responsibility. The nation's leading business schools, in particular Harvard and Stanford, have received significant gifts to support the incorporation of ethical issues into the analysis of business cases in the classroom. A colleague of mine refers to ethics as "the statistics of the 1990s"—a reference to the way in which that discipline, at an earlier time, was offered in several different forms to meet the needs of various departments. And yet the university, which offers all sorts of instruction designed to introduce the members of other professions to the ethical challenges they may face, gives none whatever to those who are planning to enter the university's *own* profession.

Of course, it doesn't have to be that way. When I left the presidency, I decided to offer a course in professorial responsibility—one that I assumed would be altered substantially by experience. A trial run during the fall quarter of 1993–94 was encouraging, although it is entirely possible that the instructor learned more from the students than the other way around. I had not been fully prepared for a number of new problems: the challenges that the computer revolution and "network publication" posed for traditional ideas about intellectual property; new sensitivities about relationships between the sexes; evolving standards in the area of grant review processes; and many others.

Teaching that class was an extraordinary experience. The students, drawn from the ranks of dissertation-level (that is, third year or higher) Ph.D. candidates planning to enter academic careers, were fully engaged. I found my optimism about the future of higher education buoyed by the conscientious enthusiasm they brought to these discussions, though I realized that I was working with a self-selected group of men and women. I also found myself stunned, every once in a while, at some of the things they hadn't considered. So many of the issues we talked about were, to me, central to life in the professoriate, but were things the students hadn't discussed before. It wasn't from any resistance on their part; on the contrary, they eagerly confronted each new topic. But it was plain that most of the bread-and-butter issues (those dealing with grading complaints, advising students who present a personal problem, confronting disputes over authorship) as well as the more complex dilemmas "just hadn't come up" in their laboratories, in their relationships to their thesis advisers, or even in conversations with their fellow graduate students.

Academic life in America, despite its diverse institutional forms, presents common experiences and challenges. Every professor teaches; most write papers or books and review those written by others; most have relationships, friendly or otherwise, with peers; many get grants to support scholarly work; many publish their findings in scholarly journals or books. And all are looked upon, by students and others, as persons somehow responsible for advancing the capacities and potentialities of the next generation. That is a very large responsibility, and it is the essence of academic duty. But the instructions for fulfilling it are left vague even for the prospective practitioners. For this reason confusion and misunderstanding often prevail inside academia, and the public is equally confused. Thus understanding the professional responsibilities that constitute academic duty is important for those who will fulfill them. But it is equally important that they be understood in the same way by the public.

By nature, universities are controversial places. Their successes and failures draw intense public scrutiny because they really matter. That they are now much misunderstood and much criticized cannot be dismissed as a temporary bump in the road, nor can it be ignored merely because other institutions in American life are also held in low regard. As our society needs higher education, so higher education needs public trust. Thus we must take the criticism seriously, and ask about its origin.

Its origin, I argue, has much to do with our internal failure to come to grips with responsibility in the university. Having been given a generous dose of academic freedom, we haven't taken care of the other side of the bargain. The struggle about the universities has little or nothing to do with Right and Left, or with cultural relativism, or with race relations, or with any of the particular matters that earn us media attention. It has to do with how we see our duty and how our patrons and clients see it. If we can clarify our perception of duty and gain public acceptance of it, we will have fulfilled an important obligation to the society that nurtures us. That obligation constitutes the highest institutional form of academic duty.

❧ 2 ❧

PREPARING

INSTITUTIONS of higher education have a responsibility to the society that sponsors and nurtures them, as well as to their students and to the people who work for them. But the institutions, both in the historical sense and at their contemporary core, are assemblages of teacher-scholars. In the way they function, universities *are*, for most purposes, the faculty.

Thus much of academic duty resolves itself into a set of obligations that professors owe to others: to their undergraduate students, to the more advanced scholars they train, to their colleagues, to the institutions with which they are affiliated, and to the larger society. That society has high expectations of the professoriate and, especially recently, is impatient with its shortcomings. The list of tasks for which the faculty are held responsible has grown from moral teaching to include knowledge production, technical assistance, community outreach, and many others. Faculty members enter an arena full of personal and professional challenges that result from that cargo of expectations. How are they prepared to meet them? What personal experiences will shape how they will fulfill their academic duty?

The ways in which faculty members are trained, find jobs, and develop their interests in teaching and research are important in determining what they will do and how they will do it. The fact that most institutional decisions represent, in the end, the collective values and aspirations of the faculty helps to explain why universities are organized the way they are and behave as they do. But institutions of higher education are so diverse, and they perform such varied functions, that any discussion of their operation must begin with some taxonomy and some history.

In what follows, I frequently refer to institutional "prestige." Despite the high quality of many colleges and universities, the perception of excellence tends to focus on a small number of places. There are many reasons for this. Age and tradition benefit some institutions, the Ivy League universities among them; the great land-grant universities of the Big Ten (once called by William Rainey Harper of the private University of Chicago the "great engines of public instruction") draw admiration for their comprehensiveness. The presence of faculty members whose writings or scientific discoveries attract national attention is important, and may be critical in the recruitment of graduate students and other faculty. Students, who often focus on selective, and thus desirable, institutions, can contribute to a school's reputation for excellence. Even athletic success can make an institution at least temporarily attractive to freshman applicants. Our national passion for rankings and ratings—"Who's Number 1?"—is a natural amplifier of small differences.

Because faculty members and prospective students care very much about prestige, it is a necessary part of the conversation about higher education. But one of the most striking things one learns about the colleges and universities in this country is that so many different kinds are so very good. My own experiences in touring higher education have left me surprised and exhilarated about the demography of institutional quality. At every level and for every conceivable kind of institution, there are inspiring examples: of superb teaching, of creative academic experiment, of faculty efforts to create powerful local traditions about the importance of teaching well. No matter where they are, how big they are, or how much prestige they possess, all institutions of higher education have, or should have, one thing in common: the primary mission of educating students. Those directly responsible for that mission are a group of highly educated, professional academicians called faculty.

How highly educated they are, and how they are credentialed, depend to some extent on the institution in which they work. The institutional prestige hierarchy is based in part on the proportion of faculty members who hold doctorates; in many community colleges and some of the less "distinguished" four-year liberal arts colleges, a significant proportion of the faculty are without advanced degrees. The majority, however, have

Ph.D.s or equivalent doctorates specific to the professional fields in which they work—Ed.D. for some professors in education, J.D. in law, M.D. in medicine, for example.

Collectively, the faculty members of an institution set the academic standards, admit the students, and grant the degrees.[1] The legal ownership of colleges and universities is vested in Boards of Trustees, if they are private, or in governmentally appointed or elected bodies with various names (regents is the most common) if they are public. But these bodies are essentially fiduciary: they own the assets and are responsible for their management on a sustainable basis. The day-to-day management tasks are delegated to a president, who appoints various deans and other administrative officers. These officers—collectively called the administration—are often from, but not quite of, the faculty. They run the place in one sense, but in nearly all American institutions the faculty retain the fundamental academic functions: admitting the students, planning and delivering the curriculum, setting degree requirements, and granting the degrees.

Faculty members across the spectrum of American colleges and universities share many of the same responsibilities, but the heterogeneity of institutional settings makes a simple description of their specific tasks difficult. The teaching "load" of a faculty member in, say, history will be much heavier in a small liberal arts college than in a research university. Conversely, less will be expected in the way of scholarly productivity. A biochemist at MIT might be asked to serve on an institute-wide committee or two, but would not have a specified "service" obligation beyond that, whereas a biochemist in the same subfield in the School of Agriculture at the University of Wisconsin might well have consulting and Agricultural Extension responsibilities. In a residential college with a highly selected student body, faculty members may be strongly urged to serve as academic advisers or even as resident fellows in student dormitories. In a large urban university such duties would be minimal.

Despite such differences in specific responsibilities, it is clear that a single issue, division of labor between teaching and research, is affecting the quality of life for many in the professoriate. This has always been a central issue for faculty in the research university, but increasingly it has become an issue even in liberal arts colleges of the second or third rank, as the competition among institutions becomes more intense and as faculty aspirations encounter an environment of increasing economic scarcity. It is a core reality of contemporary academic life, and of course it has a long history.

The first two hundred and forty years of American higher education were characterized by relatively slow change. Most of the earliest colleges—Harvard, William and Mary, Yale, Williams, and the like—were church-related. Their students were undergraduates preparing for the ministry and, later, other professions. They were tiny by the scale of modern universities: at the turn of the twentieth century, Harvard was still only the size of the larger present-day liberal arts colleges.

The transformations that led to the modern university began in the late nineteenth century, and the agent was the importation of the German university tradition. Neither serious original research nor training in scholarship had been a significant feature of the nineteenth-century American college. For that one had to go overseas; and even in the United States, the celebrated academic scholars were often European expatriates like Harvard's famous natural scientist Louis Agassiz. The few experiments in research training usually took place in special agencies or institutes like Harvard's Museum of Comparative Zoology.

Perhaps the most important milestone in the transformation was the establishment, in 1876, of The Johns Hopkins University. It was the first institution to offer graduate education on the German plan, and was followed a decade later by Clark University. Thereafter, the "new" universities of the late nineteenth century—in particular, Stanford and Chicago—incorporated both the idea of the graduate school and some of the traditions of the college.

At the same time, the two great innovations of the German system, the laboratory and the seminar, began to be adopted by the most creative of the older, well-established colleges. Harvard was the first to engage in serious reinvention, probably because its president, Charles William Eliot, was already committed to an elective curriculum and to a kind of academic entrepreneurism. The Graduate School of Arts and Sciences at Harvard was created in 1889, and its early successes appear simply remarkable in retrospect. By the turn of the century it had a philosophy department that included Josiah Royce, Hugo Munsterberg, George Santayana, and William James—surely one of the most extraordinary groups of scholars in the humanities ever gathered in one seminar room.[2] The trend to graduate education spread; Columbia was not far behind, and other institutions followed. But it would be wrong to characterize this revolution as a bandwagon upon which all existing institutions eagerly leapt.

On the contrary, there was a real struggle. At Princeton, Woodrow Wilson urged that his college "keep out the microbes of the scientific conception of books and the past." He saw Princeton as an institution in which "men are licked into something like the same shape in respect of the principles with which they go out into the world." At Yale, the resistance to research accomplishment as an indicator of academic worth was so strong that it gave rise to the following joke, no doubt repeated more often in Cambridge than in New Haven: "The professional spirit prevails in Yale athletics, and the amateur spirit prevails in Yale scholarship." Princeton and Yale deferred their transition, but not for very long. A brief counterrevolution at Harvard attempted to restore some aspects of the Wilsonian college, but it failed to dislodge the new order.

At about the same time that graduate education was becoming established, Andrew Carnegie published an extraordinary essay in the *North American Review* called "The Gospel of Wealth." It accompanied, and perhaps helped to launch, an unprecedented rush of philanthropic attention to higher education. Many new colleges and universities were founded in the late nineteenth century, most of them private and many of them made possible by large gifts from private individuals. These philanthropists were responding to a new doctrine, set out by Carnegie, about the relationship between riches and religious righteousness—one that led John D. Rockefeller famously to assert: "The good Lord gave me my money, and how could I withhold it from the University of Chicago?"

Thus both financial resources and intellectual momentum favored the emergence of a new academic entity. This new entity contained elements of the old English college, now contained within an enlarged body derived from the German graduate school. For the first time, one could speak of a university and mean the kind of institution we would recognize today.

Growth was slow in the first part of the twentieth century, but scholarship was setting firm roots everywhere. Distinguished science faculties emerged in a number of places, all working under that unique partnership by which mature scholars and graduate apprentices together attack novel problems. More and more emphasis was placed on seminar work and on the training of young academics to take their places in the growing roster of colleges and state universities.

A huge windfall came to the research universities in the period following World War II. Under the guidance of Vannevar Bush and others, a decision was made to relocate the elaborate machinery for supporting military science in the nation's universities. There were plenty of alternatives: an elaborate array of government laboratories, or "privatization" into industry through contracting. Instead, the enterprise was located in those institutions in which the next generation of research scientists was being trained, in the belief that "enlarging and disseminating knowledge are equally important activities and that each is done better when both are done in the same place by the same people."[3] Thus the special knack of the German graduate school, the interweaving of original work and training, became the postwar inspiration for the most successful national system ever devised for the sponsorship of science.

But science was not the only academic domain to benefit from the windfall. As universities used government funds to develop facilities and faculties in the sciences, general funds were released for other purposes: the social sciences benefited directly, as did even the humanities, from new grants under such statutes as the National Defense Education Act.

The government's largesse also spread to institutions that were plainly not research universities. The return of veterans and the GI bill resulted in demands for increased capacity in the entire higher education system. These demands accelerated in the 1960s with the arrival of the "baby boom" cohort, and they were met by significant federal help for both state and private institutions, and by building capacity for training the faculties to staff them. Ph.D. production grew rapidly in the research universities, and an increasing number of institutions received investments for facilities and research programs. The NSF developed an array of programs to support in-service training and research for faculty members in small colleges. In short, by the late 1960s the entire enterprise of higher education was at its zenith: new buildings, training programs, program support, and even funding for curriculum development and the arts were appearing everywhere. Between 1960 and 1967, for example, support for basic science in the United States, two thirds of which is done in the research universities, grew from about two billion dollars to about five billion dollars (in constant 1982 dollars). That is an astonishing compound annual growth rate of 15 percent!

It has been a downhill course ever since. Federal funds for facilities construction were last authorized in 1968, at which time a relative cutback in training funds began. The fellowship programs of the National Defense Education Act disappeared. Capacity was no longer an issue as the college-age population dropped. Research program funding slowed its growth and soon reached a plateau, followed by more modest growth in the 1980s. The infrastructure for academic research was being neglected, and program funds had to be spread over a rapidly enlarging pool of recipients. The result was an increasing sense of despondency on the part of faculty members about the prospects for continued support of their scholarly work.[4]

This brief history tells us something of the nature and past experience of the environments in which faculty members find themselves. More important, though, it provides the background for understanding the constant tension between research and teaching that is now the single greatest problem facing the professoriate. It is clear that higher education is in a state of compression: of enrollment, of funding, and of opportunity. There are probably more able people in academic life than at any previous point in history, but more is being asked of them than ever before, and less is being given. The first of these propositions is easy to support. A static number of professors is being asked to respond to elevated expectations: students now both want and need more academic attention and challenge than did their predecessors; universities (partially because of government regulations) require more committee work and participation in governance; and with a constant funding base and a limited number of tenured faculty slots, each aspirant has to do more to qualify competitively. Less is being given because the falling tide of federal funding has stranded all the disciplinary boats: the pinch felt in the English Department probably comes later than that in Biochemistry, but in the end it may hurt almost as much.

In a climate such as the present one, competition among institutions is intensified. More colleges talk about "marketing" themselves to students; the research quality of university faculties is judged using arcane derivative measures like average number of citations per published paper. Popular magazines rank colleges by perceived quality of faculty, or as "best buys," or even by the liveliness of the social environment.

Increasingly, institutions compete by "prestige," which is usually measured in the national reputations of faculty members. Since research and not teaching ability is the primary reputational currency, the influence of the former on promotion and tenure has increased substantially. In an expanding universe this might not generate so much tension, but the universe is contracting: not only are economic constraints and demographic realities limiting the number of new slots in universities, but old ones are not being vacated because mandatory retirement by age is now illegal. The graying of the faculty is a striking fact of academic life in America.

Young faculty, whether as candidates for junior positions or as aspirants at the tenure bar, are regularly urged by their advocates to concentrate on research and, if necessary, skimp on teaching. At the same time, however, their administrations are being forced to cut back on support staff and other expenditures that facilitate teaching—thus, in effect, making teaching loads heavier. Meanwhile, the public, which looks to higher education primarily for teaching, is beginning to express concern and even mistrust over the university's attention to its primary mission.

A major source of this problem may be traced to the nature of graduate training for the academic profession. Too often, little attention is given to the teaching responsibilities that doctoral students will have later, as they are pressed to finish their dissertations or to support their mentors' research programs. Faculty members-in-training receive little or no preparation for the range of personal and professional challenges they will face as practicing members of the professoriate. The vast majority of academic doctorates are produced in fewer than one hundred "research universities," but 90 percent of them will teach in several thousand institutions that are quite different from the places in which they were trained. They arrive on the job with little guidance about how to make the transition from expert learner to novice teacher, or even about what is expected of them as professionals.

Yet faculty careers are still appealing. Colleges and universities are, in most ways, wonderful places to be: they are intellectually and culturally rich and full of interesting and eager young people. The work can be hard if one is conscientious, but it is also flexible, stimulating, and varied. By many standards (though not by those of such rival professions as law and medicine) the pay is rather good, but of course the matter of compensation and reward is complex and often trying, because it is related in important ways to institutional and personal prestige and to discipline.

Faculty prestige cannot be considered outside the context of institutional prestige. That uncertain quality, based on perceptions more often than on reality, is important: students choose one institution over another, and faculty members move from place to place, largely on the basis of reputation. Partly because prestige seems to be an increasingly important factor in student choice, attempts to measure institutional quality have become a more serious activity. Modern efforts in this direction began with the ACE's survey of doctoral programs in every major field; the "ACE Survey," performed by Allan Cartter, became an eagerly devoured source of information, updated first by ACE and then, most recently in 1995, by the National Research Council (NRC). The importance of such evaluations is underscored by the behavior of the institutions. Many major research universities now issue press releases following each new ranking episode, choosing whichever criterion (most departments in top ten or top five, highest median ranking, and so on) will put the most favorable spin on the outcome.

U.S. News and World Report's annual ranking of undergraduate programs (and, lately, also professional degree programs) is a less careful but much more popular evaluation of institutional quality. Originally these surveys asked large numbers of senior university officials which institutions they held in highest regard. Complaints naturally followed, after which the magazine began to add various "quantitative criteria," including endowment per student, alumni giving, average SAT scores of entering freshmen, and the like. As these changed from year to year, the top rankings were scrambled, leading parents and students to wonder whether institutional quality was changing. Of course, it was not.

Leaders in higher education often criticize the *U.S. News* rankings, and they certainly merit criticism. But even the critics regularly comply by passing along the information requested by the magazine. As competition for applicants among all but the top-tier institutions has intensified, there are outcries that some places are "padding" the figures they send. Although many colleges and universities would agree that the process is flawed, not to play in the game carries penalties. In 1996 Reed College, a superb liberal arts school, was ranked in the fourth tier in its category—way below its commonly accepted quality level. A small asterisk and an even smaller footnote notified the alert reader that Reed had declined to participate; its punishment had been to be sent to the bottom of the class.

The most realistic measure of institutional prestige is faculty quality, though of course it is not easy to get people to agree on criteria for that, either. Respondents in the disciplines, whose perceptions provide the basis for the ACE/NRC rankings, are clearly looking at research productivity. Careful analysis of the factors determining these rankings shows that they correlate almost perfectly with departmental rate of publication in the twenty most highly cited journals in the field.[5]

When invited to move to higher-ranking departments in more prestigious institutions, faculty members often accept. But the picture of a marketplace in which academics willingly move upward through the ranks of institutional prestige and never move downward would be misleading. Many may answer when "Harvard calls," but many others do not. Climate, urban vs. rural location, salary, special facilities, and above all the presence of valued colleagues are important factors that influence a faculty member's decision whether or not to move to a different institution. And today, with the increase in two-career families, spousal employment may be the most important factor of all.[6] These other forces are fortuitous; the "demography of quality" in American higher education, referred to elsewhere, depends on just such a distribution of preferences.

In almost every profession, people tend to worry about what they get paid. In part they worry because they and their families need money, but concern about compensation goes beyond need, and exists even among persons who couldn't possible spend all they make. This is because salaries and bonuses are symbols of institutional regard. They announce what others think people are worth.

By tradition, academic salaries are *supposed* to be low. A prevailing public perception is that professors don't work terribly hard and live pleasant lives. They teach relatively few classes, get their summers off, and work in a culturally rich and lively environment. These rewards are sometimes seen as surrogates for salary, and even many faculty members would agree that the "compensatory differential" is significant enough to justify getting along on less.

That does not make matters easy within the academy, however. Striking disparities exist among institutions, fields, and individuals. The 1995 summaries of faculty salaries published by the *Chronicle of Higher Education* reveal that, on average, full professors at all institutions make about 60 percent more than assistant professors. This would be considered a modest differential between senior and junior managers in a for-profit enterprise, but the average full professorial salary in doctorate-granting private universities exceeds that in all baccalaureate institutions by at least that much, suggesting that institutional prestige is a major factor in determining compensation levels. The most serious (and most politically troublesome) disparity problems are those that obtain among different disciplines in the same places. For example, the average faculty salary for engineers, all ranks, in private institutions exceeds that for philosophers by twenty thousand dollars.

Plainly these differentials reflect, to some degree, outside market forces. They become even larger if one considers the graduate professional schools, as one must in the large research universities. Arguments about "salary equity" in such places are almost endless, because there is no widespread agreement as to principle. In the absence of such an agreement, most institutions maintain an uneasy balance between following outside market forces and attempting to maintain some degree of comparability within a given rank. Not surprisingly, this satisfies almost no one. "Why in the world should a professor of law make much more than I do when she doesn't teach as much?" asks the professor of English. "If he thinks he is worth as much as I am," replies the professor of law, "let him go out and practice English." It is an argument scheduled for a long run.[7]

Nor is it clear how much salaries ought to be employed as reward devices in the academic setting. Because there is a prevailing sense that in institutions of higher education the quality and relative flexibility of the environment are compensation of a kind, "merit pay" has historically not had the role it has in other settings. Increasingly, however, salary increases in universities are seen as measures of a faculty member's value to the institution. And, just as with the appointment and promotion process, compensation sends signals to the rest of the community about what is valued. Salary secrecy, once a firm academic tradition, is seldom maintained anymore. Thus it is known across the institution not only that certain fields are valued more highly than others but that certain individuals are as well.

Accordingly, there is a rich lore of speculation on most campuses about what really matters. Much of it centers on the relative importance of teaching and research, about which there is little doubt: as with the promotion process, scholarly productivity seems to be what matters most. An analysis in the mid-1970s that attempted to allocate weights to different activities in determining salary strongly supported the dominant role of publication.[8] Administrative duties also exert upward salary leverage, and they may make significant contributions to lifetime academic incomes.

Outside offers also affect salary. When institutions recruit new faculty from the outside at tenured rank, their compensation is normally above the prevailing scale for that rank. This can produce some bruised feelings, and it adds weight to the view that "the only way to get promoted around here is to get a good outside offer." This reasoning, often quite sound, is that an outside offer will be higher than the salary the faculty member is making at present, and will result in a matching offer from the home institution. Although the rumor mill probably exaggerates the magnitude of this effect, it is true that many academic salaries are leveraged in this way. One outcome is that faculty members may spend too much time courting and responding to such offers in order to improve their present situation. No one knows how much waste this actually entails, but a substantial component surely is the time faculty members spend speculating about their colleagues!

The value-measuring dimension of salary policy produces terrible difficulties for those deans who are careful to maintain salary equity. In one case, three associate professors, all successful scholars who were hired at the same time, had been kept in salary lockstep. One received an attractive outside offer and asked the dean to match it with a raise and a promotion to professor. After much reflection, the dean decided to meet the competition but to maintain equity by promoting all three. That seemed to do the trick—until the offeree discovered that her two colleagues had received equal treatment, whereupon she accepted the outside offer in a huff. Sad though it is, self-esteem may depend on peer comparison.

There is no such thing as a typical career; academic institutions are diverse and disciplines are different. Nevertheless, it may be useful to compare two faculty members of different ages in the same institution and the same discipline. Such a comparison may reveal some other, equally important differences: of seniority, of "cohort experience," and of background history and training—differences associated not with the institution but with individuals and their histories.

Our hypothetical case is set in the Department of Psychology at Stratford College, a medium-sized (enrollment 2,400) private liberal arts college. Although it has several masters degree programs, it is primarily an undergraduate institution, and most of the students are resident. Stratford is reasonably well endowed and has been able to attract both an able student body and a faculty that is unusually distinguished for an institution of its size and scope.

Professor Averill White, aged sixty, has been at Stratford for almost his entire career. A social psychologist, he is the author of a standard textbook on socialization theory. During the late 1960s his work on the integration of new managers into large and stable organizations was supported by the social sciences division of the NSF. Since NSF stopped funding such projects, he has been able to pursue his scholarly interests through occasional special assignments from industries, which he courts as a way of staying active. His Ph.D. was completed at an Ivy League university under a distinguished social psychologist. White feels somewhat nostalgic about the liveliness and intensity of the research group to which he belonged there, but he enjoys working on projects with bright undergraduate psychology majors, and Stratford has plenty of them.

White has found that in his later years, his interests are less focused on personal achievement in his research discipline and more directed toward his students. Teaching now gives him special satisfaction, and he engages undergraduates with occasional projects undertaken with and for his industrial sponsors.

White finds that he can comfortably accommodate these commitments and a demanding teaching schedule. His wife, whom he married while still a graduate student, has taken a part-time job since their children left home, but she is still able to take responsibility for household chores and the family finances, as she always has. Their home, purchased in 1963, the year they came to Stratford, is large and comfortable. Even better, the 4.5 percent mortgage has long since been paid off. Thus they have benefited from the rise in home values, as well as from the effect that the excellent stock market performance of the 1980s has had on the investments they made with some textbook royalties. Their financial security is such that White sometimes uses his own funds to get projects started when no sponsor is in sight.

Hilary Johnstone, aged thirty-eight, has just been promoted to full professor. Ten years ago she was the first woman appointed to the Psychology Department faculty. Her outstanding research and teaching record has established her as a major figure on the Stratford faculty. Her specialty is neuropsychology, and she teaches the main-line courses in experimental psychology as well as an advanced seminar on neurobiology.

Unlike most of her colleagues, Johnstone has a research grant from the National Institutes of Health (NIH) that was recently renewed with a high priority score from the study section that reviewed her application—even while some of her counterparts at major research universities were losing theirs. The grant provided the funding for a well-equipped laboratory for electrophysiology and allowed the conversion of other space into a small animal room to house a colony of squirrel monkeys, which she uses in studies on the neural basis of visual recognition. Johnstone does elaborate and challenging experiments. She must prepare the monkeys surgically so that the activity of single nerve cells can be followed with implanted electrodes, and the experiments themselves entail long sessions. Often she must conduct them on weekend days when she isn't teaching, or begin them in the early afternoon and carry them into late evening. Two undergraduate honors students have been with her for a full year and are well-trained, but she herself must be present during much of every experimental session.

This presents significant difficulties. Johnstone is the single mother of a seven-year-old boy. She has arranged reliable after-school care, but on experiment nights she still finds herself worrying about how Bill is doing. They live in one half of a fairly attractive duplex, but the mortgage payments are steep and she wonders how they would manage financially if the child-support payments from Bill's father were ever reduced. At every turn competing obligations seem to be assailing Johnstone.

Notwithstanding the pressure, Johnstone manages to find time for her students, and they respond to the passion she brings to her science and the evident love she has for teaching. Except for the time she spends with Bill, her most rewarding moments are spent working out an experimental kink with her honors students. Despite these joys, she is pondering an offer to head a laboratory at Neumatics, a growing start-up company founded by some old friends. There wouldn't be any teaching, and her research directions would be more restricted. The salary would much better, though, and she would finally have more time to spend with Bill.

White and Johnstone are among the fortunate few, and they plainly deserve to be. They are in a good institution with excellent students; each has achieved a productive and satisfying mix of teaching and research. Each is getting the rewards most academics treasure: the regard of students, the approbation of colleagues, and stimulating work. These brief biographies, in short, reveal devoted people, committed not only to their own intellectual domains but to the success of their students.

But the similarities end there. White has what men of his generation would call a "full life"—a respected career, a happy family life, and financial security. He is able to devote extra time to his students, his consulting work, and his pedagogical innovation without worrying about the next family crisis, or about some looming financial hardship. For the nonprofessional parts of his life, his marriage has provided him with an intelligent and devoted associate. Johnstone, in contrast, is besieged with doubt and worry about how things are going outside the lab—to the point of surrendering a career she loves and in which she is highly successful.

This contrast is by no means atypical. There is a huge difference between the career histories of faculty nearing retirement and those at "the lower edge of seniority." These derive in part from cohort effect. Demography is destiny, it is sometimes said, and the stark differences between these two lives provide a telling illustration. White, who was born late in the Depression, was too young to serve in World War II and had a student deferment during the Korean conflict. His age cohort was small and benefited from uncrowded schools and a wide-open job market. Government programs designed primarily to benefit veterans helped others, such as White, with housing subsidies and educational assistance. Early in his career at Stratford the availability of federal funds for student aid, research, and even course development ushered in a kind of Golden Age of academic life. The college prospered, and the atmosphere in which White grew up professionally was one in which optimism prevailed.

Johnstone, by contrast, is a baby boomer. Her experience was one of crowded schools and restricted opportunity. Admission to college was a difficult scramble, and by the time she graduated from a highly selective midwestern liberal arts college she had accumulated significant debt. Her interest in animal behavior had to be set aside for two years, during which she worked in an opinion research firm. By the time she entered graduate school, competition for funding and laboratory space was intense. Fortunately, Johnstone's graduate school experience was a good one. Her postdoctoral appointment was a long shot, because she had little experience with electrophysiology. But her sponsor was prepared to take a chance, and her two-year fellowship was both a joy and a career-altering experience. The Stratford appointment was just what she wanted.

Johnstone's career at Stratford can accurately be described as meteoric. Despite the obvious satisfactions, however, she has had to cope with an environment much less hopeful and confident than the one that greeted White twenty-five years earlier. During her training she experienced the special difficulties that women in all the professions have faced. Added to these have been changes in the academic environment that White never encountered. Johnstone's colleagues complain regularly about their teaching loads, yet they are unable to obtain outside support for the research they hope to substitute for "too much teaching." That atmosphere, coupled with the chronic challenges of her overcrowded and tense personal life, provides a constant brake against her normal buoyancy.

Johnstone and White, similar in so many respects, are each the product of special periods in the history of the United States and of its academic institutions. Their contrasting backgrounds are quite typical of the differences one might observe between faculty members in their mid-thirties (and younger) and those senior professors approaching retirement in any department, on any campus. Indeed, what is unusual about Johnstone and White is not that their experiences are so different, but that they have resulted in outlooks that are both so positive and constructive.

The examples of White and Johnstone underscore the likelihood that interests will change and careers assume new shapes as faculty members enter different phases in their lives. Johnstone's intense pursuit of her research program, against formidable obstacles, is not atypical of scholars in the logarithmic phase of their intellectual growth. White's more reflective style and his deepening interest in teaching and how to improve it are representative of what happens to many late-career faculty, though surely not to all.

One other difference is worth noting. It is unlikely that White at any point experienced serious reservations about his career choice. Entering graduate school was a natural and immediate sequel to his undergraduate psychology major, and later the Stratford job was one of two or three excellent possibilities his mentor helped arrange for him. In Johnstone's case even the first decision was a struggle. Jobs were scarce, and even though she was one of the lucky ones she was subjected to all the anxieties her labmates were feeling about the future. Two decades earlier she would not have considered a job outside academia; now it seems a distinct possibility. And for many members of her cohort, it is the only prospect.

White and Johnstone have one important piece of history in common. Their careers were launched by the same pivotal decision: to undertake doctoral study in a research university, in the hope of entering careers as scholars and teachers. That decision was made more easily and confidently by White. He applied to only two institutions and was accepted by both, and he received support from private and federal programs. He finished his Ph.D. in four and a half years, a little better than the national average in the early 1960s.

Johnstone, in contrast, was disappointed in two of her graduate school applications and had to finance part of her first year with an outside job and student loans. She served as a teaching assistant for three years before receiving support from an NIH training grant. It took her six years to earn her degree, and at that she beat the national average for her discipline, which had been steadily increasing.

As White entered the job market, a host of opportunities presented themselves. A postdoctoral appointment was one, but he quickly rejected it in favor of an immediate academic appointment. An assistant professorship at a large public West Coast university was very attractive, and White considered it seriously. He had family in the East, however, and a strong preference for a small school. Stratford, on learning of the other offer, raised the ante without really needing to, and White promptly agreed to go to Stratford.

For Johnstone in the mid-1980s the situation was vastly different. A small Pennsylvania state college asked her to interview, but beyond that there was little interest from academic institutions. A research group at a large eastern university had been impressed with her work, and through a friend there she was invited to apply for a postdoctoral fellowship. Coming at the eleventh hour, it seemed like a life preserver.

Professors White and Johnstone, in their professional circumstances as well as in their personal attitudes, reflect the influences of their very different cohort histories. In much the same way, the perceptions of those entering the contemporary academic marketplace are shaped by the conditions under which their own careers developed—by the history of what was popular and what was neglected, of what was supported and what was not.

On the supply side, we find ourselves dealing with a small but important subset of America's higher education enterprise, the hundred or so research universities labeled "RU-1" in the classification developed by Carnegie. These institutions grant a large majority of the academic doctorates in the United States, and are thus responsible for the supply of new faculty members.

The average senior scholar in the leading research universities turns out a Ph.D. student every two or three years. Suppose, then, that the average faculty member in one of the top one hundred research universities produces fifteen Ph.D.s over a forty-year career. Plainly, these students, carefully selected, successful survivors of a tough regime though they are, cannot all get jobs in the top one hundred research universities. Most will be disappointed. Furthermore, the places they are likely to go instead, the vast majority of the more than three thousand other colleges and universities in the United States, are very unlike the institutions in which they trained. Many of them, of course, will not get academic jobs at all.

Thus at each stage of early academic life an aspirant confronts a tight marketplace. What are the opportunities? Will there be a position for me? In what kind of place? These are the same kinds of questions that confront job-seekers in other sectors, but in this case there are more decision points.

In recent years, many young scholars have found the answers to these questions quite dispiriting. Economic models assume that decision-makers always act rationally; that is, that they make realistic estimates of the market for their services, and make economically sound choices to maximize utility. But in academia the circumstances are often highly complex, and the resulting view of the future murky. Nonmonetary factors may be especially important: the lure of intellectual satisfaction is often powerful enough to overwhelm doubts about one's financial future. Graduate mentors may also exert strong influences over student choice, and their objectives are not always the same as those of their tutees. Finally, the past thirty years have seen dramatic fluctuations in both the supply of new Ph.D.s and the number of available faculty positions. Indeed, the rates of change have been so rapid that faulty predictions have been the rule rather than the exception, and responses to false estimates of glut or shortage have added to the volatility of the employment picture.

It all began in the 1960s, an extraordinary period in the history of higher education. Spurred by rapid growth in the federal support of research and by expanding enrollments as the "baby boom" generation approached college age, faculties grew at an average rate of about 7 percent per year. Nearly all this growth represented additions to full-time faculty. Since most of the new appointees entered the junior ranks, turnover was relatively high; the combination of scheduled retirement at age sixty-five and tenure failures created plenty of new slots, and the average age of most university faculties was in the low forties.

It is difficult to pinpoint just when this growth period ended, but 1970 is a date that would satisfy most observers. After that date total faculty size continued to increase, but much more slowly, and the increase was due mainly to the addition of part-time, nontenure-line faculty. Turnover declined, and as the tenure-line faculty aged gradually, the proportion of faculty in the untenured ranks decreased, limiting the number of positions that were available as a result of failures at the tenure line.

In the years that followed, the demographic profile of the faculty changed dramatically, with important consequences both for programs and for institutional budgets. At Stanford between 1969 and 1994, for example, the faculty showed a net gain of 250 full professors but a loss of 60 assistant professors, and the average age of the professoriate increased by more than 5 years.[9] This "graying" of the faculty surely has had important effects on research and on teaching. Numerous studies have been conducted on the relationship between age and productivity (usually measured as publishing activity or success in obtaining financial support for research). In such analyses, research productivity shows a gradual decline with age, but studies of this kind are severely hampered by an endemic confusion between age and cohort. At a given time (say, 1995), all sixty-year-old faculty members will belong to a cohort that has had a particular history of funding, institutional support, and "culture"; that is, experiences that approximate those of Averill White. The cohort that will reach sixty two decades later may be quite different in all these respects—as different as Hilary Johnstone is from White. What we know about the relationship between age and any aspect of professional performance is thus apt to be good for one time only.

The relationship between age and teaching effectiveness is even harder to measure than that between age and research productivity. In general, teaching effectiveness varies in a more complex way and shows more variability among disciplines.[10] Some faculty members in their sixties develop a revived interest in undergraduate education, and redirect much of their effort toward it. But in most cases, the increased age difference between students and faculty is a disadvantage. In the words of Edward Shils, "Teachers over 45 years of age often seem very old to students; they seem remote and sometimes too awe-inspiring."[11]

The impact of faculty aging on university budgets is substantial, but it is often neglected in institutional planning. At a research university in the highest salary category with a faculty of about 1,500, an increase of 5 years in average age would have the effect of adding to the institution's annual budget about $20 million in additional allocations to faculty salaries. In such a place, that would amount to about 5 percent of the operating budget.

Of course a vital question is when—now, even *whether*—faculty members will end their service by retiring. Predictions about faculty demographics became even riskier when, as a result of 1986 amendments to the Age Discrimination in Employment Act, mandatory retirement was abolished for members of college and university faculties, effective in 1994. Prior to 1982, virtually all institutions had required professors to retire at the age of sixty-five. Statutory amendments in 1978 raised the national mandatory retirement ceiling to age seventy, but as a result of university objections, the amendments did not apply to tenured faculty until 1982.

In the decade or so between 1982 and the final "uncapping" of mandatory retirement, universities had a chance to examine the responses of faculty members to this opportunity to extend their working careers. In earlier days many professors were "recalled" to teach specific courses at partial salary, or to continue research projects. Now, for the first time, it became possible for a sixty-five-year-old prospective retiree to continue full employment until age seventy.

The impact of the new law depended in large part on the type of institution. In the liberal arts colleges, retirement at sixty-five or shortly thereafter was the rule. The behavior of professors in the large research universities, however, appeared to depend on economic incentive. Some public institutions had state retirement plans of the "defined-benefit" type. Where such plans exist there is no advantage in extending employment beyond age sixty-five, other than the difference between retirement income and salary. In such places some faculty members retired at sixty-five, others postponed it by two years or so, and some—a slight majority—stayed on until age seventy.

Most private universities, in contrast, have "defined-contribution" benefit plans: the majority of their faculty members still belong to TIAA-CREF, a private nonprofit fund to which the faculty member contributes annually and to which the university makes a "matching" contribution. In many university benefit plans, the institution contributes 10 percent of salary annually, and the faculty member 5 percent, though of course some institutions have more generous benefit plans than others.[12]

At the time of retirement, the investment may be used to purchase an annuity, which then guarantees the retiree a lifetime income. This is subject to an insurance calculation: actuarial tables are used to estimate the likely life span of the retiree, and the annual payment is set on that basis. The expected length of life after retirement is longer for a sixty-five-year-old than for a seventy-year-old by somewhat less than five years, so if the two have investments of equal value on the day of retirement, the annual income of the seventy-year-old will be higher.[13]

Of course the seventy-year-old retiree is also likely to have more money invested by virtue of having worked longer. Now consider the incentives facing a professor who is approaching age sixty-five and thinking about whether or not to retire. Each additional year of service will deliver the following: first, the difference between full salary and retirement income; second, one more year of the university's contribution to the benefit program; third (and by far the most significant), a substantial increment in eventual annuity income. For a senior faculty member such as Professor White, this consideration might not prove dispositive. He has, after all, a substantial income from consulting work. But if Professor Johnstone were approaching that point, her needs might make it very difficult indeed for her to consider retirement.

It is not surprising, then, that faculty members in the private research universities, more than in other kinds of institutions, have chosen to extend their periods of service. Nationally, the average age at retirement in such places has gone from younger than sixty-five to about sixty-seven; and twice as many faculty retire at seventy as at any other age.[14]

What will happen in the new era of fully uncapped employment? In a study of faculty retirement published in 1991, Rees and Smith predicted that "... the effect of uncapping will be much smaller than has been anticipated."[15] Their conclusion was based in part on surveys in which older faculty members were queried about their retirement plans, and in part on the behavior and satisfaction levels of faculty who had already retired. It may not, however, apply to retirements scheduled for the more distant future. The cohort now clustered at or just below retirement age is uniquely well favored economically compared with those that will follow it. Furthermore, the real-world behavior of faculty members suggests that they do not work out their own retirement economics carefully until the moment is upon them. Few of my sixty-year-old colleagues, for example, would be able to evaluate the impact of decreased annuity years on their retirement incomes if the question were sprung on them today. As they approach the decision point and work through the details, the attractiveness of continued employment is likely to grow.

There are indications that it may already be growing. In a preliminary survey of 1,300 faculty members from 4 colleges, Ashenfelter and Card report—"tentatively"—that the end of mandatory retirement in 1994 led to an immediate decrease in voluntary retirement rates.[16] At the University of Washington, 26 faculty members reached the age of 70 during 1995–96; of these, more than half (14) chose to remain on full-time duty.[17] Stanford and the University of Michigan are reporting similar figures.

Another important influence on present vacancy rates is the state of the economy. If one is considering retirement against the background of recent inflation, one is inclined to be worried about the adequacy of pension income. The external economy affects not only the retirement plans of faculty, however—a point emphasized by Ashenfelter and Card in their study—but also the behavior of the institutions. Colleges and universities are experiencing much more stringent resource limitations, and as a result many of them are leaving vacancies produced by retirement unfilled.

At present, then, we have an aging faculty, fewer academic openings, and the likely prospect that, from the point of view of job-seekers, things will get worse rather than better. With that gloomy prospect before us, we turn to the supply side of the marketplace.

Before briefly considering the recent history of doctoral work in American universities, it is worth emphasizing what a deep and often frustrating commitment it is. The graduate student's experience depends heavily on the good will and conscientiousness of a single mentor. It requires total immersion in a demanding scholarly discipline, yet often involves the distraction of fulfilling a research assistantship, in which the student works not necessarily on his or her own project but on the professor's, or a teaching assistantship, in which the student is responsible for undergraduate instruction with varying degrees of help and guidance. It takes a long time to complete graduate work (even in the Golden Age of the late 1960s, when support for graduate study was at its zenith, the average was more than five years), and the chances of failure are dauntingly high. Nationally, only about a quarter of the students who embark on the Ph.D. actually finish one. The experience is often lonely and may be profoundly alienating. Yet at its best, with an inspiring and compassionate mentor, it can be positive and even transforming.

As mentioned earlier, in the immediate postwar years, when my own generation of scholars was in training, the occupational horizon seemed limitless, and that did much to quell the dissatisfactions normally associated with the life of a graduate student. Universities were expanding. Federal funds were flowing to support research, and there appeared to be an abundance of employment opportunities on the post-Ph.D. horizon.

At that time, and during the rest of the Golden Age, doctorate production in the United States increased dramatically, and that growth continued until the early 1970s. After about 1973, there was a significant drop in most fields. The humanities led the decline, with a dramatic falloff; among the sciences, the life sciences alone avoided decreases, although even there the growth rates flattened out. In the social sciences, the only fields not to suffer declines were those with strong clinical or nonuniversity employment sectors, such as psychology and education.[18]

The expansion in number of programs, as distinct from the number of students produced, behaved a little differently. Program growth was rapid during the 1960s. In the early 1970s, as doctoral production declined, the number of programs continued to increase, albeit at a much slower pace. It appears that aspiring "secondary" institutions, still in the thrall of the Golden Age, were adding doctoral programs as a means of increasing institutional prestige. The fraction of doctorates awarded to the top-rated departments (those ranked in the first twenty by peer observers) declined significantly, and the proportion of all doctorates awarded by "Research I" universities decreased as well.

We are left to ponder the paradox of decreasing production despite program expansion. It is not clear why the number of doctorates granted fell off, but at least two contributing causes suggest themselves: the time required to complete the degree rose during that period, and the already high "failure" rates appear to have become even higher.

A separate question concerns the declining rates of application for graduate admission, especially for the most highly ranked programs. One possible explanation is that loss of support for graduate study restricted the supply. Decreases in the level of support for competitive national fellowships offered by the NSF and the NIH, combined with the loss of the National Defense Education Act and the privately financed Woodrow Wilson Fellowships, constricted support. Another possibility is that entering students accurately perceived the coming downturn in employment possibilities and selected other career avenues instead. Fewer graduates of the top-ranked colleges were indicating an interest in academic careers, and in fact the applicant pools for admission to doctoral programs shrank. The much better health of the "clinical" doctoral programs in the social sciences supports this interpretation.

The number of new Ph.D.s stopped declining in the mid-1980s and began a slow recovery. Between 1986 and 1992, the number of doctorates granted increased at an average of 3 percent per year—4 percent in public institutions and 1 percent in private. In 1993, it reached an all-time high of just under 40,000, which was due in part to the desire of faculty members in the research universities for graduate students to support their research programs.[19] As the availability of fellowship funds became limited, an increasing proportion of graduate students were supported by research and teaching assistantships. This had the effect of lengthening the time it took to obtain a Ph.D.: the median rose from 5.3 years in 1968 to 7.1 years in 1993.[20] And as the number of American students interested in doctoral study declined, the gap was filled, especially in the sciences, by graduate students from abroad.

A few sharp critics, notably the physicist David Goodstein, the provost at the California Institute of Technology, observe that the system of academic training preserves the illusion that things are really all right—that continued doctoral production will eventually be needed, and that the academy should only wait things out.[21] Such hopeful views were reinforced by a number of predictions from authoritative sources at the beginning of the 1990s. The NSF and its director, Erich Bloch, forecast significant shortages of scientists and engineers in the 1990s and beyond; subsequently, their studies became the subject of critical hearings in the Congress.[22] The former NSF director Richard Atkinson, in his presidential address to the American Association for the Advancement of Science (AAAS), also projected a large shortfall and called it a "national crisis in the making."[23] The official character of these predictions lent them initial credibility and contributed to the depth of the anger that followed their failure to materialize. On today's electronic Young Scientists Network one can still hear a chorus of discontent from cyberspace, much of it focused on "The Myth"—the term used for the falsely optimistic employment future portrayed in the projections.

These forecasts, of course, dealt with the sciences alone, and did not restrict themselves (at least on the demand side) to academic employment. A careful study by Bowen and Sosa, published in 1989, made projections confined to the academic sector based on anticipated retirements and underlying demographic changes.[24] The results suggested that the mid- to late-1990s would see an excess of demand over supply. That study, however, could not have anticipated either the full uncapping of mandatory retirement for tenured faculty or the economic retractions in higher education during the early 1990s. Both caused constrictions in demand that Bowen and Sosa could not have foreseen.

The function of projection is to provide a benchmark against which to observe the adaptive behavior of systems. Several responses have followed the unexpected departure from the Bowen-Sosa projection. One was a dramatic rise in postdoctoral fellowships, especially in the sciences. These appointments provide additional training for two or three years, and for the new Ph.D. they provide the advantage of a holding pattern for entry into a tight labor market. For the faculty member they yield a different benefit: an experienced junior colleague is made available at a cost that rivals and may soon fall below that of a graduate research assistant.[25]

A generation ago, a new Ph.D. in biology, for example, would have completed the degree in about five years and moved directly into an academic appointment. Today the degree would require seven or eight years, often followed by a two-year postdoctoral fellowship. The young scientist's entry into academic employment has thus been delayed for four years. As a natural consequence, the average age of first academic appointments has risen dramatically. And the large and growing pool of postdoctoral fellows and special, nontenure-line faculty represents a surge tank in the employment pipeline that will make it even more difficult for new doctorates to secure positions.

A related consequence has been a radical restructuring of the research venture, especially in the sciences. A new academic class, the quasi-permanent research scholars, has arisen. These scholars have appointments in large projects or institutes in the university, and work under the direction of a senior faculty member. Under the rules of most universities they cannot apply independently for project support, although they surely participate in graduate education and training and often even contribute significantly to undergraduate teaching. The growth in this category of employment has led to significant intellectual enrichment, but also to an array of institutional problems. Scholars in this category may view themselves as being just as able and experienced as members of the regular faculty, and that self-perception is often reinforced by their research record. In their own research groups they play vital roles, yet in the institution they are treated as second-class citizens. It is not surprising that they are frequently unfulfilled and dissatisfied, nor that they are a significant source of grievances in the university about insufficient credit, status, and the ownership of ideas.

Simultaneously, we have witnessed dramatic growth in the size of the nation's "para-faculty"—teachers, most of them would-be scholars, who supplement the tenure-line faculty by accepting employment for a short term, or to teach a single course. Some of them hold more than one job simultaneously, perhaps in two community colleges or in a comprehensive institution and a small urban liberal arts college. Others become peripatetic; on the Pacific Coast anxious graduate students speak of this pattern as the "I-5 alternative" because it so often involves positions taken *seriatim* at the dozens of institutions located along that corridor. All have something in common: they are frustrated and disappointed at being overworked, underpaid, and underappreciated.[26]

The results of the employment crunch can be seen everywhere, and the folklore is abundant. In 1994, half as many new Harvard Ph.D.s in the arts and sciences went immediately into academic employment as had entered in the previous year. At least one medical school has a special program for admission of candidates who already have a doctorate in another academic discipline, and the nation's law schools are increasingly populated with students who hold a Ph.D. but have been disappointed in their career opportunities in academia. (These multiple-degree seekers may, of course, simply be exchanging one overcrowded sector for another!)

With the decline in federal support for graduate study, doctoral students have increasingly been supported by teaching assistantships and by research appointments on government grants and contracts. As a result, graduate students now provide indispensable support for the research enterprise. Indeed, most large programs in the natural sciences, and some in the social sciences, would shrink drastically or even collapse without them. The resulting interdependence of faculty members and the graduate students who support their research entails a number of complications for the relationship between student and mentor, however. The faculty member's role is obviously in some conflict: on the one hand, there is a responsibility to the student, to give him or her the opportunity to finish the degree promptly and to take "ownership" of a piece of independent work; and on the other hand, there is a pressing desire to advance the projects of the research group. For the graduate student, it too often comes down to a painful choice: work on the professor's project so I can get supported, or work on my thesis so I can get out.

The results often lead to trouble. Over the past two decades, a number of research universities have seen efforts by graduate assistants to organize bargaining units. A serious struggle of this kind arose at Yale during the academic year 1995–96. The graduate assistants argued that resource constraints were forcing more obligations on them, without a corresponding improvement in benefits. The increased demands to teach or to do research on faculty projects confirmed their feeling that they were functioning as employees. In response, Yale and other institutions argued that they were students, fulfilling academic requirements. Whether that position will persuade the National Labor Relations Board or not, it is apt to evoke cynical laughter from those graduate students—and there are many—who feel exploited by their university. Similarly, the increasing frequency of disputes over the origin of research ideas or data reflects a tightening tension over whether graduate students are independent scholars or merely extra hands for a project.[27]

Precisely because the shortage of academic jobs is threatening to become chronic, the old standard assumption that all those entering Ph.D. programs are headed for academic careers in teaching and research now turns out to be wrong more often than it is right. In some disciplines, alternative careers in government or industry have always been possible. And sometimes new opportunities open up, converting a discipline from one of strictly "academic interest" to one in which there are alternative routes to fulfilling one's research ambitions. A good example is found in modern molecular biology and neurobiology, where an explosion of basic research activity in proprietary firms has opened up a whole new array of attractive choices for people like Johnstone.

Some well-publicized analyses, emphasizing the present glut of new Ph.D.s and taking a gloomy view of future opportunities, have tended to ignore the nonacademic avenues. A study by Massy and Goldman in 1995 found an oversupply of doctorates in engineering, math, and some sciences. The authors estimated that production averaged 25 percent, contradicting earlier predictions of long-term shortages. The press dropped the adjective "some" in reporting the results and failed to note that the study was a simulation and not an actual measure of production or vacancies. Thus its relevance to policy decision making depends on the validity of its assumptions. The study also virtually ignored nonacademic demand, and thus found the largest "gaps" in exactly those fields (computer science, electrical and mechanical engineering) in which nonacademic employment is greatest.[28]

Part of the problem with graduate education in the research universities is that, except in those fields in which industry employment is the norm, scant attention is given to nonacademic options. The high school English teacher with a Ph.D. who really wanted to teach at the college level, and the industrial chemist who longed for a position in a research university, feel abused by the system that forced them into an alternative less desirable than what they had been led to expect. Their disappointment is exacerbated by attitudes they encountered during their own doctoral studies; the best jobs are thought to be in institutions just like the one in which they were trained. Failure to secure one of these is disappointing not only for the student but also for the faculty adviser who loses an academic offspring.

In response to evidence that a surplus of Ph.D.s is being produced, the most prestigious institutions invariably argue that it is other, less excellent institutions that should cut back production by limiting admissions. The difficulty, of course, is that in the academic universe no institution can admit that it is not excellent. The result is not only a recipe for glut but an invitation to bitter disappointment.

Despite the tight competition and frequent disappointments that today's academic marketplace generates, newly minted scholars attack it resolutely—and many succeed. How they search for jobs and how they are selected for them are important matters for the future of the academic enterprise. Generalities are risky, though, because the marketplace varies widely from one discipline to another.

Sylvia Warren, a hypothetical graduate student, is finishing a doctorate in developmental biology in a distinguished department at a public research university in the Midwest. Her work has been under the direction of a well-known neurobiologist who studies the development of specific neural connections among cultured cells. The first decision Sylvia will make, with the help of her adviser, will be whether to enter the academic job market right away or to do a postdoctoral fellowship. In her field the latter is by far the likelier alternative these days.

If Sylvia decides to do a postdoc, the arrangement will probably be made through a connection between her major professor and a scientist in the same field at a similar institution. The postdoctoral adviser may well be interested in Sylvia because she brings to their work a technique in which he is not expert; or it may be that he has encountered a problem that she is especially well qualified to pursue. He will supply the equipment and support from federal training or program grant funds available to him. How much independence Sylvia gets will vary with the situation, and may be the subject of some negotiation up front. In many ways, the postdoctoral fellowship is an extension of graduate study, with a marginal increase in independence—and a high degree of utility to the senior scientist. In Sylvia's field the work, even if she does it all herself, will be published jointly. And her postdoctoral adviser will become (at least under the best circumstances) a partner with her former major professor in guiding her career.

Let's suppose that Sylvia is one of the rare ones—a biologist who has developed an outstanding thesis, already has significant publications, and wants to test the market right away. She and her major professor will communicate with colleagues in other institutions, respond to advertisements in *Science* and specialty journals, and use every opportunity to present their work at national meetings. Because her thesis results are unusually exciting, and particularly because her adviser is a prestigious scientist with substantial political clout, she may receive several opportunities to visit other campuses and deliver a "job seminar"—an account of her work intended for an audience of critical specialists.

Sylvia recognizes right away that she is competing with others who have more experience. She has received an invitation to deliver a seminar at a university where her adviser knows the developmental biologist well. Her adviser's intelligence network indicates that there are two others on the university's "short list." One has done a two-year postdoc at a research institute; the other, an unusual candidate, is turning to the molecular biology of neural development after five years at an outstanding biotechnology firm in the San Francisco Bay Area.

Sylvia's visit goes well. The seminar is followed by some critical questioning, but her responses are well-conceived and she even has the opportunity to deliver some new experimental data that she has been holding back in the hope of getting just the right question. Afterward, several faculty members take her out for drinks and are eager to probe the implications of her work at greater depth. It is a stimulating, even inspiring encounter. In one respect, however, she is disappointed in the visit. Sylvia has been a particularly successful graduate teaching assistant; she served as the head teaching assistant in the developmental biology course, and was even asked to give a week of lectures when her major professor was away at an international scientific meeting. These went so well that Sylvia hoped to have an opportunity to demonstrate this skill during her visit. But when she had suggested this to her hosts in pre-visit discussions, they had shown no interest. In fact, her efforts to discuss the teaching assignments that go with the position are met with vague, almost casual responses.

After several weeks of silence following her return, Sylvia learns that one of the other candidates has been offered the position and has accepted it. Her annoyance that no one has bothered to tell her directly of this outcome fades quickly, because she is already mulling over two other possibilities. One is a postdoctoral fellowship with a very distinguished group at another university, arranged through the efforts of her major professor. The other is a teaching position at a highly selective liberal arts college located in the Middle Atlantic states.

Her adviser strongly urges her to take the fellowship. "I know of your interest in teaching, and I respect it. But you have a real talent for research, and if you throw yourself into the kind of commitments they'll expect you to meet at the college, you'll never get much beyond your thesis work. I wouldn't even bother to go there." With some trepidation, Sylvia accepts the invitation to visit anyhow. At the college she meets a lively, interesting group of professors, though the faculty is small, with only one other person interested in development. Her research seminar is successful and the questions are interesting, often challenging, and mostly from undergraduates. She learns that of the seven faculty members in biology, four have research grants—and two of the remaining three have active programs of one sort or another. Best of all, she is asked to guest-lecture in a course, and afterward is taken out with the students to a local coffeehouse.

The conversation at the coffeehouse is only partly about the class; it touches on a range of issues, and focuses especially on the differences between undergraduate education in a liberal arts college and in a research university. She finds the students curious, even wistful, about what it must be like to be an undergraduate biology major in Sylvia's department, where there are thirty faculty members and a plethora of research opportunities. But at the same time they seem to have a fierce loyalty to their own choices, and they cannot say enough about the individual experiences they have had with the faculty at the college.

Sylvia leaves with mixed emotions. The college environment appeals to her greatly, both because the place is stimulating and friendly and because it is at the right scale. She has also grown impatient with what has seemed like a prolonged period of intellectual dependency; here, at least, she would become an adult. On the other hand, the postdoctoral fellowship is a good one, in a laboratory known to be humane as well as scientifically first-rate. Her mentor and peers expect her to take the fellowship because they see it as a fulfillment of her training up until now. She is, after all, a person of high promise. This additional investment of time should, they argue, put her in a position to choose among the widest possible array of alternatives.

Sylvia is indeed one of the lucky ones. She has choices—attractive ones.

But she is also in a quandary. She loves teaching and has an immediate opportunity to join a department and an institution that value it. There are no graduate students at the college, to be sure, but the undergraduates are wonderful; indeed, more students at liberal arts colleges go on to academic careers in science than do those at the great research universities. Research may be difficult, but plainly it's possible if one is energetic and ambitious, and Sylvia knows that she is both. But her research future will surely be more secure, and her opportunities greater, if she prolongs her training.

For the moment, let's leave Sylvia in the middle of her quandary and move across her university's campus to the English Department, where Brian Carey, a fifth-year student now finishing a promising dissertation on Chaucer, is attacking the job market for the second time. Brian's first effort took place a year ago, well before his thesis was scheduled for completion. Like a number of other students in the humanities, he had decided to run a "trial heat" by applying for a number of jobs. The results had been mildly encouraging: three institutions had written for references, and one, though hardly a top-ranked department, had invited him to the campus for a seminar.

Brian thus enters the market in this, his last and critical year, with guarded optimism. With some help from his adviser, he has selected some twenty-five institutions from the vital job source in his field—the position list published by the Modern Language Association (MLA) in early October. He has dispatched a letter of application to each. By custom, this application is actually a rather complex package. It includes a cover letter in which the candidate presents (under a cloak of appropriate modesty) an account of his accomplishments. Most humanities departments advise that this be no longer than a page. Attached is a resume (or, as it is customarily called in academic circles, a curriculum vitae). This will include, in addition to the usual information about education, jobs, and personal data, virtually everything the candidate has done that might appeal to an appointment committee. In his cover letter Brian has indicated that he has a writing sample that he would be happy to send on request; he also cites letters of reference that are available on file in his university's placement center. His letter closes with this appeal: "I plan to be at the annual meeting of the Modern Language Association in New York on December 27, 28, and 29. I would be most grateful for the opportunity of an interview with you at your convenience on one of those dates."

Brian's thesis adviser, a busy and often preoccupied medieval scholar who has been spending part of the year on a visiting appointment at an East Coast university, has told him that it would be best to wait before doing any politicking with the adviser's friends at several of the more promising places. "Now isn't the proper time," the adviser says in early November during a telephone call from Cambridge. "If the right places interview you at MLA, maybe I can make a few calls."

Brian then sits back and waits. In the two months that intervene between the mailing of applications and the MLA meeting, he receives some encouraging news. Seven institutions have asked for writing samples, and of these five have also requested his letters of reference from the placement. center. By early December he has two firm appointments for interviews at MLA, but two of the universities in which he is most interested have not arranged interviews—even though they are among those that requested his letters and writing samples. Brian wonders whether he should call, but is advised against it by two young faculty friends. They argue that as many interviews are worked out at the meeting itself as are arranged beforehand. "Go to New York and make sure they know where to find you," says one of them. "If necessary, drop them a note there. If you call now they'll think you're bugging them, and it will turn them off." Brian senses that he is hearing the voice of experience, and so he waits apprehensively for the meeting date.

On the day after Christmas, Brian boards a crowded airliner at O'Hare Airport. His seatmate in 34D turns out to be a friendly older professor in comparative literature from another university. Brian asks for some advice about securing interviews at the meeting from the two recalcitrant institutions. His seatmate suggests that he use the meeting schedule itself as a way of initiating contact. "Here, let's pull out the program. If you want to jog people about an interview, find out when the right guy is giving a paper and go to it." He scans the pages for the first day and locates something interesting. "Bingo. Professor Harbison from one of those places is talking tomorrow morning at ten. Look, just go—and find a way to ask him a question afterward. He's even a medievalist, so surely you can say something that will interest him."

At the meeting, Brian follows this advice and it pays off. The medievalist is taken with his question, and they talk for five minutes. Brian deftly points out that the position at his university is open to all fields and periods; he does not need to add how nice it would be if the position just happened to go to another medievalist. On the spot, he is invited for an interview the next day.

That leaves his other top choice unaccounted for. He cannot find an occasion for initiating a contact, and so decides that he will have to wait. His interview with Professor Harbison's institution is quick and not very satisfying: he finds himself in a room with eight faculty members who pepper him with questions, few of which suggest a deep familiarity with his work or much interest in the questions it addresses. The other two interviews, later in the afternoon, are similar. As he awaits a potential contact from the one remaining university, Brian is both tense and discouraged.

Brian never hears from the last university and leaves the meeting with a sense of failure. Two weeks later, however, his spirits are revived by a call from one of the two colleges with which he had interviewed. The chairman of the department greets him warmly and asks if he would be willing to fly back for a visit at his large, public "comprehensive" university—a former teachers' college in the wheat belt. The university has grown to a large size, and though it has only limited graduate enrollment the opportunity looks attractive. Brian visits and is surprised at how well he is treated. Not only is he asked to lecture on his Chaucer work; he also guest-teaches in the medieval studies seminar for advanced undergraduates. They are lively. To Brian's surprise three other faculty members from the English and History Departments are also present, and there are even indications that all three attend regularly. After the class the four go to lunch at the Faculty Club, where they are joined by the dean of Arts and Sciences. The dean tells Brian that there is a strong tradition of good teaching at the university and interrogates him carefully about his own experience and level of commitment.

At the end of the visit, Brian is impressed with the dedication of his prospective colleagues and the degree to which they share a view of their task. Apparently they feel the same way about him: three days after his return, he gets a call in which both the English Department chair and the dean participate. They offer him an assistant professorship, and the enthusiasm behind their persuasion efforts is obvious.

Brian's adviser has returned from the East, and Brian makes an appointment to talk with him shortly afterward. The adviser tells him that a comprehensive state university is not really a suitable place for a first-rate Ph.D.

from a research university: the graduate program is small, the undergraduates not highly selected, and the library "not at all outstanding in our period." Brian tries to describe his enthusiasm for the academic culture he found there, but his adviser doesn't seem to understand what he's saying. "Of course it's your decision," he says, "but I think you'd be much better off to stay here for another year. I'm sure I can arrange an interim instructorship for you, and you can help me with my course."

Brian now joins Sylvia in quandary-land. He might do better to wait and try again, but the prospect of being his adviser's lackey in a course he is well known for neglecting seems unappealing. Besides, there is something heartwarming and even exciting about the collective dedication he glimpsed during his visit to the university. Wouldn't it be better to get out and try something?

These two stories tell us something about institutional behavior, and even more about the situations in which job candidates in academia find themselves. They are unrealistic, however, in at least one respect: both candidates have job offers, and even a choice between alternatives. Most graduate students are not so fortunate. At best they will have one prospect, often not very appealing, and many will have to turn to other alternatives.

Job hunting under any circumstances is a trying and stressful process, and in some respects academic employment markets may be more sensitive and compassionate than others. But in a nonprofit enterprise that regards itself as having values more humane than those obtaining "outside," it is distressing to observe the lack of consideration and courtesy that appears from time to time. The lore of the academic marketplace is rich with stories of unanswered phone calls, unrevealed outcomes, and just plain rude treatment. Mentors also differ widely in their sense of responsibility toward the students they supervise. In these stories, Brian's adviser comes off as indifferent and even a little self-interested, whereas Sylvia's is commendably concerned for her welfare. Despite that contrast, both have a rather firm image of what is an appropriate academic destiny for their scholarly offspring. An institution may be viewed as unsuitable if it is oriented primarily toward undergraduates, or if it simply lacks conventional prestige.

❋ Surely it is a part of academic duty—maybe even the central part—to prepare students realistically for productive and rewarding lives. If we cannot do that realistically for our own doctoral students, we have failed a basic obligation. Yet the scientific community and the universities have both refused to face up to this problem. For the biomedical sciences, which have had the highest growth rate in Ph.D. production of any field, and which clearly have a present oversupply, the 1994 recommendation of the NRC was: "Maintain the annual number of predoctoral awards in the basic biomedical sciences at 1993 levels."[29]

Although the culture of universities is slow to change, and relatively insensitive to obiter dicta from presidents and provosts, there are some administrative devices that could help. Full and honest disclosure of the employment prospects in the field, as best they can be known, is surely one important institutional responsibility. In addition, departments should be required to tell their incoming graduate students several important facts about the history of their training programs before the students make their decisions. The first critical item of information is the percentage of students entering the program during the past decade who have earned their degrees. (It is worth noting that even the National Collegiate Athletic Association (NCAA) now publishes graduation rates for athletes; an equivalent requirement for these heavily recruited prospective scholars does not seem unreasonable!) The second is an accounting of the average time taken to obtain the degree. Finally, the department should report, for each member of some substantial recent cohort of doctoral degree recipients, his or her employment history.

In this arena, the grip of institutional prestige is both powerful and conservative. The hierarchy is maintained partly through the maintenance of a fiction—a disparity between expectation and reality. The most highly regarded institutions behave as though their graduate students can find employment in other places of equivalent rank, and believe that their own prestige partly depends on their doing so. Yet only a handful of the very best can succeed; the others disappoint not only themselves but the parent institutions. It is plainly time for a dose of reality. The research universities are a small minority of the institutions on the higher education scene, but their influence is enormous; the way they train the future faculty for the whole enterprise sets its values. No more leveraged version of academic duty exists anywhere. If change is to happen, this is where it begins.

TO TEACH

RESPONSIBILITY to students is at the very core of the university's mission and of the faculty's academic duty. In recent times, however, research and innovation have been assuming larger roles in the American university. This probably represents a transitional state, and will be followed by the gradual achievement of a new balance in which the university's primary products are people, with technologies secondary, and in which research and scholarship are more tightly interwoven with our responsibilities for educating young men and women.

Of the many expectations that society has of the modern university, the most important is that it will teach well. That expectation shrouds many different versions of what the product of a university education should be: culturally aware, analytical, intellectually curious, employable, and capable of leadership.

In interviews conducted by then-President Frank Rhodes of Cornell and a group of colleagues, business and government leaders were asked to identify their concerns about higher education in the early 1990s. There was considerable praise for the accomplishments of American universities, but among the criticisms two predominated. The first had to do with the perceived failure of the universities to hold back costs and restrain the growth of tuition. The second focused on a conviction that the primary mission of undergraduate education had fallen into neglect. Nothing could be more destructive of the prestige of higher education than a growing sense on the part of the public that attention to this function has slipped. Nothing is more restorative than the legends that grow around inspiring, imaginative, and influential teaching. And even in a world in which research seems to get most of the attention, faculty members feel deeply rewarded if they sense that they have made a difference in the lives of their students.

To be a teacher is to be many things: a communicator of fact, a coach for skill improvement, an inspirer of creative insight or a thoughtful guide to analytical thought, a professional mentor, and many more. In making lists like this we tend to emphasize the things that happen in the classroom, but if we ask young people about their lives as students, and in particular if we trouble to inquire about the influences that were important to them, they usually tell us about one or a very few special teachers who made a difference in their lives. More often than not these accounts are deeply personal and make reference to terms such as "role model." If we ask, in short, about the influence of teachers rather than about what they do, we realize that in many cases they are functioning as moral teachers, making a difference in the way students choose to conduct their lives.

As for the students, it is plain that they enter college or university expecting and indeed even yearning for that kind of guidance. This is especially true of those entering the most selective four-year institutions. Each year, the ACE and UCLA, under the direction of Professor Alexander Astin, survey the cohort of students planning to matriculate in the nation's universities. This massive research effort yields data on the ethnic and religious makeup of the national student body, on family income and previous activities, and—most important for our purposes—on the intentions, hopes, and expectations that students are bringing with them to college. The data are broken down by type of institution, and every college and university receives its own data set so that it can compare its prospective freshmen with the national cohort and with those students going to similar places.

The results are a wonderful source of encouragement for those of us who occasionally find ourselves getting a little jaded about academic work. Far from being dedicated careerists, the students entering college in 1993 wanted to improve their minds more than to improve their incomes. On a long list of objectives considered essential or very important to them, those most often listed were to raise a family; to become authorities in their own field; to develop a philosophy of life; and to help others in difficulty. Students entering the more selective colleges and universities tended to rank these objectives higher; for such students, "learning more about things" was almost twice as important a reason for going to college as was "making more money." These students came to the university with high expectations. Well over 80 percent of freshmen entering the nation's most selective four-year colleges estimate that the chances are very good that they will be satisfied with their college.

As they approach their first encounters with university faculty, then, these able, highly motivated students have some firm ideas about what they want to happen. In contrast to the popular view, they do not believe that they are pulling in at an intellectual service station. Occupational preparation is not what they're after; they hope for meaningful contact with thoughtful elders—faculty members who can help them develop as individuals. We know that such experiences are best generated through close contact.

But it is plain that many faculty members do not arrive at the university eager, or even prepared, to take up this kind of responsibility. Indeed, it appears that many of them regard it as entirely outside their domain. In this respect there is a real, and troubling, confusion about what constitutes the nature and extent of faculty work. The public and the entering students believe that faculty will be engaged primarily with teaching; not only lecturing but mentoring and counseling as well. In contrast, many of the faculty members believe that their own scholarly work will absorb much, perhaps most, of their time and their intellectual energy.

The problem is complex. In the first place, the general public is confused about university-level teaching and how hard it is. That confusion is aptly summarized in the story of the senator (who could as well be any other elected official) in conversation with the professor at the senator's state university. The senator asks the faculty member, "How many hours do you teach?" The latter, knowing that he has to make it look good, calculates his undergraduate course meetings, the once-a-week laboratory, and throws in a rather generous estimate for his small graduate seminar. "Nine hours," he replies proudly. "Long day," says the senator. "Fortunately, it's light work."

Of course it isn't. Lectures are hard to develop, especially when they are well done and supported by strong materials. Good editorial criticism of student papers is a demanding and difficult task. Then there are the added burdens of developing good examinations and grading them, writing recommendations, and the like. Almost no one outside the academy knows how heavy the workload really is.

Indeed, for the conscientious first-term teacher the workload can be daunting—especially in an institution in which the pressures to do more and better research are heavy and perceived to be rising. A not atypical new assistant professor at one engineering school regularly worked seventy to seventy-five-hour weeks; he estimated that each lecture required between eight and eleven hours of preparation time. This professor happened to be very comfortable with computer technology, and part of his initial investment was the development of more than a thousand hours' worth of computer-generated instructional graphics. Few entrepreneurs starting a new business would make a heavier commitment to the task of getting started.

Yet in launching these initiates on the sea of academic duty, we seldom set clear expectations about the work or about the quality of their performance. Admirable as is the level of self-motivation in the preceding example, it derived little or nothing from institutional direction. In the dialog among faculty members, and between faculty members and "the administration," the emphasis is clearly on rights and not on responsibilities. Teaching loads may be set, but at the vital level of what faculty members really owe their students, little is said. Indeed, there is every reason for faculty members to conclude, from signals sent by their institutions, that the expectations of citizenship are set very low. The very fact that "professional responsibility" is taught in the university to everyone except those headed for the academic profession is a powerful message in itself. The advice that newly appointed faculty members are most likely to receive, from either a department chair or a sympathetic senior colleague, is: "Concentrate on your research and forget the rest of that stuff until you're tenured." This may be wise advice, but it certainly doesn't reinforce devotion to the needs of students.

Indeed, expectations about teaching commitments have changed significantly over the past two decades. Henry Rosovsky, ending his second term as dean of the Faculty of Arts and Sciences at Harvard, noticed the change. He had an unusual vantage point: having had one extraordinarily successful term as dean and having left the position, he was recalled after a lapse of seven years. In his final report to the Faculty of Arts and Sciences two years later, Rosovsky was unusually blunt in pointing out that rules regarding absences from campus, teaching loads, and student office hours were often honored in the breach, and that in general the level of faculty commitment to such duties had slipped markedly. He said, "It is my distinct impression—'firm belief' would perhaps be a better expression—that there has been a secular decline of professorial civic virtue in the Faculty of Arts and Sciences."[1]

At present, the measure of commitment to instruction rests on "teaching load," a concept that sounds straightforward but is more complex than it appears. The phrase itself is troublesome; it portends a sense of onerousness about the duty that is at the heart of an academic appointment. A more serious problem is that no commonly understood, equitable system of academic bookkeeping permits one to compare teaching loads fairly. There is lecture and there is laboratory; there is the seminar and there is advising; there is the big course and the little one. To boil such a heterogeneous teaching universe down into dicta like "four courses per faculty member each year" is to create a strange and confusing stew—and to launch a thousand arguments.

Another problem with teaching-load calculations is that they are basically process measures, not output measures. For more than two years I found myself in charge of a federal regulatory agency, one primary duty of which was to create rules for manufacturers that would ensure that their products (drugs or medical devices or canned vegetables) did not constitute risks to human health. The most common mistake the agency made was to devise detailed technical requirements governing good manufacturing practice. The result was that such requirements froze technologies in place instead of giving manufacturers an opportunity to find new ways of meeting the objective at lower cost. An approach gaining more favor today is to set requirements for the *outcome*. In the teaching context, a useful metaphor is that the load matters less than how far one moves it.

Rather than set arbitrary teaching loads for each faculty member, the dean or provost should enter into negotiations with a department to establish what its total obligation to undergraduate students is, including the vitally important individual contacts such as advising and the supervision of independent study. In the course of the negotiations, the department would be forced to review and evaluate its curriculum, the kinds of educational opportunities it offers, and the engagement of individual faculty with different portions of the task. In the end there would be a clear understanding about what the department is responsible for. For its part, the department would be able to meet those responsibilities in a flexible way, assigning the best lecturers to large lower-division courses and the best small-group seminar leaders to courses of that kind. The administration would have a more realistic set of commitments from the department, and a clear right to monitor its progress in meeting them.

By making departments accountable for meeting well-defined obligations to students, the institution would also become more inclusive in its definition of what constitutes teaching. Here I am talking not merely about the scope of teaching activities beyond the classroom—advising, career counseling, writing letters of recommendation, and the like—but also about bridging the well-advertised gulf between instruction and research. Indeed, within the formal, curricular part of teaching there is room for a synthesis between the two.

In a valuable report from the Carnegie Foundation for the Advancement of Teaching entitled "Scholarship Reconsidered," Ernest Boyer has sketched out the terrain of this overlap. Great teachers exhibit, in their teaching, forms of creativity that may not usually be thought of as research, but nevertheless analyze, synthesize, and present knowledge in new and effective ways.[2] After all, the history of how we view serious academic and intellectual work is full of shifts and changes. Emerson's 1837 manifesto to Phi Beta Kappa at Harvard, from whose title the journal *American Scholar* takes its name, urged one such transition—from "the learning of other lands" to an approach much more oriented to the worlds of nature and action. What it means to be a scholar has varied not only with time but with place, as the broader debate over the proper locus and form of "intellectual life" in our society clearly indicates. Can we afford to be stiffly restrictive about our definitions of scholarly work at a time when one of our best American historians admits that much of the most valuable modern history is being written by journalists?[3]

In the appointments process, committees might be asked to consider some or all of the following: software designed for teaching, but unusual in the way it deals with what is known; critical or synthetic analyses of a field; textbooks, where they take a novel or especially effective approach;

case materials or studies that present a policy issue in new light; or even videos aimed at increasing popular understanding of an issue. These might be assembled by the candidate or a committee of colleagues into a special portfolio devoted to "forms of scholarship related to teaching," or—perhaps better—"scholarship beyond that reported in peer-reviewed journals." Appointment or promotion committees could evaluate such materials in a way that more closely resembles their appraisal of the candidate's research.

The question of what to teach is as controversial as how much to teach. Higher education in the United States has always been perplexed about whether the university should "teach values." Recent pronouncements, especially from the political Right, have taken the academy to task for what is often called "moral relativism"—a refusal to take clear stands on what are seen as the fundamental values of our society. This charge actually sweeps up a netful of concerns about the modern university environment: it is too pluralistic (for example, in its failure to require courses in the Great Works of Western culture); it is too soft and permissive (in its campus rules about drugs and sex); it too readily gives in to the demands of minority students (or women, or gays) to have their "communities" recognized or honored.

This debate is unlikely to end very soon. Indeed, there is some reason to hope that it won't. It has put into play strong and conflicting views about the purposes of higher education and the role of university faculties, and through its challenges it has encouraged their resolution on campus and their recognition off campus. The controversy is heightened by—in fact, would probably not exist without—the enormous changes in the student bodies of our most selective colleges and universities. It was hard not to notice, at the time of my wife's twenty-fifth reunion at Stanford in the spring of 1993, that ethnic minorities constituted only a tiny percentage of her class. In fact, six African-Americans graduated in that year of Martin Luther King's assassination. But in the freshman class that enrolled during her reunion year, only about half the students were "nonminority!"

Such environments are conducive to clashes over values, because everybody brings different ones to the campus. Differences surface all the time without much encouragement, generating one "teachable moment" after another. But with all this struggling and sorting out going on in the community, what is the faculty member's role? Those who don't try to figure that out are going to be spectators in one of the most vital growth zones to be found anywhere in the university.

Clearly, if we are to prepare students for leadership we are required to give them more than knowledge, and even more than the ability to think. Values are important as well—and here I mean the beliefs we hold about what is important, how we ought to act toward one another, and how our society ought to be composed and governed. Although values form and direct conduct, they are not the same thing. Conduct is a description of actual behavior; in the case of the college or university, it is the way in which the campus community is structured and the way people act in and toward it.

Many critics of the university also believe in the centrality of values. Often they inquire as to whether we "teach values," when in fact they mean something quite different. For example, in response to a thoughtful talk by Derek Bok, then the president of Harvard, on the subject of teaching values, Secretary of Education William Bennett said that what he thought was important in this area was getting the drugs off campus. His statement was not about the teaching of values but about the regulation of conduct. To be sure, rules of conduct reflect an institution's views about values. If they display respect for due process and for the openness that is critical to an academic community, that is an important signal. But regulating conduct is not the same as teaching about values.

Indeed, the troubling question, and a source of much confusion, is whether we teach values or teach *about* them. For example, one of the great value questions for contemporary American culture and institutions is this: What balance should be struck between the individual freedom to pursue self-interested ends and the individual's obligation to the larger society? Some would have us preselect an answer to this question and "teach" it as though it had normative status. Of course, such advocates have different opinions about which is the correct value. Libertarians would place great weight on the side of individual freedom, whereas Socialists would place it on the side of service to the state. Most Americans take some intermediate position in which freedom and responsibility, liberty and duty coexist in a delicate, sometimes tense balance.

To offer courses that simply advance a particular position would be bad policy and bad pedagogy. There has, after all, been a history of the development of these ideas. There is also a record of social experiment. We have access to both, and they are the raw material for serious academic study. To analyze the ideas of Locke, Hobbes, Mill, and Rousseau, to compare societies with varying commitments to freedom and obligation—that is the way to form one's own values securely. They can't be short-ordered; they aren't McThoughts. Rather, they have to be formed through laborious analysis, through the intellectual equivalent of gourmet cooking.

Letting students work this out for themselves requires almost exquisite restraint on the part of the teacher/scholar—a careful curb on the natural desire to display one's own convictions. A central purpose of teaching, as of scholarship, is to help students acquire that kind of detachment. Plainly, one of its enemies is too much passion for a particular point of view. That does not mean, of course, that personal belief is out of bounds. Personal and even passionate commitment to the subject is an important source of resonance between a teacher and students. But as to analysis and to the development of theory, some distance is essential.

Another argument for restraint in advocacy has to do with fairness. In this context as in others, the teacher brings formidable powers to the teacher-student relationship. It is almost too easy for a professor to persuade, to impose personal views on those whose state of expectation and relative lack of experience may make them vulnerable. The charismatic but careless professor, with a gaggle of adoring but uncritical followers, is a fairly uncommon but nonetheless troubling campus landmark. In the late 1960s it was both more common and more troubling.

At Stanford in 1971 the university administration charged a member of the English Department faculty, Professor H. Bruce Franklin, with professional misconduct; the president proposed that he be fired. This case, at the end of which Franklin was discharged, was an important one in testing university procedures and the institution of tenure. The interesting revelations for the purposes of this discussion, however, have little or nothing to do with the charges or the outcome. Most of the arguments presented in the lengthy public hearing dealt with the *rights* of faculty members. Largely ignored in the decision, because they were not pertinent to the specific charges, were some even more significant issues in the area of faculty *responsibilities.*

In the course of testimony about various events it became clear that Professor Franklin's seminar course, which was listed in the catalog as dealing with the work of Melville, often met at the site of various political "actions," and that the subject matter often had no detectable relationship to Melville. Neither Professor Franklin nor his supporters showed any embarrassment over this; nor did they attempt to argue, for example, that Moby Dick is about political revolution and not merely about whaling. Rather, they thought that the times and the issues simply justified changing the program to serve their own beliefs and ends. That sort of thing was not uncommon at the time, and I have no doubt that it unsettled and may even have permanently damaged an institutional consensus about academic responsibility.

The responsibility of the professoriate is a difficult subject about which surprisingly little has been said. Sir Eric (now Lord) Ashby, in a thoughtful address to the British Academy in 1969, raised some of the problems in what was, especially in its time, a controversial and even courageous effort to confront academic duty. Later the International Council on the Future of the University established a project on the ethics of the teaching profession, one result of which was a short book by Edward Shils published in 1983.[4] Shils's book deals with many of the issues relevant here. With respect to the academic obligations of university teachers, Shils discusses the obligation to truth and objectivity, the requirement of fairness, and the costs and benefits of informal relationships.

A clearly discernible theme in Shils's book is that the primary ethical test is the teacher's capacity to put the student's interests first. Its basis is the presumption, which I believe is beyond argument, that members of the professoriate are following a calling in which the central purpose is generational improvement. The university is an institution that exists to advance the culture, both by acquiring new knowledge and by disseminating received knowledge in ways that inspire young people to use it— both creatively and constructively. In that way professors are agents for making society better than it was, generation by generation.

In this respect, their function as "role models" is important, perhaps even as important as their function in transmitting information and inspiring curiosity. For if the intellectual enterprise is to be made attractive to students—if they are to regard the life of the mind as a life worth living—they must respect those who have chosen that life as vocation. The professor who appears overly eager to transmit his own influence, or who allows her own political agenda to overwhelm a class discussion, is bound to sacrifice some of that respect.

An even more troubling aspect of bias in the classroom returns us to the fact that the academic relationship is one of inherently unequal power: the professor is not only the older person, but the person with authority. This asymmetry of the power relationship will recur in a somewhat starker context later. Here, where the struggle is over ideas and opinions, the deployment of authority may not have such clear outcomes as in, say, playing favorites in grading, but because it is both subtler and more pervasive, it is a much more significant threat to the health of the academy. Nothing is more demoralizing to students than the impression that their evaluations will depend on their acquiescence in the personal views of their mentors.

No university can or should write rules against the expression of opinion, or even bias, on the part of faculty members in the classroom. A healthy exposure of ideological differences often yields the best kind of learning. Two criteria, however, should be met before a faculty member imposes personal views in the classroom. First, such views should pass a germaneness test; there should be an arguable relationship between the professor's views and the subject matter of the course. Second, the professor should disclose any biases. Students have a right to fair warning; biases are everywhere, and candid disclosure is their natural antidote.

A different but related set of issues surfaces when the professor presents what he or she considers an orthodox or commonly accepted view that runs against deeply held beliefs on the part of certain students. This perhaps happens most frequently in courses on religious studies, but it crops up in other areas as well. As a biologist, I encountered it in introductory teaching, when students from evangelical Christian backgrounds would occasionally become disturbed by my treatment of evolution. I recall being visited once by a small delegation of such students. This was at a time, in the early 1970s, when "fundamentalist" beliefs (or at least their expression) experienced a surge of popularity on campuses, and end-zone prayer was a common postgame event in college stadiums. My visitors were sincere, polite, and troubled. I confess a fleeting temptation to dismiss their concerns by saying that I had given them a strong scientific consensus view of the matter, and that it was their responsibility to learn it. That would have been wrong; but what was the right thing to do?

With the benefit of some hindsight, I think that there are only two choices. One is to identify and then deal with the arguments of "creation scientists." The difficulty is that these arguments are basically theological, dressed up to look like science. It is almost impossible to win over someone with religious convictions by pitting a set of scientific arguments against theological ones. (These days some scientific organizations have undertaken this approach in a careful way, so it may be a more attractive option now.)

The second approach, which I favored, is to acknowledge their feelings and to notify them that they are not required to change their beliefs. But one purpose of the course is to acquaint students with a set of facts—and, in this case, with an emergent theory that nearly all scientists now accept as proven. It is perfectly acceptable for students to object morally to this, and even to express that objection. But they still have to meet the requirements of the course.

In my experience, this seemed to satisfy most of those who objected on such grounds. I have no idea what effect the course eventually had on their beliefs, but it would be interesting to know.

Another form of objection that has become common lately is the resistance of animal rights advocates to certain kinds of laboratory work. This has had its most serious consequences in secondary schools. In several states, high school students who express this conviction are now permitted to pass through biology courses without having to do the dissections or experiments required of others.

That is exactly the wrong solution. It clearly signals that the laboratory work is unimportant. If these students are perfectly able to get along without it, then why should the other students be made to do it? Indeed, it lends credibility to one of the arguments advanced by the animal rights groups, namely, that computers or other "dry" exercises can serve as proxies for real animals in learning about their function. But in fact computers can model animals only to the extent that humans are able to equip them with previously gained knowledge about those animals. The idea that demonstrations, pictures, and computer games can substitute for hands-on work with the animals themselves is an illusion, and by fostering it we fail as teachers. To the student who asks to be released from required work on these grounds, the appropriate answer would be that if certain things are eliminated from biology it isn't biology anymore, so perhaps the student should consider another subject.

One other aspect of teaching as an activity deserves special attention. It has to do with how professors conduct their teaching, in private and especially in public, and how they express their feelings about this dimension of their academic duty. Of the complaints that I have received about faculty in this regard—and this covers seven years as a department chairman, one as provost, and a dozen as president—the majority have to do with attitudes and behavior toward students, rather than with grading, quality of lectures, and so on. A characteristic flaw (not common, but persistent) that emerges from these critiques is a form of arrogance, of indifference to the feelings and the need for support that most students bring to academic encounters. Experiences like the following perhaps best give the flavor.

1. A professor of chemistry tells a group of students in the introductory course he is teaching that he isn't enjoying the course any more than they are; he has, after all, little interest in teaching people who are just headed for medicine anyhow.
2. An instructor in a seminar class, when asked a question that seems off the point, holds the student up to ridicule by inviting others to opine on what the question could possibly have meant. Not only is the questioner humiliated; the other students feel that they have been forced into becoming co-conspirators.
3. A student's final paper in her social science class is returned by the instructor with a grade of C but no general assessment of the paper's faults or virtues. There is a marginal note beside one paragraph: "This reads as though it had been written by a sophomore in high school."

These examples, each as real as it is sad, do real damage. No one should suppose that it is a faculty member's obligation to nurture each student's ego; indeed, strong and even harsh criticism may be called for. But it must be given with respect for the exercise and for the student's feelings, and with the clear purpose of bringing about improvement. If those objectives are in plain view, even a sharp public challenge from a professor can be tolerated. If they are not, the result is likely to be a mixture of resentment and discouragement.

Thus far I have been talking about matters of commitment, stance, and attitude. Beyond these matters lies the entire, complex domain of teaching as professional work: How is it done? How do we measure its effectiveness and design ways of improving it? Are there special devices that work? The territory is obviously too much to cover thoroughly in the broader context of this book, but we do need to recognize that a remarkable transition occurs as one goes from graduate student or postdoctoral fellow to the first academic appointment. Professor Lee Shulman of the Stanford School of Education expresses it well: "There is an instant conversion from expert learner to novice teacher." A less tolerant description is found in the hilarious turn-of-the-century British essay "Microcosmographica Academica," in which F. M. Cornford describes the university lecturer as "a sound scholar, who is chosen to teach on the ground that he was once able to learn."[5]

Fortunately, the gradient is not as steep these days as it once was. In my second and third years as a graduate student at Harvard, I served as head "teaching fellow" (the Harvard term for the role called teaching assistant elsewhere) in a large general education course. I was lucky: a sympathetic and thoughtful faculty mentor was willing to give me a lot of responsibility. He let me lecture two or three times, and he provided helpful criticism. That was a lot more than most of my fellow graduate students were getting, and I was grateful for it. But even this far-above-average experience provided me with little systematic preparation for conducting a class, or formal performance evaluation.

Today teaching assistants at many universities are able to get such formal training, often both through their departments and through a campus organization called by various names, often the Center for Teaching and Learning. Organizations of this kind supply technical support to departments for preparing their own students. Various departments ranging from English to physics may have courses or workshops for prospective teaching assistants that draw on resources from the center. Such centers usually have staffs of teaching consultants who will do classroom evaluations or analyze videotapes of instructional performance, and run orientation programs for new teaching assistants.

Beginning faculty, too, have access to such opportunities. Yet few take advantage of them, either because they don't know that they need assistance, or because (especially in the sciences) research has been so emphasized in their lives that they have difficulty believing that teaching "counts." But it does. Teaching is now receiving substantially greater weight in the tenure-granting process in most research universities, as it should. This is an important trend, and will depend on the development and application of methods for fair performance evaluation—a matter neither straightforward nor uncontroversial.

Much debate surrounds the questions of which are the best and fairest ways of measuring teaching performance, and how such measures should be incorporated into the procedures for appointment and promotion. These issues have plagued those who are committed to some rebalancing of the relative weights accorded to teaching and research in such procedures because, in the end, advocates of an increased role for teaching must confront two uncomfortable facts. First, whereas persuasive and credible judgments about research quality are available from multiple sources (publication record, awards and memberships, citation data, and the testimony of an international "college" of peers), judgments about teaching quality have been available mainly from students and only occasionally from departmental colleagues. Second, whereas research evaluations have an aura of objectivity because they come from afar, assessments of teaching are by nature local and are therefore perceived as being more subjective and potentially influenced by friendship, personal loyalty, or other forms of bias.

There are real differences within the academy with regard to the importance of teaching in faculty personnel decisions. As background for a report to the Stanford faculty in 1991 on the role of teaching in appointments and promotions, I examined the dockets of twenty-two candidates for promotion in the School of Humanities and Sciences for the period 1988–91. (The school was responsible for about 80 percent of all undergraduate instruction.) Eight of the dockets were for appointments to tenured professorships from outside, and eight for internal promotions to tenure. Six were for new appointments of assistant professors, all candidates from outside Stanford. Each of these sets was divided roughly equally among the humanities, natural sciences, and social sciences.

The folders were splendid examples of care in preparation. Search procedures were followed scrupulously, and the evidence provided about research potential came from a wide range of sources. The comparison of final candidates with comparable scholars and with one another was well-documented by detailed letters from outside sources. With respect to the evaluation of teaching ability, however, three features stood out. First, there were great differences, by field and by level of appointment, in the care and thoroughness with which teaching was considered. Second, the evaluations, such as they were, for the most part involved only the narrowest measure of teaching capability, namely, performance in lectures. Finally, the intensity and imaginativeness of the efforts to examine teaching ability were modest compared with the investments made in evaluating research potential.

The differences among fields were especially dramatic. For example, in evaluating outside candidates for the beginning assistant professorship, the science departments expended far less effort obtaining teaching evaluations than did the humanities departments. In one science folder there was a single brief, rather casual letter from a faculty member who had supervised the candidate as a teaching assistant; the docket sent forward from the department said merely that the two lectures given by the candidate "indicate that he will be an effective and successful teacher." By contrast, folders for beginning appointees in the arts and humanities contained an abundance of information about teaching ability from the candidates' graduate institutions, often including student evaluations. These folders also contained analyses by Stanford faculty members of the candidates' performance in teaching roles during their campus visits for final interviews. Social science departments were more variable, but most often resembled the sciences. One folder said only that there might be difficulty because "the candidate has not previously taught in English." It may be that appointees to initial assistant professorships in the sciences have had fewer teaching opportunities as graduate students or fellows than their counterparts in the humanities, but this can hardly account for all the differences in depth of evaluation.

There were also predictable differences in the level of appointment proposed. By far the most thorough evaluations were for promotions to tenure from within: all such folders gave serious attention to teaching. But again, the most thorough and imaginative evaluations were those from the humanities departments. One docket for internal promotion to tenure contained, in addition to many thoughtful letters from past and present graduate as well as undergraduate students, careful first-person observations of the candidate's teaching from no less than five senior colleagues! There were also direct comparisons with the teaching performance of others holding similar rank elsewhere, based on the candidate's participation with the others in a summer seminar. This promotion folder was the only one in the sample in which the effort and care expended on teaching evaluation approached that given to research.

The results of teaching evaluations may also be used to help improve teaching performance. But how can we intervene in faculty members' teaching without challenging their traditional prerogatives and generating annoyance instead of compliance? And, once undertaken, how can we determine whether an intervention has been successful? There is meager evidence on which to base answers to these questions, though intuition and anecdote both suggest that we can get better.

A few direct experiments have been undertaken. For example, Dr. Kelley Skeff and his colleagues in the Department of Medicine at Stanford began by developing seminars on clinical teaching improvement for faculty members in their own department. The seminars were led by a facilitator—a recognized expert at clinical teaching with special training and interest in teaching improvement. Before and after the series of seven two-hour sessions, faculty members evaluated themselves on seven "educational components": learning climate, control of session, promotion of understanding, evaluation, and the like. House staff and students who were taught by these faculty members also rated their teachers before and after the intervention. Both groups detected significant improvement after the intervention.

These methods were then disseminated nationally, through a program in which other institutions sent prospective facilitators to Stanford for a month of intensive training. They then returned to their home institutions and offered seminars there. Over a period of several years, nearly a hundred facilitators were trained in this way. The results they are achieving in their own institutions are comparable to those reported from Stanford, and the leverage is considerable, since some of the facilitators have themselves trained more than a hundred faculty members.[6]

Attention to teaching improvement varies among the disciplines. At Stanford significantly more attention is paid to the quality of undergraduate instruction in the School of Engineering than in most other areas. Student evaluations, conducted in an unusually vigorous way by the undergraduate honor society Tau Beta Pi, which also ranks departments, have long been a regular part of the appointment, promotion, and salary review processes. Partly as a result, junior faculty in that school are among the heaviest users of the services of the Center for Teaching and Learning, which are available on demand for professors interested in improving instructional skills. One of the most compelling stories about teaching improvement comes from that school. One year in the early 1980s the Department of Chemical Engineering was ranked last. The members of that relatively small department—a proud faculty with an enthusiastic chairman—got together and decided that enough was enough. Most or all faculty members took advantage of the center's programs, and there was a determined effort to do things better. The result was a striking move upward in the rankings over the course of a single year.

There remains some dissatisfaction with student evaluation in the School of Engineering, but interestingly, it has led to an argument in favor of review by faculty peers. This attitude may reflect a practical, "let's get down to cases" orientation often attributed to engineers. Whatever the explanation, things are very different in other parts of the university, where serious reservations prevail about the evaluation of teaching performance. If a school or department proposes to undertake evaluation seriously, that is, if it decides to incorporate some kind of peer review, then collegial monitoring is almost inevitable. This could lead to a sense among the faculty that their fundamental right to teach the way they choose is being violated. The presence of faculty evaluators, or even a video recorder, indicates to many that this right is being infringed.

Beyond that, there are some native academic suspicions about the act of performance evaluation itself—a feeling that it belongs to some alien, perhaps corporate culture that is out of place on campus. For example, at Stanford student evaluations of teaching formerly included data that permitted faculty members to compare their own ratings with those of others teaching similar courses. But in the 1980s a faculty committee examining the process recommended dropping this feature; it was argued that such "normative" comparisons were unwarranted.

The increased focus on quality of undergraduate teaching has led to some serious attention to techniques and devices that might improve it. The list of promising proposals is much longer than a reasonable space can accommodate, but many of us have found our teaching transformed by rather simple changes of approach—many of which have in common one or both of the following features. First, they engage students actively in the process, even in large-class settings. Second, they use students to teach one another.

At universities all across the country, efforts are being made to gather and disseminate these ideas to new faculty and to teaching assistants. At Harvard, for example, a series of assessment seminars was organized in the late 1980s on the initiative of President Derek Bok; the annual publication resulting from these exchanges is a rich source of information. At Syracuse University, an institution-wide initiative for the improvement of undergraduate education drew national attention, and appears to have been sustained. As mentioned earlier, centers for teaching and learning in many of our institutions provide consultation and advice as well as regular publications. In these respects at least, the university environment seems much more hospitable to teaching improvement than it was ten years ago.

An important element in these efforts is the development of new teaching techniques. Among the devices that have surfaced in teaching-improvement seminars is the one-minute paper, originally described by Patricia Cross. It is worth describing because it embodies so much of what is wrong with traditional large-lecture teaching and how easily it can be made better. Cross's idea is simply that at the end of a lecture the professor reserve the final minute, during which the students are asked to write a brief, spontaneous essay that supplies feedback about the lecture. It might, for example, be a response to the question: What is the single most important point from today's lecture? Or the students could be asked to identify the most crucial information provided about some particular concept, or even to specify the lecture material that was least clear. The professor explains that the exercise is not an evaluation, but that its purpose is to improve the quality of the class by opening a dialog about how things are going. Follow-up is critically important: the results are summarized and discussed with the class at its next meeting.

I have talked with faculty members in all kinds of disciplines who are prepared to swear by this technique. It makes students more active participants in their own learning, they say, and it regularly points out unexpected areas of difficulty in the presentation of lecture material.

A host of other good ideas are currently circulating. A professor at the University of Wisconsin develops a whole suite of exciting laboratory exercises based on "fast plants"—small, flowering plants that reproduce and set viable seeds very quickly and can be used to investigate genetics, pollination, and other phenomena. A University of Texas faculty member uses virtual molecules with three-dimensional structures that can be made to combine in a dynamic way that illustrates how reaction sites work. A Harvard physics professor uses real-time computer-based interaction with his students to test their understanding of concepts in the middle of lectures. A Stanford engineer has students "dissect" small machines as though they were organisms in order to illustrate design principles. When the National Academy of Sciences (NAS) began a new effort on undergraduate science education with a convocation in 1995, a whole forest of innovations came to light. New programs at the NSF and elsewhere will aid the development of more of the same. Two key elements appear in the most successful programs: students are put in groups so that they can teach one another; and there is a strong emphasis on investigation and inquiry. In the humanities and the social sciences the same kind of ferment is beginning: in the teaching of language, in the use of computers in visual arts courses, and in the development of educational software.

Such innovation is critical to the improvement of teaching, and yet it remains an area in which, in contrast to research, communication networks operate poorly. A new finding in, say, molecular biology will be transmitted almost instantaneously to laboratories all over the world, but there is no incentive for that kind of rapid communication of a new teaching device. Despite this lack of contagion, new energy behind education reform has raised new hope. If we are lucky, good ideas about teaching could become as infective as new findings in research.

Nowhere is the challenge of teaching greater than in overcoming the inherent conflict between the two roles of instructor and evaluator. Indeed, in some old and respected academic settings, Oxford and Cambridge, for example, the roles are disentangled, so that examinations are set by a university board, and other teachers prepare the students for them. But in American higher education it is the norm for the professor to be both teacher and examiner.[7]

One often hears criticism of this mixing of roles. The same person is asked to be the student's mentor and advocate while the material is being presented, and then turn into a compliance officer when the outcome is under evaluation. Yet if properly crafted, examinations, papers, and various other graded works can become vehicles for instruction in themselves—real adjuncts to the other material in the course. Examinations set for the sole purpose of evaluation can be put in the hands of strangers, but if part of their role is actually to teach, then they had better be the responsibility of the teacher.

Most grading systems depend on numbers or letters and are fundamentally relative; that is, they compare one student's accomplishments quantitatively with those of others. It seems almost anachronistic now, but at one time nearly all large courses at American universities were graded "on the curve." It was assumed that ability and effort in any large sample of students would have a normal distribution, leading to an approximately normal grade distribution. A mean was selected, usually at C plus or B minus, and the students were numerically ranked and the grades assigned according to the distribution. A common rule of thumb was 5 percent failures; and then, of the passes, 15 percent A's and D's, and 30 percent B's and C's.

Such grading systems were open to the charge that they were arbitrary, relied upon unproved assumptions about the distribution of ability and effort, and enhanced competition among students. And in the hands of many faculty members, even grade evaluations based on the curve could be quite subjective. Over the past several decades we have moved away from the practice of assuming grade distributions and opened the way to a wider variety of evaluation instruments. The "curve" is a thing of the past except in a few large science courses. It is now more common for the faculty member in charge of a course, especially if it is relatively small, to make less comparative judgments. Indeed, many professors will set a standard (often a very exacting one), and then, if all the students meet it, award all of them A's.

These changes naturally have led to somewhat more generous grading, as well as to the charge that "grade inflation" is rampant in American universities. There is more than a wisp of politics in this charge, which is most often leveled by those who are highly critical of universities, and who favor a "tougher stance" with respect not only to grading but also to various aspects of student discipline. Thus this new system of grading has provoked sharp debate among academic fundamentalists (referred to by some students as "Grading Nazis") and progressives (referred to by some colleagues, and perhaps even by some students as well, as "Bleeding

Hearts"). A few observers have even tried to associate grade inflation with the arrival of large numbers of minority students, but that relationship can hardly be causal, because on the basis of their test scores the minority students now being enrolled in the most selective places are more able, on average, than the nonminority students admitted to those same institutions thirty years ago.

There is probably less to the grade inflation controversy than meets the eye. In many institutions the tendency to inflate grades has been magnified by a welcome increase in the proportion of small classes, which have always been graded more generously. My own observation is that students arrive at college better prepared, and work harder, than they did one or two decades ago; if faculty members are grading them more generously, it hardly seems fair to speak of "inflation." Indeed, one wonders whether we would be worried about grade inflation if A were not the first letter in the alphabet: the feature that causes the most distress is compression at the top of the scale.

On the other hand, the phenomenon is real enough: the data suggest that at many of the most prestigious, highly selective undergraduate institutions, average grades have gone up a full grade point (for example, from C to B) over a period of thirty years or so. If there is so much saturation at the high end that outsiders cannot make realistic discriminations among the graduates, then the institution is failing in a significant obligation. Society has a right to expect that colleges and universities will provide it with a reasonably accurate certification of its students' abilities. At any given time, then, an evaluation system ought to provide comparative judgments that are useful to outsiders. But the system also should meet important internal tests: it should be perceived as fair and not arbitrary, and it should provide positive incentives for creativity and imagination on the part of students.

A few "experimental" institutions have dispensed with quantitative grading altogether. They rely on deep faculty knowledge of individual student accomplishment, provided in the form of written evaluations for each course. In aggregate, these commentaries substitute for a transcript. My own experience with these is that at their best they are superb—but that they are not always, or even often, at their best. They require an extraordinary degree of faculty diligence and a high faculty-student ratio. It is unlikely that they will become a widely used substitute for the present mix of graded instruments, of which the written examination is by far the most familiar sort.

A good examination does not simply test knowledge; it tests the capacity to analyze, to use newly learned information creatively, and to apply it to unfamiliar problems. Because writing skill is so vital in the lives of educated men and women, it should not be ignored, as it so often is, in evaluating students; to grade on content and ignore the quality of language sends a message that the latter doesn't matter—a terribly misleading signal about real life. This does not lead ineluctably to an argument that only essay examinations should be used. Indeed, there are multiple-choice, mechanically graded examinations that are challenging and creative and demand real analytical thinking. But if they are used to the exclusion of everything else, they invite a kind of communication atrophy, and that is the wrong outcome.

Many faculty colleagues I have known much prefer assigning papers to setting examinations, especially in advanced courses. It is an appealing idea: the paper is more realistic in its invitation to use all accessible information; it is also more "scholarly," and thus seems more appropriate for advanced students. But papers do not demand the focused, time-limited performance that examinations require. They are a different kind of exercise entirely, and therefore should complement exams rather than replace them. I have also observed (even, I must confess, in myself) a certain "buy now, pay later" approach to the choice between papers and examinations. Exams are harder to make up but easier to grade, and in the middle of a difficult term a professor sometimes finds it attractive to announce a final paper rather than a final exam.

The chief problem with papers is that they are often graded too hastily and hardly edited at all. Perhaps the most frequent complaint I have heard from students is about just this deficiency. "Why," they ask, "did this paper get a B when the grader found so little to complain about?" Nor is this concern limited to those who have been disappointed with their grades. If anything, it is heard more stridently from those who are deeply interested in improving their work, have invested heavily in an essay of which they are proud, and who get an A but no constructive feedback. Thus to assign papers, especially in the place of examinations, carries with it a significant added burden: the professor has to take the product seriously enough to assume the task of editor.

I have heard many faculty members in different disciplines deny that they have any obligation to help students with their writing. They behave as though there were a bright line between style and substance, between communication and content. Even if there were (and I believe, to the contrary, that the quality of expression says something about the quality of thought) no more vital skill is taught in the university than the ability to communicate clearly and effectively. If we cannot make that our business across the curriculum, we just aren't fulfilling our role as faculty members.

Professor M, one of the most admirable teachers I know, does much of her educating in the margins of her students' papers. She creates a conversation in writing between text and critic that is generous and encouraging but also challenging. In it one has difficulty separating style from substance; while clarifying the prose, M is also working on the student's thinking, suggesting new avenues of deliberation as well as of expression. It takes only a small sample of her work to falsify the old belief that a paper can be graded independently on content and "writing."

No single issue raises more hostility in the teacher-student relationship than the management of grading disputes. My own undergraduate experience was colored by faculty members who refused to consider grading appeals at all. In the rather more authority-conscious years of the late 1940s and early 1950s that did not seem unnatural, though the arrogant manner of the refusals did linger with us a bit.

Nowadays, of course, expectations are quite different. Students are accustomed to a higher level of accountability; it is recognized that even faculty members occasionally make mistakes. Grades are also more important than ever. In a stressed economy, educational attainment has a heavy impact on later success—including, but not limited to, lifetime earnings. The heightened seriousness of the consequences of grading only emphasize the need for due process. Procedures for handling grading disputes vary widely, just as they did in earlier times, and no single rule will suffice under all circumstances.

Grading policy is a matter worth serious consideration, especially in large courses that are prerequisites for admission to the most competitive professional schools. The competitive character of courses in organic and general chemistry, intimidating hurdles on the yellow brick road to medical school, is legendary. Students have been known to sabotage one another's experiments and to hide vital texts in the library in such courses; surely, then, they will argue about a grade. In some introductory chemistry courses the teaching staff expects that one third of the examinations will be submitted for regrading.

Such situations naturally invite codifications of procedure. Sometimes only problems or "objective" answers can be appealed, and essays will not be regraded. Sometimes there is a rule that if a student requests regrading of one question the entire examination will be reevaluated. The hanging threat, of course, is that the eye taking the second look will be extremely jaundiced—and that any gains are likely to be compensated by losses imposed in other areas of the examination. Whether or not that is actual practice, it is firmly implanted in student folklore.

One answer to the regrading problem is the solution found in most law schools. When examinations are taken under conditions of anonymity, grading is by number. Since appeals would violate the principle of anonymity, none are allowed, although there are elaborate mechanisms for correcting errors of recording.

Although this solution has much to recommend it, it is unlikely to catch on everywhere. Indeed, there is no magic bullet solution to grading disputes; almost no policy seems capable of covering all possible cases. But there are some principles of general utility. The first is to be compassionate even when it is necessary to be firm. A second is to preserve the rights of everyone while dealing with the individual complaint. (For example, there are serious problems in agreeing to regrade one essay in a small class without reevaluating the others.) A third is always to admit the possibility of error, and to permit the student a fair opportunity to show that there has been one. A fourth is not to be arbitrary. The deepest resentments that develop over grading disagreements result from situations in which a frustrated or worn-out professor has delivered the equivalent of the Parent's Last Resort: "Why? Because I said so, damn it." And, most important, if there is to be a policy, it should be advertised up front, so everyone knows what it is.

As the foregoing would suggest, many faculty members apply some fairly simple rules of thumb to answering grading complaints: permit all appeals based on grading error; hear all arguments about confusing wording and decide them on their merits, regrading the exams if necessary; be very cautious about reevaluating essay questions or papers; always use grading appeals as another chance to teach. Above all, be consistent and don't be defensive.

Many of my colleagues agree on an explanation of why—quite apart from the economic realities outside—there is such intense concern among today's students about examinations, grades, and performance. The former are convinced that even the very brightest of students come to college so intensely focused on *information* that they are confused at the requirement to think originally. Recently I sought out an experienced, much-respected tutor about the case of a student who was desperate about a poor exam performance. He had consulted this particular tutor earlier in the year, and I asked the tutor what he thought. "Mark is like a lot of students here," he said. "He believes that he learns the material thoroughly, and that he has a special problem in taking tests. Mark's real problem is that he thinks your course is about learning facts, whereas the tests are asking him to apply them."

This is an all-too-familiar disjunction between two different facets of education. Of course it is true that one cannot hope to master any discipline (or prepare for any profession) without accumulating a factual base. But the essence of education at the college level is to help students learn to analyze, to make their knowledge work over unfamiliar terrain. In the lingo of science education reform, the emphasis has shifted significantly toward "inquiry-based" instruction. Courses that merely equip students with "knowledge," and examinations that measure its accumulation by requiring recall, perpetuate the Mark problem.

Finally, some treatment must be given to the tragic but not uncommon case in which the grading conflict involves academic dishonesty. Every college faculty member has to face a few of these, sooner or later. The suggestion that a student has cheated on an examination or an assignment provides a difficult test of the faculty-student relationship. It demands understanding, care, and due process on the part of the faculty member— just at the moment when he or she is likely to have run out of tolerance.

It is said that academic cheating is on the upswing. Faculty colleagues have assured me of this fact in each of the five decades during which I have been a university teacher, and I think they have been wrong every time. In discussing the frequency of cheating it is important to differentiate between two systems: proctored examinations and some form of honor code. In the former one can record the rate of violations, but that rate is a product of two factors: the rate of cheating and the intensity of proctoring. Any impression that cheating is on the rise will result in more aggressive proctoring, which will increase the rate of detected violations, thus confirming the suspicion of the authorities that violations are rising. So data from proctored examinations are not very trustworthy.

At Stanford several surveys of the frequency of honor code violations have been conducted since the 1960s. The questionnaires have all been anonymous. Although the self-acknowledged rates may nevertheless underestimate actual violations, there is no reason to believe that the proportion of true reports would change significantly over time. Over three decades the frequency of cheating appears to have been about constant, with the question "have you ever?" getting *yes* answers from between 6 and 15 percent of the students for forms of academic dishonesty ranging from copying through the use of crib notes to obtaining answers from a student who has already taken the exam. In the most recent of these surveys (1990), students were also asked whether they had witnessed cases of cheating by others, or if they were aware of such cases. Very few students reported having observed cheating themselves, but many more said that they had heard of instances, and that they believed there were frequent violations. It is not surprising that students (a) don't do it much themselves; (b) don't see much of it going on; but (c) hear about a lot of it. That touch of prevailing paranoia spreads readily to faculty and gives rise to occasional pressure to change the honor code; but most students at Stanford prefer it.

Not so the faculty. Serious conflicts have arisen over honor code enforcement in cases of charged violation, and on more than one occasion these have led to strongly worded disagreements between the accusing faculty member and the university administrators who staff the process of judicial review. The former have a strong and entirely justified interest in successful prosecution because it protects the community's faith that the evaluation system is fair. The latter have an equally reasonable interest in guaranteeing due process—the student disciplinary system, too, rides on a perception of fairness. Thus a lot of these cases used to reach me on appeal.

Some of them involved facts that were simply difficult to sort out; for example, a convinced and angry faculty member and an equally outraged student would disagree about whether an answer had been altered after an exam had been returned. The main problem in these cases was persuading the faculty member to let the judicial process work, and not to take action alone through the grading system. There were troublesome instances in which a colorable case could be made that material in a paper had been heavily borrowed from another source, but the similarity fell short of plagiarism. And new technologies bring new problems. The largest number of difficult cases came from the Computer Science Department, over the issue of unpermitted aid. It was difficult to tell who was right; the professors thought their instructions about permitted levels of collaboration were clear, but the students (in large number) contended that they were not. Ambiguity was, as it often is, responsible for a lot of the problem. Especially under an honor code, the most important requirement for preserving academic honesty is clear rules. The following hypothetical case illustrates the need for them.

A. is a student in Professor B.'s junior-level course, the Biology of Natural Populations. As a take-home examination, students are asked to produce and run a population model on software developed by the professor for his and similar courses and sold through the university bookstore. The exercise involves predicting the changes in density of a species population through time, varying such parameters as area, predator density, and availability of food resources. A. turns in results that are, for the most part, plausible. Some, however, are so wrong that Professor B. is perplexed. He questions A. and finds him quite ignorant about some fundamental aspects of the simulation. A. freely admits that he had difficulty with the software: "I'm actually pretty dumb about computers, but my roommate—who is also taking the course—helped me get started running it. I found I could do most of it, and I think I know the biology pretty well. But as for the program, I guess he didn't have time to give me the whole nine yards." Professor B. reminds A. that it was a take-home examination given under the honor code, which does not permit aid. A. responds that he received no aid on the subject matter; what his roommate did, he maintains, was not different from showing him how to use any other tool. Professor B. is unimpressed with this argument and somewhat annoyed. Instead of charging A. with an honor code violation, he simply informs him that he will record a failing grade for this part of the course. "That way," he says, "we won't have to activate the whole Judicial Council bureaucracy, and you won't get a black mark on your record."

This case was deliberately designed to illuminate some of the uncertainties and difficulties that surround many grading disputes. The introduction of computing as a tool in many courses has served to blur the line between what is "substance" and what is not. In discussing the above case with students, I continually met with requests for "more detail" about the simulation, illustrating the complexity and ambiguity of the problems generated in such work. But on the more significant issue, there was general agreement that Professor B. should not have taken matters into his own hands, thereby depriving A. of the due process afforded by the judicial system. In fact, the most common problems under honor codes often involve a failure, on the part of students or faculty, to know and understand the rules.[8]

A group of young faculty-members-to-be, all of them experienced as teaching assistants, wanted to know more about the required "courseware" developed by the faculty member. In the ensuing discussion a good deal of resentment emerged over the fact that some faculty members assign their own books and materials in a course and, of course, receive royalties on the sales. It is true, though perhaps only technically true, that this places the faculty member in a conflict-of-interest position. Yet the book he or she writes is very likely to be the best book for that particular purpose, and in any event the royalty yield from a single class is not likely to provide a judgment-warping incentive. The practice nevertheless does attract negative attention, and invites a certain cynicism on the part of students that is amplified by the frequency with which revised editions appear. ("I guess planned obsolescence is part of the marketing strategy," one student remarked.) For this reason a few faculty members have adopted the practice of donating such royalties to the university, and announcing that fact to their classes.

The circumstances of the foregoing hypothetical case clearly illustrate some of the problems with an honor code. It may, by encouraging unmonitored out-of-class work, provide extra temptations to cheat. And it may, as in this case, create ambiguities that are difficult to resolve. Proctored systems, by contrast, are apt to invite more careful codification. Despite these difficulties I much prefer the honor code. My view is partly

shaped by a conviction that students learn something from taking responsibility for their own conduct; even if it were to be shown that this system
yields a higher rate of cheating, I think the cost-benefit ratio would nevertheless be favorable. But in fact, the available data point in the other
direction. In institutions with honor codes, the incidence of cheating (as
measured by self-reporting in anonymous questionnaires) is significantly
lower than in institutions with proctored examinations. More recent studies confirm that finding and show that other factors are important—especially student understanding of whatever system is in place, and how
students perceive the academic honesty of their peers.[9]

My support of honor codes is also influenced by my own experience as
a student. My memory of examinations taken in Harvard's Memorial Hall
in the late 1940s and early 1950s is of a dreary vastness, overlain with the
officious bustle of proctorial oversight. The atmosphere of hostility and
mistrust was so awful that it spurred us to ingenious efforts at amusement,
such as pretending that we were consulting crib notes when we were really
sneaking food from an inside pocket. It has always struck me that a significant educational cost is associated with aggressive proctoring and the
attitude it engenders among students.

Whatever advantages the honor code offers cannot be realized absent
significant faculty belief and commitment. When faculty don't quite trust
the honor code—and display their lack of trust by proctoring when an
examination should be unproctored, or by failing to abide by the provisions for prosecuting cases of alleged cheating—faith in the system falls
everywhere. The case discussed above is realistic in that the most serious
challenges to Stanford's honor code that I encountered came when faculty
members decided to take matters into their own hands and administer
frontier justice through the grading system when they were convinced that
cheating had occurred. (Of course, the decision to do so will depend on
the way in which honor code violations are evaluated and sanctioned. If
prosecutions encounter regular difficulty, either because the standard of
proof is too exacting or because the hearing body is regularly overcome
with mercy, then faculty members are more likely to take matters into
their own hands.)

More and more faculty members are becoming convinced that exams
and papers are too limited a repertoire for finding out how students are
performing. Interesting alternatives are available. For example, the evalu-

ation of cases in class has been successful, particularly in courses that emphasize policy studies. This format makes it possible to gain estimates of the quality of the student's participation. Oral examinations often yield different measures of a student's capacity and have the advantage of great flexibility. Computer models and courseware exercises have opened up a whole new domain of evaluation as well as of teaching.

Of all the alternative methods of evaluation, I have been most intrigued by those that depart radically from the usual comparative measures. Grades, whether on papers, examinations, seminar performance, or even created works, all supply the individual student with a benchmark of his or her performance in comparison with that of others. They carry the inevitable implication of competition for rewards. But in most activities that a student will undertake later on, success will depend on the capacity to bring many minds and/or hands to bear on a single challenge. Few exercises in the contemporary academic system foster this skill, much less reward it.

Students can be assembled in small groups, encouraged to pool their knowledge and their skills, and then rewarded commonly for the quality of the joint product. This produces the expected amount of angst: students will complain about the "free-rider" problem in their group, and often exhibit frustration when the professor makes them solve it themselves. But in the end they will take enormous pride in the group effort, develop a real team spirit, and often sustain a serious interest in the topic long after the exercise is over. This technique must be used with some caution, and usually in combination with more individual evaluation methods.

Beyond their role as evaluators, faculty members must advise and counsel students, as well as determine their suitability for advanced academic work. Like all responsibilities, mentoring can be challenging and difficult. Good mentors often develop a strong personal stake in the success of their students. But that can be dangerous, resulting in a degree of emotional attachment that overtakes objectivity, yielding unrealistic estimates of the student's potential or encouraging the faculty member to push the student into career choices that gratify the former but may not suit the latter.

Academic advising begins with the assignment of a freshman adviser. This is a task that most faculty members eschew. Students at this stage sometimes have poorly formed or unrealistic expectations about themselves and their academic opportunities. They are sometimes shy, or at least reluctant to discuss their aspirations or their likes and dislikes candidly. Conversations with such seventeen-year-olds can be labored and unrewarding.

But in my experience, encounters of this kind are relatively uncommon, in comparison with the energy, curiosity, and ambition most students bring to their first university exposure. While I was president of Stanford, I took on half a dozen freshman advisees every other year, in the last few sharing the load with my wife, who herself had been advising students as a member of the university's administrative staff. We found the experience rewarding; indeed, it was sometimes an invaluable way of finding out, through the eyes of consumers, what was and wasn't working at the university. The most important benefit was the personal relationships we would develop with bright and energetic young people who constantly reminded us of what the university was really for. Their responses to their own educations were, at times, the best reinforcement I got about what we were trying to accomplish.

Almost the very first challenge an adviser will face is likely to be a conflict between his or her idea of an appropriate academic destination and the student's. It is very difficult for scientists not to insist on mathematics and/or chemistry for most first-year students ("Even if you don't choose in the end to major in science, these courses provide excellent mental training and discipline."). It is equally difficult for historians not to lean toward historical studies in recommending ways for the student to meet a distribution requirement in the humanities. A certain amount of disciplinary salesmanship is actually desirable. Students want to know that their institution has people who care passionately about their own fields, to the point of occasionally proselytizing on their behalf. And the advice may be good.

Advisers need to guard, however, against a kind of arbitrary insistence on their own recommendations. For some students the conventional dose of freshman calculus is not the right idea, no matter how much the adviser may think of it as mental discipline. For others, postponing courses "for distribution" may be not a form of procrastination but the reflection of a real need to achieve some depth before branching out.

At many universities the recruitment of freshman advisers from the faculty (especially the senior faculty) has proven difficult. Administrative staff and sometimes graduate students are often called to fill the void. They may be among the best advisers, but the participation of non–faculty members in large numbers in these roles lends weight to the impression that the faculty doesn't care about undergraduates. Part of the adviser's job is also to be a broker of academic opportunity and an advocate for his or her advisees when difficulties arise. The task may be to persuade the professor of history that student S really should be allowed to take Colonial America without a certain prerequisite, or to resolve a section-assignment dilemma with the freshman writing program. Such negotiations go much better when they are conducted by a faculty colleague.

It is usual for the department in which the student will concentrate (the "major" department) to assume the advising responsibility sometime near the mid-point of the student's academic progress. Here the same problems are encountered, but there is often less time to resolve them: in departments with large major enrollments, advisers may take on many more students than does the typical freshman adviser. And new problems also arise. At this stage in a student's academic career, plans are being laid for what will come after college; thus the adviser also becomes a career counselor.

Here the main danger comes from the dedication of the faculty member to a particular discipline and, more generally, to an academic life. Professors are often disappointed when an outstanding student elects not to undertake graduate study, or to prepare for a professional school instead of a Ph.D. program. I have heard faculty members complain that a university's admissions policy has failed because, according to them, relatively few of its graduates entered academic careers. As a member of a visiting committee at another university, I listened dumfounded as a distinguished faculty member justified the deletion of a course from the departmental curriculum by asserting that it was only taken by premedical students anyhow. Needless to say, this kind of academic chauvinism invites discouragement and hostility on the part of students, who are being told, in effect, that they cannot decide on the highest and best use of their own talents and interests, but should instead adopt someone else's normative judgments.

The culmination of advising is writing the letter of recommendation, a special form of evaluation that is especially important in the future lives of students. Some faculty members regard the letter as an entirely peripheral chore that is not part of their teaching duties at all. On the contrary, writing the letter of recommendation is to teaching what publishing the paper is to research: a vital, organic part of the process.

Writing a good letter of recommendation requires many things of the teacher: a reasonably deep knowledge of the student is important, along with the ability to make thoughtful judgments. So is a somewhat denatured attitude about the subject's personality. Character, of course, is hugely relevant; persistence, self-discipline, and integrity really matter. But charm and likability ought to enter lightly if at all. Another essential is a willingness to compare the recommended candidly with others at the same level of experience or training. Now that students' files are open to scrutiny in the event of litigation, the requirement for candor has been harder to meet. No one likes to have his or her negative judgments made quasi-public, especially if the subject is a student one likes. The Family Educational Rights and Privacy Act of 1978, which first instituted the disclosure policy, has had a dampening effect on the frankness of letters, and may well have caused a small boom in telephone usage. The natural hesitancy induced by the prospect that one's letters of reference may be read someday by the candidate makes it very difficult to be straightforward.

When asked for such letters, some faculty members who find themselves unable to be enthusiastic about a candidate may suggest another course, saying something like, "I'm sorry; I don't think I could be as supportive (or as knowledgeable) as you would want a reference to be." The Faculty of Arts and Sciences at Harvard has advised professors to decline to write under such circumstances.[10] But that policy, if adopted universally, might lead to a bipolar world consisting of uniform, breathless enthusiasm and dead silence, making discrimination on the part of the reader even harder than it is now. This is a problem not only for student letters of reference but for the even more painstaking evaluations required for faculty appointments. How to deal with candidates one cannot be enthusiastic about presents a real ethical challenge. To decline to comment may damage the entire system by transferring responsibility to someone less critical; to damn with faint praise sends a signal that is readily confused.

Recommendations for professional schools present a special challenge for the teacher of undergraduates. They tend to come in all at once, and for an unusually devoted and valued teacher the period between December 1 and mid-January can be a veritable blizzard of paper. The inundated victim can only bless those schools, such as the medical schools, that have standardized their forms so that a single thoughtful letter for a particular student can serve all. The most vengeful muttering is reserved for the graduate schools of business, which must have colluded to ensure that every institution requires its own unique response, forcing the recommender to answer slightly different questions for each form.

Recommendation writing is thus a high-volume activity, and it is therefore important to know that after a while institutions and programs develop a "book" on individual recommenders. If a faculty member at university X has ranked all of her recommendees to medical school Y over the past decade as "among the four or five best students I have ever had," the admissions committee will eventually conclude that she must be from Lake Wobegon, where no one is below average.

Indeed, loyalty—admirable virtue though it may be—is ultimately the worst enemy of reliable recommendations. All who have real affection for their students are vulnerable to it, and must struggle constantly for objectivity. Everyone knows, and sympathizes with, the loyalist who cannot help overstating the case for his candidates. Of one such faculty member, a colleague said, "Oh, S. The trouble with S. is that all his geese are swans." Overzealous support for a weak student is in fact one form of intergenerational theft: it cannot help damaging another, better-qualified student later on by damaging the recommender's credibility.

Perhaps the fundamental thing to be said about the teaching of undergraduates is that it is an important part of any academic life, and that its importance is suddenly being more widely recognized. The cynical observer will be tempted to attribute this elevated concern to popular critiques of higher education, and certainly there has been no shortage of those. Books with titles such as *Profscam* and *Illiberal Education* have appeared on the *New York Times* nonfiction best-seller list. Closer examination of the texts, however, suggests that the critique may be more political than substantive. Such books deal at length with the various phenomena of "political correctness"; all allege that conservative opinion is stifled on university campuses. References to the level of attention paid to undergraduate teaching are secondary efforts meant to gain attention for a political agenda. The authors are all well-credentialed conservatives.

But surely that is no reason to reject everything they say; after all, sources with no political ax to grind have been tough critics, too. In two influential recent publications, the Carnegie Foundation for the Advancement of Teaching has criticized the state of the undergraduate experience and offered promising suggestions toward improving it. Harold Shapiro, the president of Princeton University, gives a perceptive analysis of the predicament of good university teachers: "[It] is not that they fail to devote adequate time to teaching but that they are transmitting what they know—and love—with too little awareness of what it is that the student needs to learn. We need some ways to reorient our pedagogical efforts toward the excitement of inquiry and discovery, in addition to the transmission of knowledge."[11]

We also have to recognize that institutions and their leaders are not making their expectations about teaching clear to faculty. In his report to the Harvard faculty, excerpted earlier, Henry Rosovsky spoke of a decline in civic consciousness. Surely, however, the institution bears some responsibility for the clarity of the messages it sends. If appointment and promotion processes are seen to depend overwhelmingly on research productivity, and if salary treatment appears to ignore outstanding teaching performance, then all the exhortation and criticism in the world is not going to alter faculty behavior.

At Stanford in 1991 I thought the time had arrived to put this matter directly on the table, and I devoted my annual report to the faculty to it. I did the same the following year. A public statement about the need to restore the balance between teaching and research from the president of a major research university turned out to be more newsworthy than I expected. A local paper headlined the story "Teach or Perish." That was, needless to say, not what I had in mind.

The statement that started this ruckus was actually rather mild. I pointed out that the joint-product character of universities (teaching *and* research) has long been a strength, but that the relative weight had shifted over time to research. I argued that it was time to reaffirm that education was the primary task, and that society would judge universities in the long run on how well we performed that task. I went on to list a number of warning signs: "buy-outs" of teaching time by senior faculty in order to concentrate on research; overuse of visiting or temporary faculty members; failure to recognize particularly outstanding teaching in tenure decisions. I observed that Stanford had not been very systematic about its efforts to improve teaching, though we valued it highly and often did it well. The lack of conversation about what pedagogy meant, and what made it successful, seemed especially striking; teaching, though it was our profession, seemed mysteriously absent from our professional discourse. We were speaking of an activity vital to ourselves, our students, and our public as though it had no data base, lacked a history, and offered no innovative challenges. We were seldom focused on the vital nonclassroom kinds of teaching, like advising. We weren't even arguing, aside from the occasional spat like the Western Culture debate, about what ought to be common knowledge among educated men and women.

I believed then, and still do, that universities like Stanford can have superb research and superb teaching too. But I argued that we needed— especially in research universities—to talk about teaching more and to respect and reward those who do it well, making it a labor of love and the *personal* responsibility of each of us.

The dialog that followed within Stanford was helpful, though it did not lack a certain edge. University faculty members were understandably defensive about news reports suggesting that they may need to improve. (Indeed, in this day and age honest self-analysis can quickly be turned into self-indictment by the media, so those who thought I had taken too large a risk may have had a point.) Some others felt that the analysis was plain wrong; still others agreed with it.

But the issue became a subject for conversation and even controversy. Actions followed. By 1992 there were new teaching awards and special salary supplements for outstanding performance, and a subcommittee of the faculty committee on academic appraisal and achievement was working at a year-long study of teaching evaluation. In 1993 my successor appointed a commission—the first in a quarter century—to study possible changes in undergraduate education at Stanford. By 1995 it had introduced a new set of seminars for sophomores, revised the "breadth" requirement, and instituted a new science core curriculum.

Elsewhere there are further signs of change. The American Association for Higher Education (AAHS) and the Carnegie Foundation for the Advancement of Teaching continue to analyze the quality of teaching and to explore ways in which it can be made a more central concern. At many universities, criteria for promotion are being reformulated to give more serious attention to teaching accomplishments. In perhaps the most hopeful sign, the National Academy of Sciences (NAS) sponsored a convocation in 1995 on undergraduate education in science, mathematics, and engineering. It is in the science departments that teaching often gets shortest shrift; if the most distinguished science leaders in the nation take a serious stance with respect to improving teaching, it will be an important signal to the rest.

Perhaps the best news of all is how exciting and experimental the best teaching has become. In all kinds of places new things are being tried, and meanwhile the relationship between teacher and student is being revolutionized by technology. Teachers of creative writing edit their students' work on video monitors, and the latter view the changes in their dorm rooms. Questions about course material come in on e-mail and get answered in real time. Cyberspace is no substitute for personal contact between teacher and student, but it does make possible a level of interaction that would otherwise be inconceivable. In its highest form it may accelerate the more routine work of learning, reserving for the faculty member those forms of interaction that are, in the end, the most important and most meaningful.

Much of the innovation in teaching is being accomplished by young faculty members. It is a welcome and exciting development, but we cannot help worrying about the futures of those who make such commitments while still untenured. We cannot yet assure young academics that their departments will be as interested in their teaching as in their research. But times are changing. The day may not be far off when teaching performances are routinely reviewed by peers, when senior academic visitors conduct teaching "master classes" as well as give research seminars, and when candidates are told that teaching is important by department chairs who really mean it.

4

TO MENTOR

THE DUTY TO TEACH is transformed as the student becomes more advanced, as the venue shifts from the classroom to the laboratory, the library, and the office, and as the relationship becomes more singular and more personal. The one-on-one interaction that develops between experienced practitioner and aspirant is more like training than teaching; it resembles the journeyman-apprentice relationship that once characterized artisan guilds.

It is through those relationships that the academic profession reproduces itself. For those who value the university, there is surely no more important task than to ensure its survival by bringing in new blood. What the new faculty member knows about the university, he or she learned by absorption—in a library or laboratory, under the guidance (or, perhaps, the indifferent sponsorship) of a graduate or postdoctoral mentor. The faculty member's understanding of his or her academic responsibilities is not prescribed by contract or institutional rule; in this respect it is unlike the understanding of duty one would have as a soldier or as a mid-level executive in a large corporation. It is, rather, part of an inherited culture, and the route of transmission is thus of vital importance.

The interaction between advanced student and faculty mentor is complex, and presents its own set of hazards and challenges. Usually the advanced research student comes equipped with his or her own convictions and ideas. There are tensions between a growing independence on the part of the student and various needs that may be felt by the professor: to set standards and to be a good mentor on the one hand; and on the other, to enlist the student's help in advancing a research project , sometimes capitalizing on a skill that is uniquely the student's. Because the relationship involves close connections between people of unequal status and experience who share deep interests and high ability, it is a potential source of inspiring personal guidance. But at the same time it is a fertile seedbed for difficulties: conflicts over intellectual property and authorship, disputes over collaborative work, feelings of exploitation, evaluation problems, the stresses of developing personal intimacy and dependence, and even (you must have seen this coming) romance.

To this well-furnished suite of challenges, most mentors come entirely unprepared at the beginning of their careers. Beyond observation, doctoral and postdoctoral programs typically include nothing at all by way of training in this vital aspect of academic life. In the vacuum, the new Ph.D.s have little choice but to observe those around them and accept whatever model is provided to them by their own mentors. (First-time parents have much the same problem, but at least they have ready access to Dr. Spock and a host of other sources on how to raise children.) A colleague, the distinguished chemist Carl Djerassi, stated the problem plainly: "Young faculty members get absolutely no formal guidance, it being assumed that their own ad hoc graduate school and postdoctoral experience will turn them into skilled, wise mentors ... I was struck by the total absence (at least in those elite institutions with which I am familiar) of any formal mechanism for evaluating the mentor's performance."[1] Indeed, Djerassi proposed to send around a questionnaire to graduate students and postdoctoral fellows in his own department, inquiring whether they discussed such matters as the nature of the mentor-trainee relationship, record-keeping, and publication policies with the professor in charge of the laboratory. The departmental faculty voted not to permit the questionnaire to be circulated. Plainly, these subjects are uncomfortable ones. Given the faculty's reluctance to talk about them, it is small wonder that, generation after generation, we launch innocents into the world of academic mentorship.

Among all the interactions between faculty members and their advanced students, one kind of conflict is particularly pervasive and troublesome. It involves the very stuff of scholarship itself: data, ideas, experiments, theories. The questions that lie at its heart also lie near the heart of scholarly advancement and prestige: Who thought of it? Who thought of it *first?* Who did the work? Who should get the credit?

In thirteen years as the court of last resort for academic grievance appeals at a research university, I encountered more difficult, passionately contested complaints in this area than in any other. Indeed, the lore of scholarship is full of a kind of wry, uneasy humor about the matter of academic credit. A colleague of mine used to introduce research seminars by showing a slide that listed his postdoctoral and graduate student collaborators. After introducing them and saying a gracious word or two about each, he would say, "In what follows, when I say 'I' I mean 'we,' and when I say 'we,' I mean 'they.'" A certain false heartiness in the laughter that followed suggested how real an issue academic credit was for the members of his audience.

Virtually all the conflicts with which I have had some experience have been between faculty members and their students, either pre- or postdoctoral. The vast majority have been in the sciences. Partly, that is because the ideas in the sciences tend to take more precise forms and identities than in the humanities and social sciences; and partly, no doubt, it is because they are more likely to have economic value. In a few of the cases I had to deal with, the students turned out to have wrongly (though quite possibly sincerely) charged the faculty member with the appropriation of what they regarded as their own ideas. In others the students had a real reason for believing that credit for work they had done had been unfairly claimed by the professor. Even in some of these instances, however, the "taking" was perfectly routine under the usual customs of the discipline— even though it may have seemed quite wrong to the student and even to others called in to adjudicate the matter.

Before discussing particular situations, it may be helpful to touch briefly on the legal traditions that bear on ownership of ideas. By themselves, ideas are not intellectual property; they are ushered into property status by being elaborated into a form that establishes ownership. In the case of a written document, that means copyright. In the case of a process or device, it means a patent. The fundamental principle is that ownership is "in the hands that did the work." That is the basis of patent and copyright laws, which exist to further the social purpose of transferring technology or information—making it more widely available by protecting owners' rights so that it will not be protected instead by secrecy. Those rights may, of course, be reassigned by contract, as when a writer is paid by a publisher for a work. Employers usually claim, through contract arrangements, the intellectual property of employees when the inventions or works are made in the course of employment.

There are, of course, exceptions, and in no kind of institution are the exceptions more varied and confusing than they are in universities. In most cases, the institution claims the rights to work done by faculty members working on university time in university facilities. A few institutions do not, but the number of these is dwindling—suggesting a significant swing in policy. In either case, corporate or foundation sponsors of research may lay some additional claim of their own. Fortunately, the federal government, by far the largest sponsor of all, eased its own policies in this regard in 1980 with the passage of the so-called Bayh-Dole amendment. Through this important piece of legislation, the Congress established that even for research heavily supported by government funds, the university policies for assigning patent rights should prevail.

Even within this framework there are inconsistencies. Works subject to copyright and inventions subject to patent are often treated differently. Furthermore, universities that claim copyright or patent rights on faculty work have never pressed their claim against textbooks or literary works, or against works of art. These are immune by virtue of long historical tradition.

These precedents and policies all apply, of course, to commercially valuable intellectual property. But in the university the majority of scholarly work, including some of the most important, has no value as property. Rather, it is a free good launched by academic tradition into the public domain for the benefit of all. Yet of course it has value of other kinds. There is whatever intrinsic value it brings to the society at large. And for the author there is reputational value: credit for the work may enhance his or her scholarly prestige, and that, in turn, may have an indirect monetary impact through its effect on salary and advancement.

But the most important dimension of reputational value has less to do with these utilitarian consequences than it does with the nonmonetary satisfactions that derive from successful work: a sense of accomplishment, prestige, and professional respect. The most trying conflicts, not surprisingly, arise over just this kind of reputational value. A hypothetical case may help to illustrate the sort of dilemma that is frequently encountered.

Professor G, a tenured member of the Psychology Department, studies auditory localization ability in visually deprived monkeys. Graduate Student V has been working in G's laboratory with two animals, the gifts of a zoo, that have been blind from birth; the other deprived subjects in G's studies have all been sighted at birth, and later artificially occluded for various periods. For the longest periods of deprivation, G's other subjects have shown modest but significant improvement in auditory localization ability, as judged by behavioral and electrophysiological measures. But V's monkeys have shown dramatic improvement, and V has demonstrated by electrical recording in auditory cortex that closely spaced dichotic stimuli are discriminated at much lower thresholds than they are in sighted controls. G, excited by the results, urges V to prepare a paper for publication. V demurs, wishing to gather more data first. A protracted though polite struggle ensues. While V is gathering more data, G and V continue to meet and review the new findings. G continually urges that they publish, reminding V that it was G, after all, who supplied the resources for the research (including the two now-indispensable monkeys) as well as the original idea for the project. V continues to demur. G is preparing an article for a review journal and decides to include a figure summarizing V's data. The legend identifies V as the source, and the description in the text refers to "work from our laboratory."

V complains bitterly when the paper is published. In a grievance to the department chairman and the dean, V refers to "my work," and describes it as having been "stolen without permission." In responding, G reasserts his major intellectual role in the project and argues that V's role was properly credited. "In constructing invited review articles of this kind," G writes, "it is quite customary to make use of joint work, as long as there is an appropriate reference to its origin."

To deal with such cases on a regular basis is to gain respect for the complexity of the problems of academic authorship, and in particular for the degree to which disciplinary traditions differ. It was in part this heterogeneity of local custom that persuaded me to publish, in 1985, a discussion of the allocation of academic credit called "On Academic Authorship."[2] In it I pointed out that in some disciplines it is quite customary for graduate students to publish their own research results by themselves—

even when the work was closely supervised by a faculty member—whereas in others, the professor's name is added to every paper from the laboratory. An individual's position on the list of authors is an ambiguous signal regarding the amount of participation; in some fields the authorship sequence means everything, elsewhere it may just follow the alphabet. In most biological papers, the sequence of authors reflects approximately the extent of contribution; but another tradition places the chief of the laboratory last regardless.

I also found that the nature of collaboration was both highly variable and difficult to define. It is often very hard to trace the parentage of an idea, and in many large, multiauthor research projects, particularly in the sciences, there are likely to be divisions of labor among subspecialists. What would qualify one for coauthorship may differ widely from one discipline to another.

All of these factors play into the difficulty of cases like the one I have described. Opportunities to produce comprehensive reviews come mainly to senior scholars. Most scientists, in describing the significant developments in their field, will emphasize work done by themselves and their students and junior associates. Usually the scope of the topic is so broad that including all associates as coauthors is impractical and/or silly. Wherever the article deals with the results of others that are already published or have been accepted for publication, employing them (with appropriate citation) is perfectly proper. If the material is to be published later as a joint work, it is generally accepted that any of its prospective coauthors may refer to it, even at length, in separate articles of their own—provided that the joint origin is acknowledged, and provided that the opportunity for regular scholarly publication is not preempted. Common courtesy requires that they be consulted, and that reasonable requests be accommodated; this is especially important if the welfare of one's own students is at issue. If the material is unpublished and not scheduled to be a joint work, permission must be obtained for any extended use.

In the case under consideration, the matter of joint vs. sole authorship had not been negotiated between G and V. The guidelines on which such negotiations would have to be based are vague at best, and highly variable among the disciplines. The custom in my own laboratory was that if I had contributed significantly both to the idea and to the hands-on work, I was entitled to coauthorship—but that was subject to a more general rule, namely, that in any joint publication, each coauthor had to grasp the entire venture fully enough to be able to defend it creditably in a scientific meeting.

In the situation involving G and V, understanding is being sought too late. G should have established firm expectations about the proprietorship of data and ideas in the laboratory at the very beginning; it is too much to expect that the culture of a particular discipline will be transmitted automatically to its apprentices. G's case for coauthorship is not without substance, but most would view it as a close call.

Suppose we agree that it is, in fact, a joint work. Was G justified in including it in the review article? Possibly, but there are two major problems with the way G handled the situation. First, the citation was meager—indeed, almost miserly. It would have been more generous and more appropriate to cite the work in the text and to praise it. Second, there was no consultation. This last omission, highly suspicious in light of G's failure to win agreement on the joint publication, may not constitute professional misconduct on G's part, but G surely defaulted on an important element of academic duty.

I had an unexpected opportunity to explore how contemporary graduate students view this kind of situation. In the early 1990s the government imposed a new requirement that all institutions supporting graduate students or postdoctoral fellows through the Research Service Awards or research training grants provided by the NIH include in their applications "acceptable plans for instructing trainees in the responsible conduct of research."

In a large class offered to Stanford pre- and postdoctoral students in the biomedical sciences, I lectured on the subject of academic authorship and intellectual property, and used the case of G and V to open a discussion about the kinds of controversy that can arise between science mentors and their students. The results were surprising; indeed, I felt at the end of the hour that my own view of the matter must have sounded old-fashioned to these students, perhaps even quaint. Each of the 105 members of the class received the text of the case exactly as printed here. I read the case with them without adding new information, and then asked them to respond anonymously, with a *yes* or *no*, to the following questions on cards provided for the purpose:

1. Is G guilty of professional misconduct?
2. Has V overreacted to the situation?

Members of the class were asked to give their opinions immediately; I told them I knew that the data given were not adequate for them to adjudicate the matter in a fully satisfactory way, but that I wanted their first impressions anyhow. They cooperated cheerfully—and quickly. Those who know advanced graduate students and postdoctoral fellows in the biomedical sciences will doubtless share my astonishment that there was a minimum of litigious qualification on the cards. In fact, only 2 answers of a possible 210 had to be thrown out because they were not *yes* or *no*.

Only a quarter of the sample thought G was guilty of professional misconduct. This is perhaps not surprising; to many, the phrase has the tone of a legal term of art, and so some students may have withheld judgments toward which they were leaning. (Indeed, two who answered *no* to that question added, parenthetically, "but he's a mean guy," thus leaping, interestingly, to a conclusion about gender not warranted by the text!). But it is interesting that there was this much hesitancy on the part of students to find against a faculty member under circumstances that appear as damning as these.

The much bigger surprise was that the majority—more than 60 percent—of the class thought that V was overreacting to the events. I would have thought that most advanced students, whether or not they judged G's conduct to be sanctionable, would have found it reprehensible enough to justify anger on V's part, and the subsequent filing of a grievance. Of course, most of those who did not think his anger justified were those who answered *no* on the first question. But to my astonishment about 10 percent of the class answered *yes* to both questions; that is, 10 percent thought that the graduate student had "overreacted" even though they also thought the professor was guilty of professional misconduct! That improbable combination of responses may say something about the way in which some graduate students and postdoctorals see their own power.

What happens to these attitudes as students become more advanced and accumulate more experience—and as they approach more closely positions in which they will have their own students? Some clue may be found in the differences between the responses of postdoctoral fellows and graduate students to these questions. The former were quicker to exonerate G than were the graduate students; and they were twice as likely to charge V with overreacting.

This exercise, limited though it was, convinced me that there is, at least in the biomedical sciences, remarkable acceptance of a culture or tradition in which the faculty director of a laboratory has control over all the work that emerges from it. In a spirited discussion after the votes were in, one student argued that the faculty member should be a coauthor on all papers "even though he or she supplied one piece of equipment and nothing else." Another told me, "I've just thought that's the way it was. As a student, I do the work and the professor gets the credit; when I have my own lab, it will be my turn!"

If all the parties had that understanding from the beginning, it might be argued that things aren't so bad; at least the situation would be free of ambiguity, and students would know what to expect at the time they made their first commitment. But it is necessary to ask whether the message communicated by this understanding is the right one. It conveys the idea that student work has no standing on its own, that it derives its credibility and substance from the identity of the senior scholar under whose direction it was done. It would be hard to design a better signal for undermining confidence and prolonging dependence. The custom of automatic coauthorship also allocates rights in a way that defeats incentive. No matter how hard or how independently the student works, the credit will belong to someone else. Finally, it obliterates what might otherwise be important distinctions among students with respect to their originality and capacity to work alone. A department chair hiring a new assistant professor would be helped by knowing that Candidate A worked by herself on an idea of her own, whereas Candidate B was guided by a collaborator every step of the way. Under the system that some disciplines have adopted, the customs of credit allocation and authorship make that distinction quite impossible.

It is only fair to note at this point that the differences among the disciplines with respect to these customs are great. Even within the biological sciences, graduate students in ecology and evolutionary biology are given much more independent control over the work they do and the credit they get for it than would obtain in a laboratory of molecular and cellular biology. In the humanities there would be more independence still, whereas computer science and some of the other engineering disciplines would be more like biomedicine. There is also the special case of the paid student research assistant who is not working on an independent project but performing research duties under the professor's explicit direction. Here the rules would be quite different, requiring gracious acknowledgment but certainly not a sharing of academic credit.

As experience and these attitudes both show, the appropriation of academic credit has been a source of some strain in the relationship between faculty member and advanced student. But coercion and exploitation, subtler and more resistant to analysis, also flow out of the imbalance of power between the two. The following cases exemplify some real or perceived efforts on the part of faculty members to push student decisions in the direction of their own interests.

> Professor P, an anthropologist, has published a theory about the evolution of languages among the tribes that inhabit a large oceanic island. His theory argues for three separate, independent origins. Graduate Student S has concluded two years of field research in regions of the island not previously visited by P. S's draft dissertation proposes, on the basis of this new evidence, a single origin—though in the manuscript P's "tricladistic" theory is treated with great respect. In discussions of the draft, P repeatedly attempts to convince S that the data are equally consistent with a multiple origin.
>
> Eventually, P's criticism grows increasingly harsh, attacking the methodology and raising questions about data interpretation. S confides to friends some concern over whether the dissertation will be accepted.

> Professor M has published a series of works on colonial American history, analyzing the development of pre-Federal governments. M suggests an honors thesis project to B, a junior undergraduate who has excelled in M's advanced course. B is from rural New England and has found access to some very old community records in his own region that may shed light on the formation of village councils. M discourages this project, arguing that only events at a more regional level are of real interest. M proposes instead that B analyze some manuscripts on the early governance of the Massachusetts Bay Colony. To support this work, M promises to help arrange travel funds for B from the Undergraduate Research Opportunities Program.

Each reader of these cases will probably reach a tentative conclusion about the propriety of the faculty member's behavior, and that conclusion will depend very much on the status and personal experience of the reader. Yet one cannot really decide either case without more information. The pressure brought by P in the first case sounds unreasonable, and one is tempted to conclude that self-interest is at work. But other facts might convince us that S has, perhaps out of undue eagerness to produce a "new," contrarian conclusion, overread the data. Perhaps P is playing, entirely properly, the role of tough academic critic. And in the second case, M may well be trying to protect an inexperienced student from an overdose of enthusiasm over original but unimportant material. We just don't know.

But in each situation there is some reason for discomfort. In all too many instances professors do employ their power, in subtle and not-so-subtle ways, to press students to act in their interest rather than in the student's own. The cases both involve pressure to influence the subject matter or the outcome of scholarly work. More common, perhaps, are efforts to use students in exploitative ways—to engage them in routine tasks for the benefit of the faculty member or other senior participants in the group effort.

In some cases this may be entirely justified. In many fields, students may require lengthy exposure to library or laboratory methodology, to technical routines, or to the operation of complex equipment. Tasks supporting the faculty member's research goals may be the very best way to "teach" how to do the work of the discipline and to help the student absorb its culture. But in these cases it is an important responsibility to involve the student as quickly as possible with the intellectual content of the venture—to make him or her a serious contributor. If the student is kept at the routine tasks long after mastery has been gained, or is then used only to teach them to others, then the relationship has become exploitative.

The guiding principle simply has to be the interest of the student. Faculty members have a special obligation to foster intellectual development and independence; that is, after all, their primary job. They fail in it when they direct students too firmly into areas that happen to interest the faculty members, or use students for routine support rather than let them do creative work of their own, or—most especially—they withhold or attempt unfairly to share the credit that the students' accomplishments merit.

Personal relationships with students at this higher level of academic performance and intimacy are both rewarding and more problematic. In some fields, especially those in which the library rather than the laboratory is the primary venue of discovery, there may be rather formal and even impersonal relationships between professors and graduate students. Most surveys about graduate student life have emphasized the greater isolation and sense of alienation among doctoral candidates in the humanities. Not only are levels of financial support often more meager; contact with the major professor and other members of the dissertation committee tends to be much rarer than in the sciences. A committee at the University of California charged to examine graduate student life some years ago wondered, in its final report, how it could be that graduate education in the sciences could be so humane compared with that in the humanities!

The great advantage in the sciences, I suspect, has to do with the use of instruments. Much of the work involves experiments, and of necessity requires equipment—around which people frequently are clustered. But the vaunted "fellowship of the laboratory bench" can be an illusion. The increasingly competitive nature of science often pits students against one another, and it is more evident under such circumstances when mentors "play favorites." Nevertheless, such settings offer the potential for friendliness and even intimacy between faculty member and student, and for a kind of group collegiality that is rewarding for all.

For the most part, the closeness is helpful. Students at this level are undertaking their first major, all-consuming academic project. The prospect is often daunting, and personal support and encouragement may be vitally important. When the work is isolating, the personal friendship and support of a mentor can be a source of stability and strength.

There is no formula for discharging the academic duties involved in being a good mentor. Knowing when to be demanding and when to be flexible and forgiving is a skill possessed by the best. But there are successful mentors who are either consistently tough or reliably supportive; the important feature is that the same message is sent all the time. The research supervisor who is warm and friendly one day and punitively critical the next creates confusion in the student. Nothing is more discouraging than an unsystematic mixture of positive and negative reinforcement.

Apprentice scholarship is a time of trying out new ideas and testing creative limits. Sometimes the new ideas are bad or even silly. Veterans become used to the harsh public fate of bad ideas, but neophytes can be scared into a kind of unproductive trance if one of their first real creations is treated roughly. Criticizing with respect and turning a poorly structured question into a good one are among the skills that good mentors are able to utilize regularly.

A different kind of challenge arises when graduate students or postdoctoral fellows develop personal problems that reach the crisis level. Two of the more successful Ph.D. students I had in the 1960s and 1970s—successful, that is, in terms of subsequent research productivity—experienced real personal crises in the course of their graduate careers. I suppose that the testimony of most research supervisors would be similar. The graduate years can, after all, be a time of real hardships, in personal as well as in academic life. Often there is a first marriage, and sometimes a first divorce. The burden of independent work is difficult, and periods of doubt and insecurity are almost inevitable. When these coincide with difficulties in a student's personal life or if they are amplified by some form of clinical depression, work can seem almost impossible. Under these circumstances an insightful adviser is often able to give friendly support and even broker some professional help. But often the best solution is merely to take the pressure off for a while. A student finishing his doctorate told me recently of a series of difficult personal episodes that had delayed completion of his thesis. I asked whether his major professor had been helpful to him in a personal way. He said, "No, but he did what I really needed: he cut me some slack."

In a closely knit group setting, a perennial danger is the establishment of "favorites." If one student appears to be getting most of the time and attention from the professor, some resentment is bound to develop. The problem is much worse if the extra investment is seen to depend on personal relationship rather than on professional criteria or some particular individual need. Research groups can become almost dysfunctional if jealousy develops over special attentions paid to any one member on the wrong basis. Yet in a well-integrated group everyone will rally in support of the student who has a real need, even if it involves the personal rather than the scholarly domain. Mentors need to be aware that their treatment of individual students at this level always has an impact on their relationships with others.

A special kind of damage is done when the relationship between the faculty member and a student goes beyond the level of friendship and becomes something else. The entire area of romantic and sexual relationships between faculty members and their students is fraught with complexity. It is a tempting domain in which to issue firm dicta ("No faculty member shall establish a romantic relationship with any student who is enrolled in a course or under his or her academic direction"). That is a clear enough rule, and it has a great deal going for it. The trouble is that it is overbroad and yields difficulties when one begins to take inventory of the exceptions. When Henry Rosovsky, then dean of the Faculty of Arts and Sciences at Harvard, proposed to consider a rule on this subject, he received the following response from the distinguished economist and former ambassador to India, John Kenneth Galbraith:

> I was, as you will presently understand, both enchanted and distressed by your recent communication on behalf of the Faculty Council, entitled "Sexual Harassment, Related Matters." My pleasure had to do with the eloquence and delicacy of the language in which, in keeping with Harvard standards in such matters, your letter is couched. The reference to "amorous relationships" in the "instructional context" is superb and reflects an acute sense of Harvard faculty and even New England sensibilities. My distress is personal. Just over 45 years ago, already a well-fledged member of the Harvard faculty on a three-year appointment, I fell in love with a young female student. It was not in an instructional context; however, non-instructional amour is a "situation" against which you also warn. A not wholly unpredictable consequence of this lapse from faculty and professional decorum, as now required, was that we were married. So, and even happily, we have remained. But now my distress. As a senior member of this community, I am acutely conscious of my need to be an example for younger and possibly even more ardent members of the faculty. I must do everything possible to retrieve my error. My wife, needless to say, shares my concern. What would you advise?[3]

The wit and candor of this response do not, of course, lay this difficult matter to rest. There are real problems here: other students are unlikely to be charmed into tolerance of one of their number who is engaged in a flirtation with the faculty member who is teaching or training (and will be called upon to evaluate) all of them. Excesses can develop in an atmosphere that treats such matters too casually, as many institutions did in the late 1960s.

Thus it is tempting for universities to initiate restrictive legislation. Whenever they do so, however—as the University of California at Berkeley did a few years ago—there is a predictable public reaction. The media and many casual observers, on learning that there are professors who develop sexual relationships with their students, react as to a startling revelation. There follows a quickly developing appetite for strict, even Draconian regulation of romance spurred by public outrage. Once the matter is thoroughly discussed by whichever legislative body is handling it in the academy, however, difficulties and complexities appear. First, the proposed rules for dealing with the problem look more and more unadministrable. Second, charming exceptions such as Professor Galbraith's show up occasionally, reminding the rulemakers that, after all, young people can't always help falling in love and that in most cases attachments are handled conscientiously. So the faculty legislative body ultimately decides against regulatory intervention, whereupon the media and the public react as they do when the Congress votes itself a pay raise.

The temptation to intervene is also driven by occasional revelations of truly egregious behavior. Few academic images invite public loathing more than that of the faculty Lothario, and not without reason. There is usually a significant age difference in a professor-student relationship, but the real concern is that it has the taint of coercion about it. The argument offered in defense of such liaisons is that consenting adults should be permitted freedom to follow their own wishes. Apart from the difficult question of whether the student's consent in such cases can ever truly be informed, there is the matter of collateral damage to the student. When what begins as a supportive, presumably academic interest turns into a sexual interest, the student is entitled to wonder whether the early support and praise weren't conditional. Even in affairs that end with minimal regret, that sense of betrayal can linger. No student should be forced to wonder whether the appraisal of his or her intellect by a valued mentor was not, after all, based on something quite different.[4]

The costs of such entanglements, in short, are potentially so great that the right course for the faculty member is to avoid them scrupulously. This is sometimes easier said than done: uninvited approaches do happen, and they can have considerable emotional power behind them. Young people are never more vulnerable than at such moments, and the right mixture of compassion and firmness is required.

The more serious problem of faculty members who press romantic attentions on unwilling students has arisen in several institutions. Sexual harassment is by no means an academic problem. It is receiving more and more attention in the workplace generally, partly as a result of highly visible confrontations in the early 1990s: the testimony of Anita Hill in the Senate confirmation hearings for Justice Clarence Thomas, the charges made by various women against Senator Bob Packwood, and a number of other high-profile cases in law firms and large corporations. To say that sexual harassment is not an academic problem, however, is not to say that it doesn't happen in institutions of higher education. It does. In colleges and universities, female students encounter a predominantly male faculty whose members are older and often in a position of power; and the setting in which they work can be almost charismatic. (Some cases of sexual harassment on the part of female faculty against male students have been reported, but they are relatively rare. So are homosexual approaches.)

Temptation and opportunity thus may go hand in hand in this situation. In the most egregious cases, faculty members have employed the grading system as an incentive for sexual compliance; in others, scarcely less troubling, there have been hints of career support or other favors. With such cases it is not difficult to reach a conclusion that professional misconduct has occurred. But there is a gray zone, and it is getting larger. What constitutes sexual harassment in the more ambiguous cases can launch endless debate.

Most of the difficulty in defining sexual harassment has to do with speech. Local custom and tradition have an enormous influence over which kinds of comments are considered acceptable in certain instances. At one pole, then, lie behaviors that may be offensive under some circumstances but not others. For example, in some places it is a risky business for a man to compliment a female student or colleague on her clothing or hairdo, whereas in a more traditional venue such comments may be entirely welcome. Context is important. If the setting and the subject matter are serious and scholarly, then a male remark about any aspect of a woman's appearance will be jarring—although the same comment might be perfectly acceptable in a different conversation. The exercise of good taste and gentle social correction will have to suffice in this area; it is not a domain for regulation.

At the other pole are the cases of direct invitation, fondling, or the introduction of blatantly sexual references into a conversation contextually devoid of them. It is hard to find an excuse for behavior like this in any situation, least of all when directed by a faculty member to a student. The persistent forcing of attention, even when the overtures are polite, belongs in the same category. In most institutions actions in this category would be the basis for charges of professional misconduct, resulting at least in censure of the faculty member and some persuasive commitment to corrective action.

In between these poles there are some truly difficult cases. The following example is only moderately modified from a real incident.

Professor P has a small group of Ph.D. candidates in organizational behavior in the business school. S is a first-year graduate student who has come to join P's program. They have worked out a plan for the first year, and P has suggested that S take his own course as preparation. P gives a very difficult mid-term examination designed to diagnose deficiencies in the students' preparation. A week after it is given, P invites S to come to his office to discuss her performance.

P begins by offering S a cup of tea, which she declines. He then asks her about her background in the social sciences. She reminds P that she majored in economics and sociology in college before joining the Peace Corps. "I'm afraid that two years of community public health work in Costa Rica taught me something about organization and behavior but caused me to forget some economics," she explains ruefully.

P smiles sympathetically. "I'm sure it was a rewarding and challenging experience for you." "Yes, it was really worth it," S answers. "But," P continues, "it must have been hard to leave family and friends."

S, not certain of the relevance of all this, nods and mentions two siblings whom she missed especially. P continues solicitously, "I was wondering whether this performance on the exam could have resulted from some emotional state. When you came back last fall to begin your work here, had you perhaps broken up with a boyfriend or something like that?"

S has now become uncomfortable with this intrusion but finds it ambiguous and does not wish to alienate P. She concedes, because she is flustered and because it is on her mind, that she had a relationship with a fellow Peace Corps volunteer in Costa Rica that had ended sadly on her return. "That must be very difficult for you," P responded. "I can understand now why the course is presenting problems for you and I'd like to give you some special help. Could we get together for lunch later this week and talk about it?"

S is by now alarmed, and responds by saying, "I really don't think that would be appropriate, but I do want to do well in the course and to be accepted in your group. I hope I can ask you for help in a non-social way." She rises and leaves.

That evening she tells her roommate about the conversation. The roommate, in her second year, laughs and says, "Welcome to the club. P is notorious for that stuff. I bet he leaned across the desk and gripped your forearm when he told you how difficult it must have been for you." S, surprised, confirms that he had indeed. At a meeting of the Women's Student Association later that week, the two roommates conduct an informal survey; they find a third-year student who had a similar experience, and secondhand accounts of others. The women decide that the situation is intolerable, and begin plans to see the dean and disclose their concerns.

The likely outcome of this scenario is that the dean will appoint a committee to investigate the facts, interview these students and others, and then make recommendations as to whether a charge of professional misconduct should be lodged. The facts in the scenario indicate only that there is real cause for concern; the case for professional misconduct, and for any subsequent sanctions, would rest on the answers to several open questions. First, how frequent was this conduct? Did other students report the impression that P was issuing sexual invitations? Were there implications that acceptance would enhance the possibility of academic rewards, or that refusal would carry the risk of penalty?

Quite apart from the variable and often ponderous course of formal institutional investigation and sanctioning, this kind of behavior is likely to have informal consequences. Women's groups on many campuses have been publicizing the identity of men thought to be guilty of sexual harassment. Sometimes the names are listed in women's rest rooms; sometimes they are published in the form of posted leaflets or letters to the editor in newspapers, or even advertisements in campus periodicals. They reflect women's rapidly changing and strengthening views about this subject and also betray their dissatisfaction with the procedures in place on many campuses for dealing with sexual harassment problems. On my own campus, the School of Medicine was the locus of complaints on the part of women faculty members that sexism is so much a part of day-to-day life that real cases of sexual harassment may pass almost unnoticed.[5] Some of the complaints about general institutional problems of this sort, to be sure, are couched in extreme terms, and the informal "naming" methods employed to identify suspected harassers sometimes smack of vigilantism. But the experiences of academic women in this regard entitle them to a sense of frustration, and it would be wrong to cast the complainers in the role of feminist zealots.

Sexual harassment and sexism are not the same thing. But sexism is surely a part of sexual harassment, and acceptance of it probably does enhance the probability that the other will occur: an atmosphere that is intolerant of women in small ways is likely to be permissive with respect to larger abuses. Both sexism and sexual harassment, I think, relate to some more general attributes of academic communities. In the debates over these matters in the School of Medicine at Stanford, I was struck by the degree to which uncivil conduct based on hierarchy contributed to the problem. To be sure, male faculty members were guilty of sexist remarks and, in a couple of cases, of outright harassment. But it was part of a larger pattern, in which many professors felt free to deprecate residents and residents turned the same attitudes on medical students. In an environment in which civil discourse is a regular casualty, it cannot be surprising when the offenses become gender-related.

Sexism, even of the most subtle kind, is a particularly troublesome problem for developing female scholars, and it can have serious adverse effects on their futures. No one, and particularly no male, entering academic life can afford to be unaware of this potential for damage. It is especially significant in the sciences, where women confront unique problems. As undergraduates and even before, they frequently encounter low expectations on the part of teachers and may even be urged to "leave science." Under the circumstances, many do not even need urging. Yet surprisingly, at the same performance level women are no more likely than men to switch their majors from the natural sciences to other fields. This persistence occurs, in many places, against a background of subtle discouragement—which makes it all the more remarkable. Women students handle their negative experiences with faculty by avoiding certain classes or contacts, or simply by laughing them off. What seems more significant is the frequent failure of faculty members to provide individual help and support. Indeed, for both sexes a primary cause of loss of interest in scientific careers is faculty disinterest.[6]

It is clear from this evidence and much more that a level of personal caring and interest makes a large difference in academic outcomes, not only at the advanced level, where mentorship is the rule, but earlier as well. Advising relationships, career counseling, and guidance in independent study are the interactions from which the most meaningful and memorable influences arise.

These are also the relationships that many faculty members find the most rewarding. There is a special joy in watching a student succeed brilliantly with a difficult problem; and sometimes an equal joy in helping a limited or troubled student overcome a handicap. Long before there were colleges there were journeymen and their mentors. There is both lore and truth in the old aphorism that the best education consisted of Mark Hopkins on one end of a log and a student on the other. But the log can't make the right things happen. The one-on-one academic relationships, however informal they may seem, require at least as much planned effort and special skill as the lecture and the seminar. They represent the highest form of academic duty, but they also embody the greatest risk of failure.

5

TO SERVE THE
UNIVERSITY

SERVICE IS an important academic duty in all colleges and universities. In the context of the large state-supported institution, it embraces a wide range of public obligations: outreach to community groups, service to industry and practitioners of the professions, and participation in efforts to make the academic community relevant to important state or regional constituencies. To the professor of animal husbandry at a midwestern state university, participation in the institution's "swine day" is as natural a part of the job as teaching an undergraduate class.

Service as a feature of academic life is far less visible in small colleges or in the private research universities. But it is nevertheless important. In all kinds of institutions the faculty play significant roles in a kind of service enterprise. They help to run the place by governing their departments, participating in legislatures that conduct the business of fulfilling tasks delegated to the faculty, and helping in the formation of institutional policy.

Those tasks are vital. But they also help to foster a certain kind of academic ambiguity. Because faculty members participate in the most vital university functions, they see themselves as much more than employees. Indeed, they are, but they are also paid salaries by an institution that, in the legal sense, is "owned" by someone else. Hence the ambiguity.

Because many of the university's academic powers are delegated to the faculty by trustees or regents, faculty members have significant influence in the determination of institutional policies. They are responsible for the organization of academic departments, for hiring their colleagues, for the curriculum, and for establishing rules about the conduct of research and the requirements for graduation. Individual faculty members may attain significant management responsibility while still holding faculty status. And in special cases, professors may find themselves in charge of individually led projects of considerable magnitude. Thus at some times or in some cases, professors may resemble the leaders of small entrepreneurial ventures; at others, managers in a large, somewhat bureaucratic organization; at still others, simply employees. Seldom, however, do faculty members behave as though they consider themselves merely employees, and in fact they are quite unlike employees in most other sectors.

In some respects, though, professors *are* like other employees. They are, after all, salaried, with compensation and benefits determined by officers of the university on the basis of their performance. They can be terminated for cause (for neglect of duty, for example, or moral turpitude); and even, as long as the protections of tenure are observed, for reasons of financial stringency or a change in program need. In theory at least, faculty members can be required to perform designated tasks, just like workers in other settings.

The ambiguity of faculty status naturally leads to occasional conflict. This is sometimes played out in the courts, when faculty members attempt to form unions. The law requires that in order to form bargaining units for the purpose of negotiating with employers, groups demonstrate that they are labor and not management.[1] Wherever unionization efforts have been subjected to legal test, the arguments are revealing. Such a case, involving a faculty organizing effort at Yeshiva University in New York, reached the Supreme Court in 1979.

In the Court's decision in that case, the dialog between Justice Powell (for the majority) and Justice Brennan (for the minority) perfectly captures the inherent ambiguities of faculty governance.[2]

Here is Justice Powell:

The authority (of faculty members) in academic matters is absolute. They decide what courses will be offered, when they will be scheduled, and to whom they will be taught. They debate and determine teaching methods, grading policies, and matriculation standards. They effectively decide which students will be admitted, retained, and graduated. On occasion their views have determined the size of the student body, the tuition to be charged, and the location of a school. When one considers the function of a university, it is difficult to imagine decisions more managerial than these.

But now hear Justice Brennan:

Unlike the purely hierarchical decision-making structure that prevails in the typical industrial organization, the bureaucratic foundation of most "mature" universities is characterized by dual authority systems. The primary decisional network is hierarchical in nature: Authority is lodged in the administration, and a formal chain of command runs from a lay governing board down through university officers to individual faculty members and students. At the same time, there exists a parallel professional network, in which formal mechanisms have been created to bring the expertise of the faculty into the decision-making process. Whatever influence the faculty wields in university decision-making is attributable solely to its collective expertise as professional educators and not to any managerial or supervisory prerogatives. The University always retains the ultimate decision-making authority ... and the administration gives what weight and import to the faculty's judgment as it chooses and deems consistent with its own perception of the institution's needs and objectives.

This judicial dialog introduces another view of faculty roles with which Justice Powell would doubtless concur: the professor as manager/governor.

In circumstances like the one that gave rise to the Yeshiva case, the professoriate defines itself as a laboring class only for the limited purpose of obtaining the protections of collective bargaining. Faculty members think of themselves not as working for the institution, but rather of having responsibility for the institution's work. Because they are responsible for the academic work of the institution, and because that is, after all, the university's central purpose, their version of "who owns" (or, often, "who *is?"*) the university makes sense. But the claim also brings to the surface two different and often conflicting notions of institutional ownership and governance. One might be called the communitarian vision; it holds that the faculty (with whatever student and staff participation it chooses to cede) ought to make the truly important policy decisions since, after all, these are at bottom academic matters. The competing notion, perhaps best identified as the fiduciary vision, puts that responsibility on the trustees as the legal owners of the institution. It will be helpful to take a closer look at each of these visions of the university.

The university is first and foremost a community that is devoted to learning and that exists in real space and in present time. Since everything that happens in the university is fundamentally academic, that is, involves teaching and research directly or involves activities that support teaching and research, it follows that faculty (and students) are the ones most deeply affected by policy decisions. An argument deployed frequently during the academic ruckuses of the late 1960s was that those who will live closest to the consequences of decisions are the ones who should make them. This was greeted with enthusiasm by many, especially the young; after all, the prospect of setting the conditions of one's life is tempting. In the more realistic climate of the 1990s, that proposition seems a good deal less reasonable in its original form—though few would deny that in an environment as collegial as the university, some weight ought to be given to the views of those most affected by the outcome.

But faculty members have another, stronger case for their involvement in institutional governance. It is that the university's practicing academic members are in the best position to evaluate academic merit, and thus can best judge the consequences of the university's decisions.

Although these arguments surely have some merit, they are firmly rooted in the present, and the university has a strong time preference for the future; that is why there are governing boards. The logic is firmly expressed in the arrangements made to preserve the value of public trusts, of which the private universities are the oldest and best-known example. A philanthropist (Leland Stanford or John D. Rockefeller) decides to endow a new institution (Stanford or the University of Chicago). The state, in recognition of the fact that private wealth is being devoted irrevocably to a public purpose (one for which the state, absent private philanthropy, might have to pay itself), places its legal authority behind two commitments: first, that the trust will be managed so as to conserve its value in perpetuity; and second, that it will be managed in a way faithful to its original purposes. This is a vitally important arrangement. Indeed, the founding of Stanford University had to be delayed until the California Legislature developed and passed, in 1885, laws providing that public trusts would be so managed.

Permanence and fidelity are more than the devout wishes of founders and legislators. They are binding legal requirements on trustees, that is, matters of *fiduciary duty*. In a different way, but for the same reasons, the governing boards of state universities are committed to permanence and fidelity of purpose. This encourages, indeed compels, a certain level of devotion. As one trustee once put it: "You pay pretty serious attention when you know that it's your house and your car."

If, for example, a governing board were to decide that some external social purpose was more important than higher education, and therefore devoted university resources to that purpose, it would be a breach of fiduciary duty. That scenario is not as improbable as it might sound. In the mid-1980s there was an intensive campaign to persuade regents and trustees of U.S. universities to engage in blanket divestiture of the stocks of all companies doing business in South Africa. (This movement called itself the Anti-Apartheid Movement, in an effort to persuade people that ending apartheid required the withdrawal of American firms.) Some universities responded with full, blanket divestiture; Columbia was a particularly prominent example. Others undertook a selective review of their holdings, divesting the stocks of certain companies that failed to follow the Sullivan Principles.[3] The Board of Regents of the University of California took a well-publicized vote in favor of blanket divestiture, and was thereby relieved of further student and media pressure. But the divestiture never took place. Sources close to the board report that regents opposed to the move had received a legal opinion asserting that blanket divestiture would result in significant financial losses to the university's endowment, thus exposing board members to legal action.

Indeed, the South African issue served to highlight the question of fiduciary duty in an entirely new way. Endless analyses appeared, even in financial journals, about whether divestiture—or any other form of concentration on "socially responsible" investment—would penalize the total return of institutional portfolios. The debate trailed off inconclusively, partly because political attention drifted, as it will, and partly because, given the complexity of the asset mix in large portfolios, the question is very hard to answer.

Perhaps the best conclusion is this: if investment strategy is influenced by any purpose other than maximizing returns, there is very likely to be an adverse effect. One result of the debate is that the fiduciary responsibility of trustees became more sharply focused in the public mind. It is probably better understood now that part of that responsibility is to maintain the real purchasing power of the university's endowments, and thus to practice a form of intergenerational equity.[4]

In this way the board takes responsibility for the students who haven't been admitted yet, the faculty who haven't been appointed yet, and the experiments that haven't been thought of yet. This is a natural source of tension between the two versions of university "ownership," because the loyalty of faculty, students, and staff to contemporary plans and programs often conflicts with the fiduciary desire to husband resources for the future.

In several institutions, such conflict flared into open hostilities over budget reductions that had to be imposed in the recessionary conditions of the early 1990s. During the 1980s there was almost unprecedented growth in university endowments. Corporate and foundation giving grew as institutions prospered, and individual giving was stimulated by the same strong economy. But the biggest factor in endowment growth was the extraordinary market performance of those years. Thereby hangs the tale of this particular conflict.

Most private universities have policies that restrict the spending of endowment income to a portion of total return that, over the long haul, will preserve the purchasing power of the endowment. Suppose, for example, that the endowment earns 6 percent in nominal terms, and inflation is 3 percent. The institution should spend only the difference if it hopes to preserve intact for the next generation the programs supported by that endowment.

In practice the calculation is much more difficult. In the first place the meaningful figure for inflation is not the Consumer Price Index (CPI) or some other commonly used indicator; it is the rise in cost of the "market basket" of goods and services that the university purchases. Because universities are service enterprises they are very salary-intensive, and inflationary growth in salaries is faster than that in the consumer goods on which the CPI is largely based.[5] Other important cost items for the university (such as travel, books, other publications, and scientific instrumentation) are also notoriously inflation-sensitive. Thus the standard economic measures will understate what the university needs to do to stay level—and the right ones are not easy to derive.

During the 1980s, annual total returns for the major private university endowments were extraordinarily high, averaging well over 10 percent and in some years reaching even higher values. (The numbers fluctuate wildly over time, and thus even ten-year average rates of return are highly dependent on the time frame chosen.) Inflation during this period, measured by CPI, averaged perhaps 4.5 percent. Even assuming that the higher education deflator outpaced CPI by 2 percent, there was still real endowment growth of around 4 percent over the decade.

This was fuel for controversy. Some faculty members who saw numbers like these, just as budget reductions were beginning in the early 1990s, wondered how institutions could possibly justify sequestering "profit" at a time when professors were being asked to sacrifice current programs and even to accept salary cuts for themselves. The university administrations responded that a decade-long bull market is an aberration, and that the formula for determining endowment payout must work over the long term—that is, over several business cycles. In other words, the formula (which builds in the recent history of endowment return) may favor the future in good times, but in bad times, which will inevitably come, it will favor the present.

It is very difficult to make those arguments stick in an environment of intense and unanticipated privation. Indeed, although the theory is technically correct, it is nevertheless true that over a twenty-year period that included the bad investment years of the 1970s as well as the bull market of the 1980s, the major private university endowments grew significantly in real terms. (They increased in part because new funds were raised for new programs, and in part because existing endowment investments grew with the market.) Faced with strained budgets and faculty skepticism about the issue, several private research universities did increase their endowment payout rates in the early 1990s, as a recessionary economy and falling federal support began to bite into the gains of the 1980s. The debates preceding these decisions were really struggles between the two versions of the university. And, like all issues of intergenerational equity, they aroused strong passions.

Having explored two different versions of university ownership and governance, we can return to the Powell-Brennan debate about what the faculty's role is in relation to those others who take ultimate responsibility for the university's assets. As the differences between the justices suggest, some powers are clearly assigned, yet others are distributed according to institutional tradition and/or the sway of practical politics. Power can be real or residual, *de jure* or *de facto*. In their conflicting descriptions of how university governance works, the justices made thoughtful analyses. They reached different conclusions because they had different visions of how the university is supposed to work, and no certain knowledge of how it *actually* works.

On a broad range of matters, the university's fiduciaries yield their power to the community of the present, in particular to the faculty. In part this practice arose in recognition of the faculty's expert knowledge. In part it derives from ancient tradition: the academic profession is, after all, a kind of guild in which only members can certify others for membership. Thus the granting of degrees and the establishment of requirements are plainly faculty responsibilities.

It also derives from the more recent tradition of protecting the role of the university, as the source of new and sometimes threatening ideas, from outside political interference. Were trustees or regents to have responsibility for the academic substance of the university's work as well as for its economic health, the temptation to patrol it for unhealthy or unwelcome notions might prove irresistible. As this tradition was becoming established early in the twentieth century, some landmark cases illustrated what might happen if trustees were to interfere in academic decisions.

Perhaps the best known of these was the firing of Professor Edward Ross from the Stanford University faculty in 1900. Ross was a distinguished economist who had a record for heterodoxy and was often criticized for his public support of William Jennings Bryan, the Free Silver movement, and the Populists. Jane Stanford, then president of the Board of Trustees, demanded that President David Starr Jordan fire Ross. After a considerable effort to talk her out of it, Jordan acquiesced. The case became a national academic *cause céleldebre,* and is frequently cited in histories of the period as a classic example of a trustee's willful interference with academic decision making on political grounds. Jane Stanford is represented as strongly opposed to Ross's support of Populism and his public advocacy of Bryan's candidacy.[6]

But in fact, Ross had supported Bryan publicly for years without interference. What triggered Jane Stanford's ire was not Ross's politics but his xenophobia: in a speech in San Francisco opposing Asian immigration to the United States, he had said, "And should the worst come to the worst, it would be better for us if we were to turn our guns upon every vessel bringing Japanese to our shores than to permit them to land."

At the time, Jane Stanford had written of her outrage that a Stanford professor would associate himself with such political demagoguery. She was especially outraged at Ross's anti-Asian prejudices; Stanford had been making special efforts to include Japanese and Chinese students in its first classes.

Seen in this historically accurate light, the Ross case becomes a "hate-speech" case, perhaps the first. It is interesting to speculate what would happen today if a tenured professor at a modern American university, responsible for teaching classes with large numbers of minority students, actively advocated the use of military force to halt the immigration of a particular ethnic group. Doubtless there would be some arguments that such statements constitute professional misconduct—countered by vigorous rejoinders to the effect that freedom of speech on the campus deserves even more protection than the First Amendment gives it elsewhere.

In the years since those turn-of-the-century tests of academic freedom, the faculty collectively have gained substantial authority in faculty appointments (and unappointments). The American Association of University Professors (AAUP) actively monitors institutions for violations of tenure and academic freedom policies, and censure from that group is a substantial disincentive to cavalier institutional treatment of these matters.

And of course, with respect to curriculum, admissions, assignment of grades, and the granting of degrees, the legal owners of the university almost from the beginning put the power squarely in the hands of the president. As the academic leader of the faculty, the president received those responsibilities by formal delegation. At Stanford the delegation is expressed in the following powers, set out in the university's Founding Grant:

1. To prescribe the duties of the professors and teachers.
2. To remove professors and teachers at will.
3. To prescribe and enforce the course of study and the mode and manner of teaching.

4. Such other powers as will enable him to control the educational part of the University to such an extent that he may be held responsible for the course of study therein and for the good conduct and capacity of the professors and teachers.

Even in 1904 this seemed like too much power for a president to have. So as a check, the trustees approved the Articles of Organization of the Academic Council. This document established a form of governance that persisted until 1977; more important, it made the president the executive officer of the faculty and vested in the council the powers and duties "usually vested in the faculties of similar institutions." The phrasing was perhaps deliberately vague, but what it meant was responsibility for curriculum, admissions, the granting of degrees, and related academic matters.

There are, at least in some places, other delegations as well. Students, for example, are often given responsibility (or at least a large share of it) for making various community rules and for student discipline. Academic or social conduct may itself be the subject of a special delegation, through the adoption of an honor code that places responsibility on individual students.

In addition to those powers formally delegated to them by trustees, the faculty have a broad array of *de facto* governance responsibilities: for example, rules for the conduct of research; policies for libraries or academic computing; regulations regarding health and safety; athletic policy; benefits planning; and—last but surely not least—that perennial generator of disputes, parking policy.[7] Even with respect to matters ultimately decided by trustees, the faculty's voice is important. Faculty and administrative staff therefore participate jointly in committees that develop recommendations regarding the siting of academic buildings, benefits policies, and the like for presentation to the president and, eventually, the board.

I have thus far scarcely mentioned the process of faculty appointment, yet it is the single most important agent in sustaining the institution's quality. The question "Who appoints the faculty?" has various answers, depending on when it is asked and how it is meant. The turn-of-the-century phrase giving the president the power of "appointment and removal at will" falls on modern ears with almost Draconian harshness. Not surprisingly, that kind of language has vanished, and it is here that the gulf between *de jure* and *de facto* authority is widest.

In practice, as President Kingman Brewster once said in the heat of a late-1960s controversy at Yale, "the faculty decides who shall be on the faculty." His statement sounds as if it might have been a wry concession of some presidential prerogative. Not at all; Brewster was explaining a decision on his part not to intervene in a matter over which he felt the faculty *should* have the final say. That view is the predominant one in the modern American university.

Surely the composition and quality of the faculty is the single most important determinant of the character and prestige of the university; thus the power of appointment, formally delegated to the President but *de facto* a matter for faculty decision, is the most important power there is.

How does it work in practice? Let us follow an example from the perspective of the hiring institution. Suppose that the Department of Biology is making a new faculty appointment to replace an ecologist who has just retired. The department's Policy Committee has a protracted debate over the field of the replacement; the population biologists argue that the billet was, after all, in their domain and that the retiree has left a teaching vacancy. But a coalition of neurobiologists and molecular geneticists wants to appoint a person in the burgeoning field of developmental neurobiology. Eventually the population group wins out, partly because the committee understands that the neurobiologist will require several hundred thousand dollars in one-time capital set-up costs. A debate with the dean then follows, because the department has its eye on a distinguished mathematical ecologist who will require a tenured professorship. The dean insists, however, that given the resource constraints affecting the institution the appointment has to be made at the beginning assistant professor level.

Accepting this decision, albeit with ill grace, the department appoints a search committee consisting of three population biologists and, just to keep them honest, a geneticist and an immunologist. The committee scours the nation, calling leaders in the field, writing to all important Ph.D.-granting departments, and advertising in the *Chronicle of Higher Education* and *Science*. Of two hundred applicants for the position, a dozen or so are considered seriously. After further evaluation and checking with sources, four are invited to campus for the ritual recruiting visit and job seminar. (In certain departments, especially in the humanities, it would also be usual to ask the candidate to teach a class, and to have that performance reviewed. In the sciences that practice is increasingly rare.)

One candidate stands out. She gets the unanimous vote of the search committee and then of the department, and is made an offer by the department chairman. The dean has been consulted, and approves the offer. But the candidate must be told that the offer is not final until the appointment papers prepared by the chairman have been approved by the provost, the university's Committee on Appointments and Promotions, and the president and the board. The committee will typically be composed of distinguished senior faculty elected from across the university. But in some universities, school-level committees make the final recommendations, and in a few there are special *ad hoc* committees for each tenure appointment.

These layers of approval are all composed of faculty members. The provost—who is nearly always drawn from faculty ranks—may occasionally turn back appointment papers to a department. But in most cases that is not a serious reversal; usually such action is in the interest of reconstructing the case so that it will pass committee scrutiny. Once past that level, it is virtually unheard of for an appointment to be rejected. Indeed, the president usually simply presents a long list of academic appointments as part of the board agenda, and the docket is then approved without discussion.

Thus Brewster is right in practice; the faculty decides who is to be on the faculty. Of course, there have been occasional exceptions: appointments have from time to time been disapproved by presidents or by trustees on political or other extraneous grounds. These exceptions create enormous fuss whenever they occur, partly because they are so rare. If the practice recurs in a single institution, the AAUP will review the cases and may decide to censure the institution. Although no legal or financial penalty accompanies listing by the AAUP, it is nevertheless a strong deterrent because of the public blow to the prestige of any university so censured.

Faculty members also play key roles in deciding who shall be on the faculty in other institutions. Participation in the process, whether at one's own or in another university, entails stern tests of objectivity and fairness. In one's own department, it is often hard not to place undue weight on the needs of one's own subdiscipline, against the interests of the group as a whole. In evaluating candidates for positions elsewhere, it may be difficult to avoid the same kinds of personal rivalries that may unduly influence the reviewing of grants and manuscripts.

In a faculty member's own department all kinds of pressures are likely to attend the choice of which field gets the next appointment. This is difficult enough for a relatively young professor to deal with. Should he or she vote "with the discipline" or risk collegial displeasure by deciding this time to favor breadth? More difficult still is the trial of evaluating final candidates objectively and fairly—especially if they are close to one's own field. Past differences, present rivalry, or some personal attribute of the candidate may exert influences that tend to unbalance judgment. Worst of all is the situation in which a choice must be made between a candidate who is thought to be very slightly better than another but appears much less "collegial." Often, sad to say, this last descriptor is a code word for something far less acceptable: it may signify that the candidate is more "aggressive" than the department's male members like a woman to be, or that the candidate is overweight and dresses badly, or has unorthodox political views. It is all very well to say of this process that the candidate should be evaluated strictly on his or her merits, and leave it at that. But the matter won't stay put. In what universe is "merit" being defined? Isn't it possible that a particular personality trait may make a candidate a less effective teacher? Is the notion of "collegiality" so irrelevant after all, in a department whose work depends heavily on consensus? These are deeply divisive matters, and they frequently cause misunderstanding and even enmity among colleagues. There are no firm guidelines, save the not very useful observation that candor combined with restraint often makes the debate go better.

Evaluating candidates for positions elsewhere raises a whole new set of challenges. Some of them we have met before, in connection with the writing of letters of recommendation for one's own students. A new one arises directly in this connection: how should one advise another department about a new appointment when one of the candidates is one's own student, and one is being asked to evaluate a competitor as well? The temptation to favor one's own progeny is very hard to resist, and I know of few scholars who can manage complete objectivity under such circumstances.

Beyond that, there is the recurring question of how much candor to employ. Like other modes of discourse, "recommendese" tends to develop its own traditions and codes. Damning with faint praise is common, leaving the recommender in deep doubt as to whether honest but narrow reservations in an otherwise favorable letter may be deadly. Worse still is the prospect that the contents may under some circumstances be made public. Letters about prospective faculty members are not subject to the disclosure laws (the "Buckley amendment") that apply to letters about students. Unfortunately, in today's litigious world many failures to achieve appointment or promotion result in lawsuits against universities, sometimes even naming faculty members as codefendants. Plaintiffs frequently demand disclosure of letters of recommendation as part of the discovery process. In general, universities have resisted, sometimes yielding, as a compromise, bowdlerized versions that may or may not successfully conceal the identity of the author. Case law in this area is still being formed, but in a number of states legislation now compels the release of such letters on demand. Thus a veil of caution—some would describe it as a straitjacket—has been drawn over the recommendation process.

Equal Employment Opportunity Commission (EEOC) complaints and civil lawsuits have become a regular part of faculty appointment. It is important that legal recourse be available to those who are unfairly damaged by the process, but a significant proportion of those who do not make tenure now seem to feel that the fault lies with the system. Indeed, at some major research universities it is the exception when a woman or a member of a minority group does *not* file an EEOC complaint following a disappointing decision.

We are now even seeing litigation over failures to appoint persons from the outside who had no particular claim to candidacy. At Stanford, for example, a visiting professor in the Department of History was proposed for appointment as a tenured member of the faculty. After a lengthy evaluation process, the members of the department decided against making the appointment. Although no commitment had been made to the visitor, he nonetheless sued Stanford and the members of the History Department *as individuals.* The plaintiff charged that the decision not to appoint him was made on political grounds, citing criticisms made by some faculty members that his book was anti-Semitic. In the hands of an aggressive and highly visible plaintiff's attorney, well known for his critical stance against Israel, this case made Bay Area news for several months before it was decided in the university's favor.

The sternest tests of the process come not when appointments are made but when it is proposed that they be undone. Can faculty members—especially faculty members with tenure—be fired? Of course they can. If an institution decides that a particular department is no longer relevant to its programs of research and instruction, it may eliminate it, along with the appointments of its faculty members. In practice, departmental elimination, whether under financial duress or for strictly programmatic reasons, has normally been accompanied by efforts to find other homes for those professors whom the institution wants to keep.

In addition, the tenure policy statements of universities set out the conditions under which professors can be fired for cause. Stanford's cites "substantial and manifest incompetence, substantial and manifest neglect of duty, or personal conduct substantially impairing the individual's performance of his appropriate function within the university community."

One must suppose that the framers of this and similar regulations had in mind the professor who has fallen victim to Demon Rum, as sometimes still happens, or who is chronically irresponsible about meeting classes, or who simply cannot resist a pretty face. There is a voluminous literature on academic freedom and the protection of appointment; in it, incompetence and moral turpitude are seen as "adequate causes" for dismissal.[8] But such rules do not really provide secure grounds for firing a professor on the basis of laziness, or for inactivity in his or her research area, or for lecturing in a monotone from ten-year-old notes. The public perception that tenure protects "deadwood" is, alas, correct. Henry Rosovsky, in *The University: An Owner's Manual,* recites a story he says comes from Stanford. In it the provost presents the university's new early retirement incentive program to a faculty member who has been unpublished and unappreciated for years. He announces that this splendid new program will permit Professor Deadwood to retire immediately at half salary. Why, Professor D wants to know, should he do that when he is already retired on full salary?[9]

Of course, the protections of tenure were intended to confer institutional benefits in quite a different area. They were meant to protect the institution and its faculty from political assault—to make the university a safe haven for ideas, even heterodox ones. From that viewpoint the accumulation of a few sticks of deadwood is a modest price to pay for the freedom so treasured by the academy.

In the late 1960s new challenges to the principles of tenure protection appeared. Institutions were faced not just with the occasional instance of professorial incompetence or moral turpitude, but with faculty members who joined with students to challenge the values and sometimes the rules of those institutions.

In a case at Stanford in 1971–72, President Richard Lyman proposed to fire a tenured professor of English, H. Bruce Franklin, on the basis of four specific charges. The most serious alleged that he had led a student occupation of the university's computer center, subsequently urged a crowd outside the building to ignore a police order to disperse, and later made a speech in which he incited students and others to make "people's war" against the university.

Because this was a celebrated case that drew heavy media attention, and because it was so controversial inside Stanford, the huge investment of effort made to resolve it fairly was probably a good one. But in fact that investment was required by the level of due process guaranteed under the university's rules, which, like those in most institutions, afford extensive protections to faculty defendants. At Stanford the rules require that the president present formal charges to the faculty member accused, and propose a penalty that could range from formal censure through fines or restrictive conditions to discharge. If the faculty member accepts the penalty, that is the end of it. But if he or she does not, then the Advisory Board—a seven-person faculty committee elected from across the university to evaluate appointments and promotions—hears the case and makes its recommendation to the president. The faculty member may elect to have the hearing public or private.

In the Franklin case the president proposed dismissal. Franklin, a self-proclaimed revolutionary with an active campus movement behind him, elected to have the hearing public—and promised to use it as an occasion for making his views and those of his followers widely known. A large classroom was converted to a hearing room capable of holding more than two hundred people, and at least in the beginning it was always full. Both the university and Professor Franklin were represented by counsel, the university by a patient litigator from the Los Angeles law firm of Tuttle and Taylor, and Franklin by a changing cast that initially included the well-known defense attorney Michael Kennedy and, for a time, Professor Alan Dershowitz of Harvard Law School (who withdrew promptly upon seeing a picture of Stalin above the defense table but invited himself back in as an *amicus* near the end). There were also a number of talented amateur volunteer lawyers! The hearings lasted six hours a day, six days a week, for six weeks; The Advisory Board heard from more than a hundred witnesses between disruptions and guerrilla theater, and after it was over had to sort through a million words of testimony. As the chairman of the Advisory Board at the time, I presided over the hearings. I learned that being a judge isn't easy—especially when you have neither bailiffs nor a sergeant at arms.

The Advisory Board consisted of unusually busy and committed scholars. One was the director of the world's largest linear accelerator. Two went on to become presidents of major foundations or universities. Three were department chairmen at the time. It seems almost inconceivable now that an academic community would invest such resources in so trying and unpleasant a task. But to all of us then it seemed as though the very fabric of academic life was under unbearable stress, and that cases such as this one would decide whether the great universities of this country could remain livable places.

The three main charges, having to do with the computer center occupation and its aftermath, all involved incitement. Because this was widely seen as a "speech case," the Advisory Board had to decide whether it would adopt the applicable Constitutional interpretations, as though Stanford were a state institution, or claim private status. We decided on the former course.[10] Professor Franklin then argued that what he did—advocating occupation of the computer center, trying to get people not to disperse following a police order, and urging various actions against the university—was in fact constitutionally protected speech. The Advisory Board held to the contrary, finding that under the most liberal Supreme Court standard Professor Franklin's speech constituted incitement in that it increased the risk of imminent lawless action and injury to others. The board held that Professor Franklin's pattern of conduct in these incidents violated not only the Policy on Campus Disruptions but the general conditions regarding faculty conduct set out in Stanford's tenure policy. By a vote of five to two, the board recommended dismissal. The dissenters (I was one) did not differ with the majority on the basic speech issues, but believed that the university failed to sustain its burden of proof on two of the charges. They recommended serious penalties short of dismissal.

The American Civil Liberties Union (ACLU) of Northern California was persuaded to take Franklin's case into the courts, where it was argued that he had been dismissed for constitutionally protected speech. After a tortuous eight years of decision and appeal, during which every ruling went against the ACLU, the case was finally decided in the university's favor.

Several years after the Advisory Board's decision, I was asked how I felt about my own investment of time and energy in the case. I replied that I thought I had wasted half a year of my life. That was in the late 1970s; peace had returned to the nation's campuses, and in some ways it seemed hard to recall what all the fuss had been about. Since then I have spent nearly three years in government and more than a dozen in university administration, and I have a different view of the matter. At Stanford, the Franklin case was influential in reshaping the faculty's view of its own role, leading to a new Statement on Faculty Discipline, adopted in 1972, in which more precise definitions of sanctionable activities are provided. More important, I now believe that this case and others like it proved that faculties can take hold of the values of their institutions, defend them successfully, and make a reality of the vision of the academy under even the most stressful challenges. The Franklin verdict, whether one agrees with it or not, represented a real triumph of due process. Thus it spoke volumes about the capacity of the faculty to fuse the different versions of university governance, reinforcing the communitarian vision while guaranteeing the institution's survival into the future. At this vital moment the faculty *were* the university.

❧ Mention of the word "tenure" almost invariably draws an irritated response from those who do not work in the domain of higher education. It elicits questions like "Why in the world would anyone adopt a policy that gives lifetime job security to thirty-three-year-olds?" To inhabitants of the for-profit sector, it seems an unwarranted and foolish withdrawal of performance incentive.

Of course, tenure originally had little to do with performance. The institution arose first out of a concern for political independence: tenure is no ancient institution, but was first established at the University of Wisconsin in the early part of this century. The locale is well-matched to the purpose. Wisconsin at the time was a stronghold of "LaFollette progressivism," and life tenure for professors was viewed as essential if they were to be able to express heterodox views without fear of political reprisal. The idea spread, and is by now ingrained in the fabric of American higher education.

New stresses on tenure have arisen very recently and bid to generate a serious reappraisal of policy. The driving forces are three: financial stringency, the "demographic profile" of university faculties, and the uncapping of mandatory retirement. The first means that each faculty billet is more precious. The second has produced a gradual but inexorable increase in the average age of university faculties.[11] The last has extended the length of time a faculty member may occupy a billet. Thus many observers have suggested that tenure must be reevaluated, and possibly replaced by multi-year employment contracts.

Several arguments have been raised in response to these proposals. First, although studies on current faculty members' intentions with respect to retirement have yielded conflicting results, it is widely believed that most professors intend to retire voluntarily at or around the age of seventy, eliminating some of the fears generated by the uncapping of mandatory retirement. Second, it is argued that the freedom-of-expression functions of tenure protection are no longer needed, because the idea of free speech on campus is now so firmly implanted in society. That may be true for the major universities, goes the reply, but in a number of smaller and more regional places there have been troubling incursions on academic freedom. Thus tenure at the University of California, Harvard, and Stanford might be abolished without adverse consequence to those institutions, but if abolition spread widely, as it surely would, orthodoxy and even political control might climb into the driver's seat elsewhere. Finally, there is a practical argument: there may be little real effect of substituting, for example, ten-year contracts for tenure. High achievers would simply negotiate for rolling extensions, like today's successful football coaches, thus leaving the institution in nearly the same position it was in under the tenure system.

Normally, tenure is conferred after a "waiting period" that, according to custom and principles laid out by the AAUP, should not be longer than seven years. The intention is to discourage exploitation of tenure-line faculty in junior positions by leaving them hung out to dry, waiting for a permanent position that never comes.

Usually tenure is conferred at the line that divides the assistant and associate professorship. But that line has been blurred by a number of institutional experiments. Many universities now have nontenured associate professorships, while still observing the seven-year rule. Some years ago Yale University considered a proposal to make the associate professorship an entirely nontenured rank. The story goes that when this was presented to the Yale faculty, Professor G. Evelyn Hutchinson, the world-

135

renowned ecologist, made the following counterproposal. There should, indeed, be only one tenured rank, said Hutchinson—but you have the wrong one. Confer tenure on the associate professor. Then, when he or she is ready for promotion, offer everything: a handsome salary with bonuses, an "A" parking sticker, 50-yard-line seats in the Yale Bowl, and so on. To get all these things, all the new professor would have to do is give up tenure.

This story, apocryphal or not, speaks volumes about the institution of tenure and how people feel about it. It has taken on a life larger than its own real dimensions; it has become a label that embodies more than security and more than simple economics. It is, in short, so much a part of the American academic fabric that it exists all by itself, as a symbol of accomplishment and seniority that might be needed even if it were empty of real significance.

The structure and function of academic departments in universities depend significantly on how they manage their appointment strategies in light of the tenure distinction. There are two basic patterns. Some departments (and in a few cases entire institutions) have a deliberate policy of making all or nearly all of their tenure appointments from the outside: that is, they bet on proven quantities. We will call these Type I. Others, and they are the majority, try to screen carefully for appointments to the assistant professorship, with the expectation that they have a good chance of achieving tenure.[12] We will call these Type II. Harvard, for example, has traditionally been a Type I institution, but has recently shown more willingness to promote through the ranks. At Stanford most science departments are Type II, although one (Physics) is clearly a Type I.

From this pattern, naturally, important cultural features of institutions or departments are derived. Type I universities or departments arguably make fewer mistakes at the top, since they are seldom tempted to promote for reasons other than nationally established research excellence. But their assistant professors are apt to be less enthusiastic about the common mission, since they know that they are not stakeholders in the university's future. Indeed, morale in Type I departments is often low at the junior level, with complaints about undemocratic management and poor access to "shared" resources predominating. Type II departments are happier places, in my experience. But as the internal promotion rate drops, as it has for strictly demographic reasons, it becomes harder to convince junior faculty that their prospects justify full investments in the institution's future. And failures are much more damaging than they would be if expectations were lower. Type II departments are thus likely to generate more litigation.

Important advantages are gained from setting a firm time line for tenure consideration. It forces the institution to make tough, up-or-out decisions rather than postponing them indefinitely, to the disadvantage of both the university and the candidate. There is a real element of fairness in the insistence that after seven years of an assistant professorship, the decision is going to be made. But it also has the effect of heightening tension—increasing, as it were, the perceived height of the hurdle. This "tenure bar" is the major obstacle to an academic career. To fail to clear it often produces a complete change of direction; in an earlier time those who did not receive tenure in the leading research universities could hope for "good" academic appointments in lesser places. Now the result is often a career change.

There is a growing impression that the bar should be lower. It now looms as an overdominant expression of the value the institution places on its individual faculty members. The contrast between the extensive evaluations in the tenure process and the weakness of evaluation afterward disturbs many. In response, some institutions are strengthening post-tenure assessments of faculty and managing salary administration policies more aggressively so as to provide an alternative way of signaling value. Some would go further. In a stimulating essay, the chairman of the Astronomy Department at Columbia University describes how he negotiated with his university a series of fixed-term appointments, with merit reviews, as a substitute for tenure.[13] He proposes that faculty approaching the tenure line be offered the choice between a long "life-contract" (the equivalent of tenure) and a series of five-year appointments. The former would include university retirement contributions that would give the faculty member a postretirement income nearly equivalent to his or her salary, and some guaranteed sabbatical leaves—but, because there would be no provision for merit reviews, annual increases would be based on the cost of living. The latter choice would entail five-year merit reviews, with the possibility of significant salary increases and extra leaves. The choice, in short, would be between job security and the prospect of significant financial gain.

Finally, we must confront the question whether the institution of tenure as we have come to know it is likely to survive its present trials: uncapped mandatory retirement, financial stringency, and public disapproval. There is a powerful reluctance to abandon it, for reasons already stated: it does provide protection against political interference, and arguably leaves senior faculty members freer than they would otherwise be to pursue creative but high-risk lines of scholarly investigation. On the other hand, it exacts a price in productivity that many find unacceptable in hard financial times.

In fact the argument may be moot. In many places, especially the large research universities, tenure may be slowly dying of natural causes. The most striking change in faculties over the past thirty years has been a gradual but inexorable increase in the number of faculty members who not only lack tenure but will never get it—and in many cases don't expect it. The "parafaculty," known by titles that disguise without quite deceiving, such as lecturer, senior lecturer, clinical associate professor, professor (teaching), and the like, now perform a vast array of academic work once accomplished by tenure-line faculty, including the teaching of many undergraduate courses. Many of them are excellent teachers; indeed, on many campuses it is a source of tension that they receive accolades from students that are denied their tenured colleagues.

Although this situation may be partly the result of the "regular" faculty's retreat from responsibility to students, as many of the academic muckrakers contend, there is a better explanation for it. After all, downsizing and outsourcing have become the battle-cries of corporate America as it contends with what is essentially a problem of too much job security. In dealing with the "tenure problem," as some administrators are inclined to call it, universities face the same thing—as the result not of a legacy of collective-bargaining negotiation, but of a policy adopted many years ago for purposes having little to do with traditional "conditions of employment" issues. The growth of the parafaculty, seen in this light, is the academic equivalent of outsourcing, adopted as a result of similar economic incentives. The two-class faculty is now a fact of life in many places, and that will doubtless give rise to its own generation of new problems.

✺ The disparity between the faculty's role as governors of the institution and their role as salaried employees delivering services invites a question: who is making up the rules of engagement for faculty? The answer is not nearly as clear as most people would suppose. Indeed, the level of control faculty members have over their own conditions of employment once led a university trustee, used to more hierarchical settings, to exclaim, "The inmates are running the asylum!"

In that unflattering metaphor there is a grain of uncomfortable truth. Faculty commitments are governed by tradition and understanding rather than by firm rules; there are no time clocks, and nobody checks up. The difficulty is that whereas understanding was once widely shared and conformity nearly universal, the press of outside activities and the increasing heterogeneity and complexity of the university have tended to dissolve both. Writing of the presence of faculty members at Harvard during reading and examination periods, Henry Rosovsky claimed in his 1991 report to the Faculty of Arts and Sciences: "In the past [that need] was a well understood aspect of our social contract. Judging by the empty corridors and the difficulties I used to have in reaching my colleagues in January and May, we can safely assert that this aspect of the social contract is no longer honored."[14]

Later in the same report, Rosovsky described the crux of the matter. The faculty, he claimed,

> has become a society largely without rules, or to put it slightly differently, the tenured members of the faculty—frequently as individuals—make their own rules. Of course, there are a great many rules in any bureaucratic organization, but these largely concern less essential matters. When it concerns our more important obligations—faculty citizenship—neither rule nor custom is any longer compelling . . . as a social organism, we operate without a written constitution and with very little common law. That is a poor combination, especially when there is no strong consensus concerning duties or standards of behavior.

Critics of the modern university have, not surprisingly, leapt on this lack of administrative or external control as evidence that the academy is indeed an asylum in the hands of the inmates. Yet there are powerful reasons for the degree of freedom that faculty members enjoy. Creativity does not prosper, nor does entrepreneurial initiative flourish, under firm bureaucratic control. Scholars need a loose rein if they are to be at their best.

Furthermore, our colleges and universities are full of conscientious, dedicated people who manage, without visible rules, to fulfill and exceed their obligations both to their students and to their own intellectual interests. Nevertheless, given the present level of external criticism, it is likely that more efforts at specifying obligations and enforcing compliance will be forthcoming. The alternative to internal reform, with active faculty participation, is apt to be an intensified drive for external accountability. Most members of the academic community will surely prefer a social contract revived from within.

In addition to fulfilling the responsibilities already mentioned, faculty members at almost any large research university will serve on administrative committees for the purpose of developing a remarkable range of policies. A partial list of such committees (the actual titles might vary) will suggest the breadth of the issues attended to and also indicate how dramatically the task has expanded over time: Athletics, Benefits, Health and Safety, Land and Building Development, Parking and Transportation, Human Subjects, Laboratory Animal Care, Outdoor Art, Investment Responsibility.

This list illustrates the degree to which external forces and agencies have added to the burden the faculty takes on in helping with institutional decision making. For example, intercollegiate athletics has become a more complex and perilous domain, though we tend to forget that it has always been large and often controversial. (It is said that at the turn of the century gate revenue from football at Yale exceeded the combined budgets of medicine, law, and divinity!) Today the major conferences and the NCAA have complex rules for student eligibility, program staffing, and financial accountability. The NCAA rulebook alone is a maze of complex regulations; for a single annual meeting, the docket of proposed legislative changes is nearly an inch thick. Each major conference also has its own rules, and will develop conference positions for the NCAA meeting. University faculty athletic representatives and their institutional committees thus spend much of their time on policy matters that are essentially extra-institutional in character.

In other areas—health and safety, buildings, and the panoply of panels that deal with the conduct of research—the source of the burden is government regulation. Everything from earthquake codes to housing standards for laboratory mice, from the storage of laboratory chemicals to the design of research questionnaires, is the subject of a state, federal, or local rule that requires institutional oversight. Faculty participation in designing the procedures for that oversight is essential if the latter is to work, as many universities have discovered the hard way.

In response to the increase in federal and state laboratory safety requirements, most universities establish a health and safety office, notify the faculty of the requirements, and then schedule inspections. There may be no tradition of independence stronger than that of the faculty member as master of his or her own laboratory. It does little good for the inspector to announce that the order to dispose of acids in a certain way, or to label everything in the refrigerator, actually came from a government agency. In this domain, messengers are shot with regularity. As faculty members have been brought more prominently into the process and as local safety committees have extended the work of central committees and panels, resentment has gradually subsided and compliance has improved. But the initial cost, in terms of faculty effort, has often been substantial.

To make matters worse, this rapidly escalating involvement with government-mandated functions has been taking place at a time when other burdens are growing heavier as well. In the years between 1975 and 1990, for example, the number of grants that a Stanford faculty member needed to hold in order to maintain a constant real revenue stream increased by 50 percent; at the same time, the reporting requirements and the extent of justification needed to win the grants also grew. So it is not surprising that the appetite faculty members feel for having a say in the governance of the university is tempered by the reality that there is simply not enough time for everything.

Although it is true that the average faculty member who serves on a committee is surrendering time to some purpose that holds no special interest or reward for him or her, it is important to keep in mind that the faculty of a modern research university is a truly extraordinary repository of special knowledge and expertise, on everything from cost accounting and earthquake engineering to the economics of publishing and construction safety. A well-run committee process can engage such knowledge with the institution's problems in a way that rewards both. For example, for three years Stanford's Faculty/Staff Benefits Committee was chaired by Professor Alain Enthoven, one of the nation's leading experts on the design of health care systems. During his chairmanship, the committee led the way in conferring certain benefits on unmarried domestic partners and achieved a spectacular success in revamping health benefits plans so as to introduce competition among plans.[15] And as we were considering revisions in the appointment and promotion process that would place more emphasis on teaching performance, Professor Lee Shulman of the School of Education agreed to chair a subcommittee to look at new ways of evaluating teaching. Although it was a standing subcommittee, it was given staff resources and a grant to study teaching effectiveness measures, in which Professor Shulman also had a scholarly interest. Thus it served to advance scholarship as well as to do some important business for the university.

In some areas, however, the faculty role raises troublesome questions. Consider, for example, the issues of siting academic buildings, setting faculty retirement policies, and making decisions regarding the use of the university's nonacademic lands. In each of these cases, either a special problem or some larger interest surfaces on close examination. A department badly in need of a new facility, for example, might not get one if too much weight were given to other faculty claimants for the same resources. Retirement policies clearly affect the age and character of the future faculty, and thus are vital to the fiduciary version of the institution, yet these policies may run directly against the interest of many present members. When Congress was first considering the full uncapping of mandatory retirement, Stanford was among the many universities that communicated their deep concern about the problems this would impose on institutions with faculty tenure. I reported that position to the Academic Senate, and there were strong objections from some members who thought that no view from "the university" on this matter should have been communicated without their legislative approval. There was a clear conflict between their interest and that of a much younger generation of faculty members—a conflict in which the fiduciary version of the university had to find in favor of the future.

More recently, my successor presented to that same Academic Senate a proposed university policy on sexual harassment. He had followed a procedure quite standard for university rulemaking: the policy, which would apply to staff, students, and faculty, had been thoroughly worked through with senior university officers, including the deans, and was being presented to the Senate for discussion before being taken to the Board of

Trustees. Members of the Senate repeatedly tried to reword and amend the document by legislative action. They had to be reminded that although their views were certainly being sought, they had no mandate to legislate unilateral revisions in a policy that would apply to about twenty thousand people who did not happen to be faculty members.

Perhaps the best illustration of the kind of conflict that can arise in this sensitive area is provided by land-use decisions. Stanford is almost unique among American universities in having quite a lot of land: several hundred miles of streets, some of them used more by the public than by the campus community; open space in the foothills; nearly eleven hundred units of on-campus faculty housing; and a shopping center. It is perhaps only natural that decisions about how these lands are used produce controversy, since so many faculty members are in fact part of the neighborhood. Like neighbors everywhere, they are concerned about zoning and land use.

The difficulty arises when these political impulses come into conflict with the legitimate fiduciary purposes of the university. In the late 1980s Stanford built a new graduate housing complex; one of the main entrances to its parking lot was scheduled for an intersection near the edge of a faculty housing area. This location was fought tenaciously by a group of faculty members who lived in the neighborhood, on the grounds that it might increase traffic on residential streets. At least one site review and a major traffic study had to be done in order to satisfy the objections, which eventually proved groundless. But this and other land-use issues, essentially neighborhood zoning matters that belonged before a county authority (Stanford is part of unincorporated Santa Clara County), were on occasion brought up at faculty Senate meetings—as though they were eligible for debate in a forum dedicated to academic policy.

Perhaps such conflicts are inevitable when the university tries to be too many things for its faculty. If the university is landlord and lender as well as employer it is not surprising that the most valued employees will seek to exert influence in these other areas. If a quiet negotiation with the provost after an offer from Harvard can result in more help with the mortgage, faculty members may logically conclude that pressure of that sort might reduce traffic in the neighborhood, or place a dormitory at a greater distance, or even change the lease terms on a family-owned restaurant in the university's shopping center. (This last request, strange as it may sound, was once actually made.)

It may be time for universities to work their way out of these rather paternalistic relationships. In the meantime, however, for the health of the academic community, some boundaries should be respected. Faculty members should express their views on matters that involve the fiduciary version of the university (that is, the university as legal entity), but they should steer clear of using the arenas of delegated academic authority to resolve those matters, and—short of a crisis of principle—should not import them into negotiations about employment.

Although the boundaries of proper engagement may not always be clear, as the preceding section illustrates, there is no doubting the central postulate that the faculty *must* be involved in the process of institutional governance. This engagement is not merely an essential one for maintaining faculty prerogatives and protecting academic freedom, although that is often the motivating force behind it. It is equally essential to the university in its legal or fiduciary version, because the faculty is the heart of the institution, and if its members are not active participants and stakeholders in any proposed change, then change is unlikely.

Appropriate forms of academic governance are essential for providing that engagement, and they have undergone significant changes in the decades since World War II. At Stanford, for example, the governing body until the mid-1960s was the faculty as a whole, called the Academic Council. It met at least quarterly, but its important decisions were made by an elected Executive Committee that met more frequently. In addition, the faculty elected an Advisory Board, which served as the institution's appointments and promotions committee and was consulted by the president on a variety of other matters.

The Academic Council grew much too unwieldy when the number of regular faculty began to press a thousand members, and at a critical point during a student protest in the late 1960s it proved absolutely unable to cope with crisis. What followed was an extraordinary exercise in the creation of government. Professor Kenneth Arrow (later the winner of a Nobel Prize in economics) chaired a committee that wrote the charter for a legislature, and then got it approved by the Academic Council. The Senate of the Academic Council, elected from major academic divisions of the university, meets every other week. Not only does it have a broad span of responsibility over delegated matters of academic policy, its part of "shared governance," but its members are able to question, and often to challenge, the president and the provost on all matters. Having to "stand for questions," though it is occasionally uncomfortable, is a good thing for university administrators as well as for the faculty.

The legislative solution is probably the dominant one when a large institution, rather than a separate faculty, is the governed entity. But there are others. Smaller faculties (and sometimes even larger ones) prefer the plenary style of decision making and shun representative governance. Indeed, Stanford resisted the latter until a precipitating crisis made it clear that under pressure decision making by large bodies simply doesn't work. After that, the change gathered the political support it needed.

Whatever method is employed, it is essential that faculty members have a way of deploying trusted representatives to participate not only in the committees that carry out the regular delegated functions of the faculty, but also in the committees that act for it in major university policy decisions. In no kind of institution is the consent of the governed more vital to success—or more difficult to obtain—than in a university. Because the faculty's work *is* the university's work, it is essential that faculty support be behind the decisions that vitally affect it.

Nowhere is this need more vividly demonstrated than when a university proposes major budget reductions or significant restructuring. During the early 1990s such moves were common in the major research universities, both private and public. In some places these caused tremendous tension, with threats of faculty revolts and even votes of no confidence in university administrators. In other places the reductions—even rather painful ones— were made almost without dissent. My sampling, informal and modest thought it is, suggests that the single most important differentiating factor was the level of participation by respected members of the faculty in developing the plans. Wherever there was significant involvement, the process was somewhat more difficult and time-consuming, but the results were much more palatable.

The extent, and even the desirability, of faculty engagement in institutional reorganization and budget-cutting will depend very much on the size and custom of the institution. In a small liberal arts college, where the degree of intimacy among faculty members even of different departments is high, it may be nearly impossible to obtain consensus on, say, the elimination of a department or a program. And institutions differ widely in their traditions of faculty participation, and thus in faculty expectations.

In places where there is a high degree of participation, those faculty members who did most of the work might well say, "It was a good process, but never again!" Such involvement is time-consuming, and it now comes atop an expanded array of faculty roles in institutional management. Professors are asking themselves with increasing frequency whether their present level of participation in university governance is worth it.

One hopes that the answer is yes. The past two decades have been marked by an increasing attenuation of institutional loyalty on the part of the professoriate: it is said, with some justification, that many of the most distinguished research scholars owe their primary allegiance to the invisible academy of their discipline rather than to their university. To the extent that is true, it seems likely that it can only be reversed by the sense of shared responsibility and common purpose that comes from meaningful participation in the institution's future. Surely that is a central part of academic duty, and its restoration will be vital to the re-establishment of the *entente cordiale* between the university and the society.

6

TO DISCOVER

IN RECENT YEARS, research has come to lie very close to the heart of academic duty. The increasing premium placed on scholarship, both within the academy and outside it, has raised new problems for the university and for society's perception of it. Scholarly production across the disciplines is now in a contentious relationship with other dimensions of academic duty, especially the teaching function. Modern scholarship costs more than other academic responsibilities, not only in terms of money to support it, but also in terms of time expended on it. These costs are often justified on the grounds that better scholars are better teachers, and that those who leave original investigation behind quickly become teachers of the obsolete. Although there is some truth in this argument, the perception is growing that the focus on scholarship comes at the expense of teaching and training.

The focus on research achievement is intensified because our institutions of higher education are in competition for the best students, the largest shares of foundation and government sponsorship, and the most public attention and regard. Although this is especially true of the research universities—who vie with one another for top ratings in the serious surveys and who yearn for membership in the AAU—the search for research-dependent prestige trickles down into the top tier of liberal arts colleges and "comprehensive" state universities.

Competition is a good thing. It certainly has strengthened the excellence of American higher education in a variety of ways. It has helped new and aspiring universities find their way into the top rank, and it has captured the public's interest in following how the established institutions are faring in comparison with one another. It has doubtless increased faculty salaries, on average, through bidding wars for highly recognized scholars. The coexistence of an independent sector with public higher education in the United States has provided, many claim, a powerful drive toward improvement in both. But even those with strong faith in market forces may pause to wonder about the extent to which the desire for institutional and individual prestige has become a hallmark of our present system. The level of competition for distinction, for awards, for priority, and for money is high enough to induce neglect of other duties, or worse. As the stakes get higher in the race for funding and the pickings get slimmer, it becomes more difficult for individuals to adhere to the highest standards of objectivity, and even of integrity. Institutions, too, may make overreaching claims in the struggle for higher rank. At perhaps the greatest risk is comity; among the effects of intensified competition is an erosion of collegiality and of civility. And there has been a marked tendency for faculty commitments to the institution and its duties to fall away, to be replaced by loyalty to a specific discipline and its national agents, committees, and academies.

Research in a university conjures up a smorgasbord of subject matter, working styles, and intellectual product. Most humanities projects are lonely efforts, conducted by dedicated single individuals in library carrels. There are some large-scale efforts, however. Among massive historical assessment projects the Martin Luther King Papers project at Stanford is large but perhaps not atypical. It involves a team effort under the direction of Professor Clay Carson; over the course of a decade the project has engaged 16 senior scholars, many of them visitors, 48 graduate students, and 106 undergraduates, one of whom has published not one but two books based on his work.

Science, by contrast, is seen as a group-oriented venture, heavily dependent upon instrumentation. Indeed, it often is: high-energy physics and now, increasingly, molecular biology and organic chemistry depend on very expensive capital facilities around which large numbers of people cluster. Program-project grants and multiauthored papers are the rule in this domain. But there is lonely scientific scholarship as well—the paleontologist at the dig, the mathematician working away on the next theory. Any effort to put the problems and challenges of research in a single format is defeated by the very pluralism of the venture.

Yet all research is alike in a few fundamental respects. It depends upon support; even the loneliest work requires funding, if only the modest, marginal help available from departmental and university general funds. It requires protections and, because it poses risks, frequently generates concerns about how it should be regulated. Because it is so central a part of the work of the American university, research has required, and received, special protection and care from the institutions in which it is done.

Modern academic research, transformed as it has been by massive infusions of support from government, industry, and other sources outside the university, has created extraordinary opportunities for academic scholars as well as for the institutions in which they work. The new pattern has given rise to the term *sponsored research*—faculty scholarship supported from externally derived funds allocated specifically to that work.

Sponsored research in the sciences, and in many of the social sciences, has supported more and more doctoral training and even independent study by undergraduates. Even when research sponsorship is aimed at faculty projects, the equipment and technical help it provides yield fallout benefits for students. Faculty members sometimes speak of "bootlegging" support for doctoral dissertation research or undergraduate honors projects on instruments bought on government grants or contracts. More directly, graduate students are often supported on sponsored project funds as "research assistants," that is, as technical staff paid to help on particular projects.

At the same time, external project funding contributes to the overproduction of doctorates by providing incentives for enrollment. Graduate students are real assets in the laboratory, and some faculty members depend on them to get the work done. This may tempt departments to take on students to meet their research requirements, even in the knowledge that there won't be enough jobs for them after they finish. In the humanities and the "softer" social sciences, external support has also often waxed and waned, providing an uncertain base for extended scholarship and discouraging students who might do well in these fields from entering them at all.

As mentioned in Chapter 2, the government's support of academic basic research slowed after the 1960s and was about the same in the early 1980s as it had been in 1967. There was some growth in the 1980s, but it was accompanied by a large increase in the federal deficit, which drove all "discretionary expenditures" downward. By the mid-1990s, the future for government support of university research looked bleaker than it had in forty years.

Other aspects of the university research picture are as grim as the status of program support. Since 1968, there has been no government funding whatever for the construction of new research facilities on university campuses. Many scholars must work in a decaying infrastructure; others, more fortunate, do their experiments in buildings provided by state funds or private donations. Both these sources have risen significantly as federal support has waned, but many of their funds have actually been shifted from other purposes. Foundations, which have traditionally "filled in" with support for the sciences and have provided the lion's share of funding for the humanities, are increasingly devoting their resources to community-based projects or to internally originated ones. And corporations, though they provided an increasing share of university sponsored research budgets through the 1980s, never accounted for more than about 10 percent of the total, even in those places, such as MIT and Stanford, that have traditionally strong links to industry.

As funding in the major basic research agencies of the federal government—primarily the NSF and the NIH—declined, hard choices were pressed on the policy-makers. NIH, in order to satisfy the demands of the "research community," established targets for a minimum number of grants to be funded in the ensuing year. Because of pre-existing commitments to continuing grants, little money was available for funding new ones; as a result, the targets had to be met by underfunding each award, so that the scientists managing those grants and contracts were forced to choose between people (technicians, research assistants, and the like) and facilities and equipment. Naturally, they chose to preserve the people. As a consequence, to quote a statement by the then-president of the AAU, "the number of applicants for grants grows faster than the available resources, the success ratio declines, unrealistic demands for university matching accompany reduced grant support, good research goes unfunded, good researchers become frustrated, young researchers leave the field, infrastructure problems are deferred, and the price for it all will be paid in the future by people who are not around now to assert their interests."[1]

This mournful assessment accurately describes the state of mind of many university researchers in the 1990s. Support from government and the major foundations is far stronger than it ever was in the prewar period, but the expectations of most of those who occupy senior faculty positions in the 1990s have been conditioned by expectations generated in times of unprecedented growth. It is difficult for them to accept that for scientists, just as for inhabitants of the American West, drought is historically a more probable state of affairs than high water.

Although there are many sources of funding for research, such as gifts from individuals, grants or contracts from industry, or support from private foundations, the main supporter of university research, dwarfing all other sources, is the federal government—especially in the sciences. Indeed, about two-thirds of all basic research done in the United States takes place in the universities, and of the funds supporting that work about 90 percent come from the government.

Thus getting a research program up and running entails a series of interactions with organizations outside the university. It is surely the most daunting experience in the life of a scholar, particularly a young one, and perhaps most particularly in the expensive and highly competitive world of the sciences. There is enormous pressure to succeed; the application process for funds is complex, and it takes a great deal of time. This quest for research support has assumed a dominant role in the academic duty that faculty members owe to the institution, and it has impinged on the time they have for other duties.

To illustrate this demanding process, let us follow Dr. G, an assistant professor of biology at a southwestern university, as she attempts to obtain funding for her work on the evolution of caste in social insects.

Professor G's studies on a genus of primitive ants, begun during the first three-year term of her assistant professorship, have already suggested a new way in which genes that favor more rapid development encourage the differentiation of "soldiers" from "workers." She was supported entirely by the NSF during that period; now, however, that agency's growing commitment to engineering centers and other large projects has forced cutbacks in its support of scholars like G. Her NSF grant is up for renewal, but she knows that if she is to add the equipment for chemical analysis of the ant pheromones and travel to New Guinea for essential fieldwork, she will have to obtain funds from other sources as well.

G's strategy is to try the National Geographic Society (NGS) to support the fieldwork. The NGS gives only small grants, in the range of $10,000, but her field site is of interest to them. The NSF continuation proposal is more problematic. G has learned that the two disciplinary panels to which she might apply have funding rates well below 10 percent. Indeed, she and her colleagues believe that the situation is so tight that the success of a proposal in the top 20 percent is largely a matter of luck. Because there are no other major funding sources for which she is eligible, and because she has passed the age at which she might qualify for one of the several "Young Investigator" awards, she has no choice but to persevere. The application must be superb if it is to succeed, so she spends about six weeks in preparing it, giving a careful account of her research objectives and their relationship to her past results. She even proposes one experiment that she has already had preliminary success with, knowing that if her project is funded she will need to show some positive early results. (This makes her acutely uncomfortable; it is, after all, a form of deception. But since the success was so preliminary, and the practice is so general, she justifies it.) She then prepares a careful budget, shuddering briefly as she adds the university's "overhead" rate to the cover page of the proposal.

G submits the NSF grant before the deadline and then prepares a smaller and simpler proposal for the NGS. While still engaged in that work, she learns from a colleague that for more than fifteen years the U.S. Department of Agriculture (USDA) has had a "competitive grants" program, one designed to supplement the agricultural research program conducted through the system of land-grant universities and state agricultural experiment stations by reaching out to other institutions. She obtains the forms and finds that the requirements are about the same as those for NSF grants. Undaunted, she turns to the task of preparing an application, carving out a limited part of her program and including summer salary for herself as well as support for her technician and a graduate student—all items she had been forced to eliminate from the NSF proposal.

After some months of waiting, G hears back on two of the three proposals. The Geographic has come through—at least she can count on another summer of fieldwork. Alas, the USDA reports that the group of ants on which she is working contains no species classified as "pests," and that although the reviewers have much admired the basic science in her proposal, it is too far from the department's mission to merit support.

Now she is pondering, with heightened anxiety, what may be going on with her NSF application. She knows that her fate is in the hands of scientists—some of whom are friends, or at least acquaintances—in the field of evolutionary biology and animal behavior. In short, she is undergoing *peer review.*

The role of peer review in the allocation of public funds for research projects and facilities is vitally important, and the obligations of peer review are significant (though probably quite positive) burdens on faculty time. When large-scale federal support for the basic sciences began to develop in this country just after World War II, a fundamental decision was made—in most though not all of the mission agencies, as well as in NIH and NSF—to employ the judgments of other scientists as quality controls in the allocation process. As this process was being put in place in the 1950s and early 1960s, selection for the peer review panels was considered a signal scientific honor. The enterprise was smaller then, as well as both less formal and less time-consuming, than it is now. Understandably, the most distinguished scientists were asked to serve on the review panels and study sections, and almost all accepted. As a young investigator in those days, I had the sense that my early proposals were being conveyed into the hands of giants. The whole venture reeked of stateliness and reliability; indeed, it was the creature of a trusted establishment. Thus at its birth peer review was really not "review by peers" but review by scientific elders.

Of course that couldn't last forever, and it didn't. We are not a very elitist society, and soon there were persuasive arguments for broadening the membership of review groups to include younger scientists, women, and members of minority groups. A more important influence was the gradual exhaustion of the elders: the distinguished names were used up, and meanwhile the size of the task was expanding rapidly as the scientific enterprise grew. Pretty soon the review panels really were composed of researchers whose average publication records and perceived distinction were not very different from those of the average applicant. Ironically, "peer review" began to lose respect only when it began to live up to its name, that is, when faculty began to object to being evaluated by colleagues whose credentials were no more impressive than their own.

Peer review was also being subjected to heavy criticism from politicians for an entirely different reason. Those representing states with few prestigious institutions resented the concentration of resources in a small number of states that were more favorably endowed in this regard. This will be of concern to G and her colleagues, because the argument has been used to justify a dramatic change in the way government funds are allocated. The postwar development of federally funded basic research leaned heavily on peer review, or at least on competitive evaluation processes carried out by each funding agency. Soon, however, a few resourceful legislators began to realize that large research projects were beneficial to their regional economies and made constituents deeply grateful. By the early 1980s legislative add-ons to research agency budgets for specific, earmarked projects had become fairly common. Institutions with friends in Congress built impressive facilities: Tufts University in Massachusetts, where President Jean Mayer was close to Senator Kennedy, was a big winner, as was the Oregon Health Sciences University, to which Senator Hatfield was notably friendly. During the 1980s the practice became epidemic. Ex-congressional staffers such as Gerald Cassidy went into the lobbying business, helping institutions like Columbia and Catholic Universities promote their need for capital facilities. Senator Alfonse d'Amato was a relentless champion of pork-barrel funding for his constituent universities. By the end of the decade nearly half a billion dollars in pork-barrel funding could be identified, mostly in the budgets of the Departments of Energy and Defense.

The AAU and the NAS both attacked the practice, as did several congressional leaders known for their friendship for science, such as Senator Sam Nunn (D-Ga.) and Representative George Brown (D-Calif.). But that has not slowed the growth of a system that, in the view of some, has changed science appropriations into a modern reincarnation of that old-time congressional favorite, the rivers and harbors appropriation. Nor has it been easy to gain acceptance of peer review among contemporary legislators as a fair and objective way of finding the best science. As Senator Russell Long is said to have remarked, "Ah don't rightly know what a Peear is, but Ah know we don't seem to have many of them down in Louisiana." The success of American science, most observers believe, has been achieved partly through the use of merit-based, competitive evaluation of proposed programs. To the extent that good scholarship is a strong element of academic duty, allocation for other reasons threatens it.

A somewhat similar version of this outcry comes from members of the public who doubt that researchers ought to be deciding what other researchers get anyhow. A different objection comes from self-styled "fringe" scientists, who claim that the peer review system promotes orthodoxy and penalizes unusually creative or novel ideas. But the most important reservations about peer review are those held silently within the research community itself. A process that is controlled by peers does not, perhaps cannot, command as much respect and trust as one that is controlled by elder statesmen. Part of the price is a heightened level of conflict and mistrust within the scholarly community.

G is experiencing some of that now. She knows that one member of the NSF panel is a rival in her research field, and a person she has reason to feel may be untrustworthy. For her, that raises some fundamental questions about fairness.

Much is asked of grant reviewers by way of restraint, for there are built-in conflicts of interest in the arrangement itself. One researcher is being asked to evaluate objectively the work of a competitor. Obviously, the reviewer is expected to praise or to damn based upon a serious, sincere evaluation of the merits of the project. Equally obviously, it would be wrong for the reviewer to appropriate the ideas or methodologies of the applicant. Alas, real situations are seldom so clear-cut. The reviewer learns a slightly different approach that can be applied to his own work in the same area, or he discovers that a problem being pursued by one of his graduate students is a blind alley. Is he entitled to act on that information? And what of ideas? Are they in fact so clear-cut that their precise point of intellectual origin can be identified? Should we take the position that a reviewer who is exposed to a new approach must remain entirely unaffected by it?

Although the line is fuzzy, there is a reasonably clear zone of egregious violation. Grant reviewers have made use of information gained from the proposals of others for their own benefit often enough that NIH and NSF have adopted policies to warn peer reviewers of their obligation to respect the privacy of authors and to specify penalties that will be imposed on those who fail to do so. Still, some researchers have claimed that NSF fails to inform applicants fully about their rights, and on occasion procedures at the granting agencies are ineffectual in helping applicants cope with a problem when one arises.

P, a professor of neurobiology at a large state university, submitted a grant application to one of the National Institutes of Health. It described experiments designed to test a hypothesis that ran counter to an accepted theory about synaptic transmission. R, a major figure whose results form one of the main supports for that theory, had been engaged in a spirited debate in the literature with P. NIH has a policy whereby if an investigator has reason to believe that another has a strong bias against his work or has a conflict of interest, he can request that the second investigator not be asked to review the grant. P was certainly concerned about R's hostility to his views, but he also remembered an occasion on which R had taken ideas from an informal discussion and represented them as his own in a review article. Accordingly, he asked that R not be included among the reviewers. NIH sent the proposal to R anyway, and it was returned with a highly negative review. Somewhat later, at a scientific meeting attended by both, P heard R describe in a formal paper one of the experiments laid out in his own proposal. He immediately contacted the executive officer of the study section and described the circumstances. The NIH official was sympathetic; she told P that he was entitled to file a formal complaint. But she also advised him against doing so, explaining that it was NIH policy not to continue processing any grant applications from a complainant until the matter had been resolved. Since R's application was critical to the continued functioning of the laboratory, and since it was still under consideration, R decided not to proceed with the complaint.

Professor G had heard of such cases, and she had considered bringing her concerns about the panelist to the NSF. In the end, she decided against it. But the unresolved issue of the treatment she would receive from the referee caused her considerable worry during the pendency of the grant application.

Fortunately, her worries ended when she received the welcome news that her project had been funded. Unfortunately, the budget was cut by 10 percent, making it impossible for her to purchase one of the major pieces of equipment she needed for the pheromone analysis. But she emerged from the process with a feeling of relief. Her sense of accomplishment as a scholar, her confidence in her teaching, and even her relationships with her departmental colleagues were profoundly affected by her success in this trying experience. Had it gone a different way, she might well have been lost to the profession.

Were we to examine the entire breadth of research at her university, we would find Professor G about in the middle of a wide range of situations. At the neediest and leanest end would be scholars in the humanities disciplines and some of the social sciences. (The latter is a heterogeneous area; economists fare quite well, others rather badly.) Rarely do scholars in the humanistic disciplines find outside funding for research assistance or summer salary or computer time during a regular academic year. Most external support comes in the form of fellowships for a year's study away from the institution, from organizations such as the NEH, the Guggenheim Foundation, or the American Council of Learned Societies.

The search for support in one of the humanities disciplines will look quite different from Dr. G's. John D, an assistant professor of history at a California university, has been in his present position for five years. During the third of those years, he received a special six-month leave from his institution to complete the book that was originally based on his doctoral dissertation. The work traced the development of water policies in the American West during the second half of the nineteenth century and met with immediate critical success. It was awarded a prize from the American Historical Association (AHA) as the year's best book in the field of environmental history. Plainly, D is in the top rank of young scholars in his discipline, and—although the department at his university is one of the best and has a reputation for being highly selective in its faculty appointments—he has high hopes for tenure.

D's university is also unusually generous to young faculty. D's research leave came from a special endowment designed to make sure that young faculty receive opportunities to develop their scholarly work before reaching the tenure line. D spent much of it in his university's Center for Humanistic Studies, interacting with half a dozen senior scholars and advanced graduate students from other places and a few colleagues from his own institution. It was an invaluable opportunity to finish one promising project and get started on another.

His second project, now quite well advanced, is to be a study of the earliest stages in the development of a "conservation ethic" in late-nineteenth- and early-twentieth-century America. D must spend at least two months with Library of Congress materials, so he will require support to live in Washington during July and August. He will also need some graduate assistance for library work at his home campus during the academic year. Fortunately, many of the materials he will need are located in California (John Muir, Joseph LeConte, and other Sierra figures are important foci for D's study), so little additional travel will be necessary.

In the year following, however, D hopes to finish the writing, and his main need during that year will be time off. He has an offer to visit a small research library with an important collection in his area, where he will have good facilities and all the privacy he requires. His university has given him a two-quarter leave without pay, even though he already enjoyed a half-sabbatical. This he regards as generous, but he still has to find a salary.

At this point, D's grant-seeking comes to resemble G's more closely. He begins by consulting a document prepared annually by the AHA that lists a wide range of funding opportunities. He first applies to the American Council of Learned Societies for one of their grants, only to discover a provision that eliminates all applicants who have had a supported leave within the past five years. D then completes applications for the Guggenheim Foundation and the NEH and waits hopefully.

During this period of waiting, he meets for lunch at the Faculty Club with two colleagues who serve with him on the University Committee on Research. They are trying to allocate some small "incentive grants" that the university's dean of research has made available to support new and innovative projects. One of the other committee members, an organic chemist, complains that the whole exercise is a waste of time. "Imagine," he says, "investing all this effort in parceling out grants worth about five thousand a year." D, who had received one of them several years ago and was thereby ineligible this time around, is nonplussed, and even a little annoyed. "That is about the amount of support I get in a year. Most of it comes from discretionary funds made available to my department by the dean, and I'm damn grateful for it." His colleague reacts with amazement. "I couldn't support one graduate student in my lab for three times that, and my total research budget this year is over $200,000." "Well," D replies, "there's an old saying. There are two routes to richness. You can have great means, or small needs."

D goes on to argue that needs in the humanities are much smaller because scholarship is generally more individual, and labor- rather than capital-intensive. Compared with the equipment purchases, facilities remodeling, and other expenditures required to set up scientists, the needs of humanists appear modest. He points out, however, that at his institution and places like it, the investments for humanistic scholarship are mostly indirect, applying broadly to all users. The computer networks that support electronic mail, word-processing, and bibliographic research, and of course the library, are the shared equivalent of the more person- and project-specific facilities and equipment expenditures that support scientists. Indeed, the library budget—now exceeding forty million dollars annually at his university, and growing dramatically—represents a huge institutional investment in scholarly work, and especially that of humanists.

D reminds his colleagues that all of them are supposed to spend half their time on teaching and the other half on research; as long as their teaching loads are reasonable, he argues, the university is really supporting research of both kinds in a direct and even generous way. The scientists feel less kindly toward the university. One of them claims that through indirect cost recovery—the payments made by outside sponsors to support those institutional research costs that cannot be allocated to particular projects—the sciences are actually subsidizing the humanities. The other agrees, adding that in his view the university is downright stingy in its failure to support faculty research more generously.

The author of this last complaint is at the other end of the scale, one to which I have given little attention so far. There one finds big-project science: the physical sciences, much of engineering, and some of the biomedical sciences. Large laboratories, with up to forty or fifty workers, are supported by major research contracts with the Department of Defense or the Department of Energy, or by program-project grants from NIH. Practitioners of science at this level are most likely to be dissatisfied with the institution's research policies and most critical of other disciplines. This is partly because the "Big Science" programs bring large amounts of overhead money into the institution. Their grants and contracts earn a disproportionate share of the indirect cost revenue, which flows directly into the university's general fund. There is thus at least a surface plausibility to their claim that they are "bringing money into the university."

Their pursuit of that support is different from either G's or D's. There may be complex negotiations between the funding agency and the institution, in which the former is represented by the manager of a research division or a specialist in the administration of outside projects called a contract monitor. Although the university has a research administration of its own, the actual discussions about the project are carried on by the faculty member who will be the principal investigator on the research contract or grant. Of course the university has to sign off on the contract and be certain that the institution's rules are followed, but it is not always privy to understandings that may have been developed between the investigator and the sponsor. Partly because of the nature of this funding process, Big Science in the universities is a particularly fertile field of disagreement between universities and the government. As federal support wanes and the interest of the commercial sector in "basic" research waxes, Big Science will become a centerpiece in the relationship between the university and industry—just as it has been at the crux of the relationship between the university and the government.

The major facilities in which research in some of the Big Science disciplines is done—high energy physics, astronomy, oceanography—are so large and expensive that they require government support. Sometimes the facilities are government owned: the large space flight centers of the National Aeronautics and Space Administration, at which numbers of academic scientists work, or the National Center for Atmospheric Research, are examples. Other centers are GoCo—Government Owned, Contractor Operated—like the Stanford Linear Accelerator Center (SLAC). There Stanford faculty run a high-energy physics facility that is overseen by a national committee of users and is host to collaborative experiments by physicists from all over the world.[2]

As science continues to develop, more and more fields will require such large, centralized foci for research. That trend will continue an argument that has already become intense: How can a nation with limited resources support an increasing agenda of big projects and continue the tradition of individual, investigator-initiated grants that has proven so successful? The debate was sharpened in the 1980s by the plan to build the next-generation high-energy physics machine, the Superconducting Supercollider (SSC). Despite strong support from the high-energy physics community, the SSC was opposed by a number of scientists who felt that the cost of such a facility would funnel too much financial support away from numerous smaller projects. Eventually the SSC was killed by Congress, though not before massive expenditures had been made. Nevertheless, the argument it generated will only become more intense, as sophisticated science becomes more capital-intensive and as the government continues to concentrate more funding on large projects and facilities.

The increasingly capital-intensive character of research is by no means limited to Big Science. Indeed, it is not limited to science at all. Scholars in the humanities require large libraries and employ computers not only in manuscript preparation but also in textual analysis. Large databases and computer models are increasingly common requirements in the social sciences. In the natural sciences laboratory equipment is more sophisticated and more costly than could have been imagined a decade ago. Inflation has impacted every item in the university's research budget, at a rate of growth far higher than the CPI. In the meantime, government and industry support, especially for the small, individual projects, has become more limited. The result is an intensified emphasis on getting funding for research and greater pressure on institutional policies for obtaining and managing those funds. Because sponsored scholarship has become such a fundamental part of the university's life and work, it is necessary to look deeply into the sources and patterns of outside support.

The money needed for research comes from various sources and is given in different ways with special understandings. In the simplest case, let us suppose that Mr. X, a grateful former patient of Dr. Y's, wishes to support Y's research at the university into the causes of adult-onset diabetes. Mr. X makes a gift subject to certain legal restrictions: it is to be used only to support the expenses of Dr. Y's research program. The money is placed in a special gift account by the university, and Dr. Y has wide latitude about his expenditures—as long as they are demonstrably research-connected and as long as he stays within the university's rules with respect to such matters as flying in coach class. Such gifts are distinguished from grants or contracts in several important ways. They do not require a plan of work. Neither do they require regular reporting of progress; rather, they rely upon the faith the donor has in the faculty member. They do not include overhead payments to reimburse the institution for the general expenditures (for example, libraries, electricity for the labs, the salaries of research administrators) that it makes in order to support the organized research venture as a whole. In effect the university subsidizes projects funded in this way by meeting the overhead costs from its general fund.

Government grants and contracts, by contrast, are awarded on the basis of elaborate proposals that outline the scope of the work and the investigator's plan for doing it. These are considered competitively through the process of peer review, discussed earlier; once awarded, they obligate the investigator to make regular (at least annual) reports of progress. The awards may be for a period as short as a year, or as long as five, with three about average, and renewal depends on performance. Contracts are more formal and legalistic than grants, and the contracting agency generally issues rather specific requests for proposals. This form of support is more common among the mission-oriented agencies, such as the departments of Defense and Energy. The NSF and the NIH tend to issue grants instead, which are more "open" invitations for the investigator to lay out a research plan.

For both grants and contracts, an indirect cost rate to cover overhead is negotiated between the university and the government. These costs arise because the university is in the business of performing sponsored research; the rate is arrived at by calculating the proportion of each expense (the library, administration, and so on) that is attributable to research as opposed to instruction. The rules are complicated and will be explained below. Corporate research sponsors are nominally charged the same rate as the government, although the latter insists on certain exclusions that may make the actual corporate rate higher.

In between the gifts of individuals and the highly structured forms of federal support are grants from private foundations. The largest and most sophisticated of the foundations may have grant-giving policies almost as elaborate as those for a federal agency, but in general they are much more informal in terms of both application style and reporting requirements. Most foundations permit only a fixed and very modest overhead charge—far less than the rate paid by the federal government and industrial sponsors. Fortunately for the university, foundations have a wide range of academic interests and support scholarly work in many domains outside the sciences. Moreover, many foundation grants are institution-building in ways that most federally sponsored research grants are not. They often include construction costs, and sometimes even program endowments. It is thus not reasonable to expect that foundations should pay the same indirect cost rate as does the government. This raises delicate and difficult issues with respect to which sponsors should pay for what, and how these rules affect equity within the institution.

Problems have arisen as a result of the way the different funding sources are treated by the university, and they go to the very heart of faculty rights and responsibilities. How one views the economics of sponsored research depends so much on where one sits. The university research administrator believes that each project ought to bear its share of *all* research costs, including those directly associated with the project, and the full indirect costs. A faculty member, by contrast, is likely to see each gift or grant as an allocation to his or her program, and will understandably resent any policy that reduces that support in an attempt to reimburse the university for the overhead cost of supporting the enterprise as a whole. The donor wants to be certain that the donation goes directly to Professor Y, every bit of it, since that's where he intended it to go.

Nor does that exhaust the list of possible perspectives. A government official responsible for the research budget of an agency is likely to worry about how the university treats foundations. Why, he asks, are they getting a break on indirect costs when they ought to be paying the government rate? The foundation executive is upset that she is paying 15 percent overhead while individual donors aren't paying at all. And the dean of the medical school is unhappy because Professor X has lots of research money contributed by grateful patients yet is not contributing financially to the support of the infrastructure in the school where the research is taking place.

How can the university possibly deal fairly with these conflicting claims? Revealed truth is in short supply in this complex and often hostile arena, but a few principles and some economic facts may help.

It costs universities a lot of money to be in the sponsored research business. Laboratories consume more power and cost more to clean and run than classrooms. Libraries have to subscribe to more journals, and the Personnel Department has to employ more people to deal with the benefits, compensation, and other problems of those supported on grants and contracts. The university's administration must devote time to the management of sponsored research and establish laboratory safety panels and other bodies required by government regulation. These are all burdens added by sponsored research.

As the federal programs for funding basic university research developed in the postwar period, the government adopted the policy of paying the full costs of research. That involved a specific commitment to support the indirect costs as well as those specifically associated with the running of each project, and it required ways to estimate those costs and then to audit actual expenditures in order to justify reimbursing the university for them.

Universities actually underrecover these costs, even at the highest rates any of them have been able to negotiate. The reason is that the government's rules, contained in an arcane document called OMB Circular A-21, have numerous exclusions and permit unrealistically low allowances for the depreciation of research buildings and equipment. Ironically, research contractors in the profit sector recover from the government much more overhead for the same amount of work than do the universities. By tradition, procurement regulations for industry permit the inclusion of items in the overhead rate that may not be recovered as indirect costs by universities. Rates well over 100 percent are common, whereas no university rate has exceeded 75 percent.

The categories of research costs and the way indirect costs are calculated are best shown by following an application for funding through its course—first from the viewpoint of the investigator, then from that of the research administrators and accountants who are responsible for certifying to the government that the university is fulfilling its responsibilities.

Professor B in the Department of Chemistry at a midwestern university studies the molecular mechanisms underlying heavy-metal enzyme catalysis. He is applying to the NIH for a grant to support his work because his findings may be relevant to understanding detoxification mechanisms in the human liver. He wants to support a half-time graduate research assistant, a full-time technician, and one month's summer salary for himself (at his university and at most other places, faculty are paid a nine-months' university salary from the institution's general funds and may supplement that with grant support during the three summer months). He enters the standard half-time graduate assistantship stipend (in this case $15,000) and a $30,000 salary for the technician. His summer month is an additional $7,000. To the $52,000 salary total he adds the institution's staff benefits rate, which reflects the university's costs for retirement and medical benefits, sabbatical leaves, recreational programs, and the like—at 26 percent, another $13,250. B adds $5,000 for travel to the European conference he will attend and for his society's annual meeting in New York. Another $15,000 is budgeted for expendable materials and supplies; the reagents he uses are expensive, and there are substantial glassware requirements. Publication costs add $2,000 more. But the most expensive budget line is for several pieces of major equipment that Professor B needs to perform his assays. These total $60,000.

Now B must add the "indirect cost" line. Following the instructions, he calculates the modified total direct cost (MTDC) by eliminating the cost of all items of capital equipment above $1,000. That means he deletes the entire $60,000 major equipment line, since each item was above the threshold. That leaves $87,250, against which he applies the university's current indirect cost rate of 65 percent, adding $52,813 to the total.

In this case, indirect costs account for a little more than one-quarter of the grant request, primarily because the exclusions for equipment are larger than average. Nationally, the proportion of total government research payments to universities accounted for by indirect costs is about one-third of the total.

At the research administration and accounting level, the establishment of that 65 percent rate is an important matter. Each function in the university that contributes to sponsored research is classified as a "cost objective," and for each one, studies are performed to determine how much of the institution's financial activity is related to research and how much to instruction. For example, the library is used for both, but by analyzing the traffic and looking carefully at the pattern of book and journal purchases it is possible to arrive at a reasonable estimate of how much activity is research-related. For a university with a graduate student population as large as its undergraduate student body and a research-intensive faculty, the number might be something like 30 percent. That percentage is then treated as a cost "pool" for convenience in auditing. In other words, the auditors do not go through the library book by book, allocating all the cost of *Huckleberry Finn* to instruction and all of the *Journal of Neurophysiology* to research. Rather, the government assumes that 30 percent of *all* library costs will be attributable to research. (At the end of a year, the government audits the actual costs to see whether they have conformed to the results of the studies used in the negotiation.)

The same procedure is applied to all other cost objectives, from operations and maintenance through departmental administration. In the end the overall rate for the institution is negotiated. At the beginning of the 1990s, the indirect cost rates (as a percentage of MTDCs) at most of the private research universities were clustered in the high 60s and low 70s.

Few foundations will provide overhead payments in excess of 20 percent. Government policy-makers ask, reasonably enough, how universities can justify letting other sponsors "ride free" in this way. The university's answer is that they aren't riding free, at least not primarily on the taxpayers.

The indirect costs have already been incurred, that is, they have been paid for by the general funds of the university. If there is a shortfall in reimbursement, it simply means that general funds have subsidized some research. Why would the university want to accept such a shortfall? The answer is that foundations support a great deal of scholarship, particularly in the humanities, the "soft" social sciences, and policy studies, that the government isn't interested in supporting. The university wants the work to be done, so it is willing to absorb about three-quarters of the overhead cost.

As for individual gifts that support research, it is true that they don't bear *any* of the indirect costs. But it is also true that they don't demand the accounting, reporting, and auditing effort that government grants and contracts require. The same donors who give money for research also give for other purposes, and they are insistent that their gifts all go to the specific purposes that they designate. It would be difficult to generate one rule for taxing gifts destined for research and another, more liberal one that applies to nonresearch purposes. In fact, most universities do impose a small "tax" on restricted gifts so as to reduce their burden on the general fund. But the tax level is not even as high as foundation grant overhead, although the entire matter is doubtless being rethought everywhere in these straitened times.

The fact that indirect cost rates, in comparison with direct costs, increased steadily before and during the 1980s has been a constant source of controversy between faculty members and university administrators. Stanford's rate, for example, was 58 percent in 1980, whereas by 1990 it had risen to 73 percent. Many people outside the university think this means that if, for example, NIH approves a grant whose direct costs total $100,000 per year, the university will recover an additional $73,000 in indirect costs. But as Professor B's budget shows, the indirect cost rate is applied to direct costs after some exclusions, so the recovery is in fact significantly less.

Formerly, the indirect cost portion of the research grant was veiled when the applications were being examined: the added indirect costs appeared on the budget sheet, but peer reviewers didn't see them. More recently, the research agencies have removed the veil, and investigators have come to fear—perhaps rightly—that their applications might be punished for their institutions' high indirect cost rates. And in many agencies, divisions are given a fixed budget; their leaders may favor universities that are "bargains." The "bargains" exist because different institutions have different cost factors. For example, many state universities have lower average rates than private universities. Often this is because indirect cost recovery flows directly into the state treasury and is not returned to the university. Thus there is little incentive for these institutions to do the careful (and expensive) cost studies and auditing that are required to justify perfectly legitimate recovery.

It is commonly assumed that if the indirect cost rate is rising, the proportion that the government pays to universities as indirect costs must also be rising. Paradoxically, that is not the case. Although the rates have been rising, so has the fraction of direct costs that is subject to exclusion. For example, large projects are making use of subcontracts; and expensive capital equipment, excluded from the "MTDC base," is an increasing fraction of most grant applications. The result is that over a ten-year period the proportion of all government funds paid to universities in the form of indirect costs stayed constant, at a little less than one-third, even though the indirect cost rate rose by more than a dozen points.[3]

At Stanford, the issue of indirect cost rates had already produced significant controversy among the faculty by the beginning of the 1990s, during my tenure as president. It eventually gave rise to a congressional hearing and to heavy media criticism of the university. These events, followed by similar but lower-key investigations at other institutions, eventually produced a sharp shift in the way university science relates to federal funding agencies: the accounting rules established as a result of that controversial episode more closely resemble product-procurement regulations in the Department of Defense than the procedures that have traditionally been applied to basic research in not-for-profit institutions.

Because the outcome is important and because the controversy raised critical issues for the government-university relationship, I give that history here. For several years after the events themselves, I was reluctant to discuss them in a way that might affect, even marginally, the university's efforts to repair its relationship with the government. Then the Justice Department told Stanford that it had found no basis for a legal proceeding; later, in a settlement with the Department of Defense, it was recognized that Stanford's agreements with the government were reached fairly and that no university officials were guilty of improper conduct. The huge predictions of Stanford's liability that made headlines in 1991 and early 1992 (they ran as high as $400 million) shrank to a settlement involving about $1.5 million. This amount is equivalent to the usual "error margin" for the ten unaudited years, and was paid by Stanford to close those years without audit.

It was a relief to have these risks off the table, but substantial damage was done to the reputation of a university and its people. The vindication did not repair that damage nor reimburse the institution for the financial losses it suffered as the result of interim reductions in the indirect cost rate. So questions hung in the air, persisting amid the relief: How could this have happened? What produced the premature and heavily publicized judgments that were so damaging to universities, and what does the answer tell us about the roles of government and the media? And does this case have an important lesson to teach about institutional academic duty, particularly in regard to research relationships with the government?

Perhaps the right place to begin this narrative is in late June 1990. Stanford was still recovering from the first visit of then-Soviet President Mikhail Gorbachev to an American campus. One afternoon Stanford's dean of research, Bob Byer, came into my office with an uncharacteristically worried look. The new Office of Naval Research (ONR) representative, he said, had been claiming that Stanford was "ripping the government off." Bob thought the new man, Paul Biddle, had somehow been put off by the controller or his staff, and that we might improve the relationship by giving him another primary contact with our institution. He urged me to meet with Biddle, and so I soon invited him over for a cup of coffee and a chat.

During that occasion Biddle seemed pleased with the meeting, and our conversation was friendly. I sensed neither hostility nor the kind of righteous outrage that was to characterize his later discussions with the press. I listened, gave him a different port of call at Stanford for his technical concerns, and asked him to bring any difficult issues to me. The discussion ended amiably.

Shortly afterward, I learned that a reporter for the *San Jose Mercury News* had filed a Freedom of Information Act request with the ONR to obtain a large volume of correspondence concerning the negotiation of indirect cost rates with Stanford. We then filed a similar request, realizing that Biddle's concerns must have been transmitted to the press and perhaps elsewhere. Subsequently, it became clear that contact had already been well established among Biddle, the reporter, and the staff of the Subcommittee on Oversight and Investigations of the House Commerce Committee. The subcommittee's involvement surfaced in August, when Stanford received a letter from Chairman John Dingell, announcing that he had requested that the Government Accounting Office (GAO) undertake an investigation of indirect cost accounting practices at several universities, starting with Stanford.

The GAO team arrived late that summer for its pre-engagement briefing, at which we explained the arcane subject of indirect cost negotiation and accounting. It seemed then that we were to deal with a tough but conventional experience in regulatory oversight.

Staff investigators from the Dingell subcommittee soon arrived in the wake of the GAO team. One of them, a young woman named Leila Kahn, was brought around to my office by our government relations people. After some pleasantries she made what struck me as an odd remark. She asked about "Stanford's yacht." I said that I didn't think we had one, but she announced that a yacht had been pointed out to her in Alameda, on a Bay Area tour. I professed ignorance, but she knew more than she was saying.

An inquiry revealed that the Athletic Department had indeed received a yacht as a gift to benefit its programs, and that it was berthed in Alameda—waiting to be sold. The controller's office was then asked whether any charges related to the *Victoria*, as we learned the yacht was named, had found their way into indirect cost pools. We wrote to the committee and said they hadn't; but later, the *Victoria* popped up in a pool on which depreciation was partly charged through the indirect cost rate. We wrote a letter of correction to the subcommittee that was leaked to the *Mercury News*. The result was a page-one story that dwelt heavily on the *Victoria*'s luxury features; a headline read "Stanford Bills US for Jacuzzi on Sailboat." Eventually, the vessel itself was billed in the media as a site for entertaining administrators and VIPs, and in several press accounts it was even referred to as a presidential yacht.

The Dingell subcommittee staff members charged Stanford with "stonewalling" on the matter of the yacht. A contemporary news story had them describing the university as "unyielding." More than any other incident, this one established a picture that Stanford's practice was to deny everything until pressed to the wall. This perceived resistance was useful to the congressional investigators, who professed to be infuriated by it. At a public meeting in Washington a year or so afterward, a subcommittee staff member charged that Stanford had "lied about the yacht." He then explained the hostility of the subcommittee in these terms: "Our motto is 'if it struggles, kill it.' "[4] The audits began late in 1990, with the GAO strongly reinforced by the Defense Contract Audit Agency. Work concentrated heavily on what were called by the subcommittee staff the "sensitive accounts," especially involving those connected with Lou Henry Hoover House, the home of the former president of the United States, and for more than fifty years the official residence of the Stanford president. By early 1991, the normal complement of two government auditors at the university—a number quite usual for an institution with a sponsored research budget of around $200 million—had risen to about thirty-five, twice as many questioners as we had professionals to provide answers for. Negative findings were leaked to the press immediately, although it was sometimes difficult to know the exact source; press accounts typically referred only to "a member of the subcommittee staff."

As the audits proceeded, we were contacted by the ABC program *20–20*. A producer named Bill Wilson, who had done previous programs associated with subcommittee inquiries, announced that they were considering a segment on the indirect cost problem at Stanford. It would, he asserted, be the "savings and loan story of the nineties." That did not encourage us to expect objective treatment, but we cooperated, knowing that a refusal would be subject to adverse interpretation. We even agreed to let ABC photograph inside the president's residence. The yacht in Alameda and particular items in the house (furniture, flowers for official entertaining, and the like) that had been placed in one of the cost pools were given special attention on the program. The interview was made particularly difficult because results of the federal audits had been given to the network before having been made available to the ONR or to Stanford.

The program was damaging in its implication that government funds had been used improperly to benefit the president and his family. It aired merely two weeks before the congressional hearing and created an environment that was unusually hostile. We had hoped to focus the subcommittee on the research values involved, on the complexity of the regulations governing indirect cost recovery, and on Stanford's record of compliance with them. Instead, the committee members focused on the so-called sensitive items. The chairman's opening statement referred to the following purchases for Hoover House, a National Historic Landmark that is the site of all official university entertaining: "a pair of George II lead urns at $12,000"; "$7,000 for sheets for Dr. Kennedy's bed"; "cedar lining for closets"; a "$1,600 shower curtain"; and "a $1,200 early-nineteenth-century Italian fruitwood commode."

Because expenses of the president's office and the official residence are legitimate parts of the indirect cost pool for "general administration," these items had been included in accounts along with secretarial salaries, maintenance, and the like. OMB Circular A-21 provides for studies to determine what portion of such administrative expenses is attributable to research, and this determination is made for the pool as a whole. Twenty-three percent of each item in the pool is in fact charged as indirect cost, even though, of course, some items are more directly related to research than others. According to the government's own rules, these were legitimate, recoverable costs—and indeed the Defense Contract Audit Agency had actually reviewed and approved some of them. In the media, however, the story was that the taxpayers had bought flowers for the president's house and paid for the furniture. We removed these costs because we decided that however allowable they might be technically, they were simply inappropriate.

The problem, of course, lay in the concept of pool accounting. Under that principle, expenses that most citizens would quickly conclude should be eligible for full government reimbursement as research costs are treated the same as ones that sound outrageously irrelevant to research. Certainly, the government shouldn't pay 23 percent of the cost of flowers for university entertainment. But 100 percent of the salary of the staff member serving the Human Subjects Committee would sound quite legitimate. The pool includes both research-related and unrelated items; on average, 23 percent of all the expenditures were shown by statistical studies to be research-related, and as a matter of auditing simplification they all carry the same reimbursement.

The revelations were damaging, and made more so by the way in which the "sensitive items" were misrepresented. For example, there was no $1,600 shower curtain and no $7,000 bed sheets. The government's auditors failed to recognize that vendors often lump purchases. The shower curtain was one minor item in a bill for a large amount of upholstery and drapery work, and the sheets item was actually an extensive one-time replacement of all the house's table linens. The urns were expensive, but the chairman had somehow mistakenly put the decimal point one place to the right, transforming a $1,200 purchase into a $12,000 purchase. As for the fruitwood commode—actually a cherry chest of drawers—the chairman could not resist a wry reminder of the costly toilet seat made famous in his earlier hearings on defense contractors. By innuendo and creative imprecision, he made his contempt for the university clear.

The political climate in which the university had to sail for the next months was thus established not by the major issues surrounding indirect cost policy but by the carefully crafted public impression that at Stanford we were living high at public expense. Such impressions are difficult to reverse; once newspapers have learned something, they can't unlearn it. It is as though a computer virus lives in their word processors, seeking out the name of a particular person or institution and then attaching its own boiler-plate. "This was an additional embarrassment for Stanford, which already faces the loss of millions of dollars in federal money for items like furniture and flowers for the home of its president, Donald Kennedy," is the text of a passage added by the *New York Times* to a story about a physician at Children's Hospital at Stanford who, it was discovered after his death, had had several wives.

The more serious issues for the university, during the hearing and afterward, had to do with assertions that Stanford officials and ONR personnel had conspired to develop memoranda of understanding (MOUs) governing cost and rate negotiations so that the university was favored. Paul Biddle was quoted frequently in the press saying that the university's liability, for ten years of unaudited indirect cost recovery, could amount to $200 or perhaps $400 million. The source of these charges goes back to a time long before the hearing.

Among some science faculty members at Stanford, there was dissatisfaction with the rise of indirect cost rates during the 1980s. In an article published in *Science* magazine late in 1989, several of them made angry statements about the situation. Paul Biddle, unbeknownst to us, had begun to meet with some faculty members over hamburgers at a local restaurant called the Oasis—in order, he said, "to see if we can do something about the indirect cost rate at Stanford."

Biddle formulated the notion that his predecessor at ONR/Stanford, a navy employee named Rob Simpson, had formed (along with his superior) a cozy relationship with the university. These suspicions were voiced at the hearing; Biddle asserted that the MOUs developed by Stanford officials in cooperation with Simpson allowed the university to recover more indirect costs than it was entitled to. Representatives of the Defense Contract Audit Agency added testimony to the effect that their agency had not been consulted on the development of these memoranda and had not approved them. Chairman Dingell then praised Biddle, criticized the navy for its sloppiness, and urged ONR to cancel the memoranda forthwith.

That was done within a few weeks following the hearing, leaving Stanford at a provisional indirect cost rate of 55.5 percent instead of the 74 percent that had been approved for the previous year. It was a costly decision, one that the university later appealed to the Armed Services Board of Contract Appeals. After many months of legal back-and-forth, the issues were finally settled in 1995. As part of the settlement, the navy agreed that the memoranda were legally binding contracts, absolved Stanford personnel of any wrongdoing, and closed ten unaudited years of indirect cost recovery in return for a payment by Stanford of $1.5 million. Two features of Stanford's case were decisive in the settlement. One was the plainly political circumstances that caused the cancellation of the contracts—in particular, Chairman Dingell's direct instruction to the navy during the hearing. The second was the demonstration that personnel of the Defense Contract Audit Agency, contrary to their testimony during the hearing, not only participated in the signing of many of the memoranda, but repeatedly conducted audits on the basis of these agreements in a way that plainly acknowledged their validity.

The vindication was gratifying if belated. But the action did not end there. While he was still a civil servant assigned by the navy to Stanford, Biddle filed a private legal action against the university with the Department of Justice. Under the *qui tam* provisions of the False Claims Act, a citizen may file such an action, which the Justice Department must hold under confidential seal. If the department decides to prosecute, the private plaintiff may receive up to 30 percent of a treble-damage award—a substantial prospect in this instance, since Biddle's estimate of the damages ran to $400 million. Stanford argued that a government employee should not be permitted to use his official position to obtain information or take actions that could produce such an extraordinary personal financial windfall. The Department of Justice apparently agreed, because it had earlier asked for legislation to outlaw the filing of *qui tam* suits by government employees.

Stanford also repeatedly requested that, in view of this conflict of interest, Biddle be transferred from his responsibilities at the university. The ONR declined to act on any of these requests. Eventually, the Department of Justice refused to file the *qui tam* suit on Biddle's behalf. He pursued it by himself for several years, but in August 1996 his lawsuit was dismissed in its entirety.

The government employee most directly implicated in Biddle's charge of conspiracy with Stanford was his predecessor, Rob Simpson. Simpson was castigated by the subcommittee in the hearing and soon afterward fired by the navy. As for Biddle, he received a special medal and a commendation from then-Secretary of the Navy Garrett. Simpson appealed to the Merit Systems Protection Board, the judicial body that reviews personnel decisions. Depositions were taken, but just before the hearing was to take place the navy settled with Simpson—re-employing him, giving him back pay with interest, and reimbursing his attorney's fees.

Some of the adverse consequences were more wide-ranging and, unlike those involving the MOU and the Biddle charges, have not been reversed. The Office of Management and Budget imposed new rules that limit indirect cost recovery. Stanford's rate under this new regime, for example, was set at 63 percent, even though the university's calculations showed that a recovery near 80 percent could be justified on the basis of its real costs. Similar reductions were put in place in other institutions, with the result that universities are cost-sharing even more extensively with the government in the sponsorship of research. For understandable reasons, some of these institutions still harbor some resentment against Stanford for its unwanted role in bringing this troubling matter to a head.

Several months after the hearing, realizing that the furor had made me more of a lightning rod than my university needed, I announced my resignation a year hence. It is difficult for someone who is seen as part of the problem to become part of the solution, and the hearing and its aftermath created circumstances in which the university would clearly be better off with new leadership.

There are lessons on both sides of this unfortunate episode. I learned—the hard way—that universities have to earn public trust and not simply count on it because they are doing good things for society. We let the important matter of how public research funds are accounted for slip into a swamp of obscurity. By failing in our duty to explain what we were doing and why, we left ourselves open to a painful trial-by-media. Long before there was any interest in indirect cost accounting, we should have recognized that the agreements between the universities and the government were so arcane and so private that they were bound to raise troubling questions. Pool accounting, mixing as it does reimbursable and nonreimbursable items and relying on statistics to get the right outcome, is an invitation to public misunderstanding.

There is also a lesson to be had from the political circumstances and relationships that gave this matter its coloration. The triangular trade among congressional investigators, a "whistleblower" with a personal agenda, and the selectively fed media had a powerful impact on public opinion and frightened federal agencies into some hasty and unfortunate decisions. Commenting on the Dingell subcommittee's *modus operandi* in another case, the *New York Times* columnist Anthony Lewis wrote, "A shameful mark of the long years when Democrats controlled the House of Representatives was the abusive record of John D. Dingell of Michigan, chairman of the Energy and Commerce Committee. In the arrogance of his power, he terrorized individuals and institutions that he wanted to humble."[5]

Those sentences came from an editorial following the resolution of the academic misconduct case against Thereza Imanishi-Kari, in which David Baltimore, the president of Rockefeller University during a critical part of the proceedings, was prominently involved. The role of Chairman Dingell in the two cases was strikingly similar. He and the same set of staff members pursued agency bureaucrats relentlessly, leaked interim documents to the press when they had content that might be damaging, and turned the full investigative powers of the government to the task of embarrassing individual targets. Clearly, this raises a question of congressional duty to citizens and society that invites inquiry and reform.

Except during bouts of exceptional publicity like the one at Stanford, the details of indirect cost recovery are little noted in the world outside the academy. Inside it, they are a source of constant controversy and friction between faculty members who often do not understand the role of indirect cost recovery in the institution's economy, and administrators who may be less sensitive than they should be to the faculty's competitive position in a tight research market. These tensions, too, should have warned me that we were not meeting an important institutional duty to faculty and to society. The universities are now counted on for knowledge production to a degree that was not envisioned as the nation's postwar research policies were being developed. Along with the duties to provide for the faculty and to guarantee that society will benefit from their research, the university has another obligation: to remain a center of free inquiry, resisting overtures that promise too much governmental control of the direction of inquiry or too much influence over the institution's affairs.

The lesson of the indirect cost controversy itself is twofold. The university does owe the public a careful accounting of how it spends public monies. Research funds represent an unusual national commitment to intellectual exploration—one that few societies have made. Part of the bargain is that the beneficiaries, faculty and institution alike, treat the investment with scrupulous care. At the same time, the government must acknowledge the special character of universities and of investigator-initiated research. The latter is different from military procurement, and it needs a different and more sensitive treatment.

Issues of another kind arise when the sponsor of a project is not the government but a commercial enterprise. This form of support is much more common than it once was, and it encompasses a range of disciplines, nearly all in the sciences. The multicenter controlled clinical trial sponsored by a pharmaceutical firm, the support of semiconductor research by a consortium of microelectronics companies, the funding of a beam-line from a synchrotron radiation source by Lockheed, the support of a molecular biologist by a biotechnology firm for which he also consults—these are real elements of the research environment in the most active research universities. Some of the issues raised by corporate support are new and challenging. There may be issues of conflict of interest on the part of faculty members. Proprietary or other considerations may come into conflict with university rules regarding open publication, and there may even be pressure to influence the outcome of research. These problems direct our attention to the same issue that engages the university with respect to government funding: does the sponsorship threaten other academic duties by opening the door to an undesirable level of external influence or control?

Thus far commercial funding has had a relatively good record, except for some differences over intellectual property. For example, sponsoring companies sometimes ask for up-front guarantees of patent rights or exclusive licensing provisions. Wherever research support is mixed, as it often is, problems have emerged. A more serious issue arises when the sponsoring firm wants a particular outcome. In a recent case at the University of California at San Francisco, a drug firm sponsored a clinical trial in which one of its products was to be compared with several competitors. When the results showed no difference, representatives of the firm charged that the science had not been well done and demanded that the study not be published. They then revealed an agreement with the university—one that never should have been made—in which the company had been given the right of approval over publications arising from the research. The university declined to take the legal risk of publishing anyhow, and the result was a spectacular failure of academic duty.

✳ Freedom of research is important, but research cannot be entirely free. There is a clear distinction between two different forms of regulatory control. The first, a variety of process regulation, deals with the *conduct* of research. It seeks to reduce risks to those involved or to others, and to deal with possible "externalities" of the research process. No matter who is paying for the research, the government has the right—indeed, the duty—to be sure that proper protections for the health, safety, and personal welfare of participants, subjects, and the general public are in place. That mandate may be somewhat stronger if the government is also funding the research, but at bottom the case for process regulation does not arise merely from sponsorship. This government function has been growing dramatically in the past two decades, and the growth of federal regulatory intervention has produced strains in the relationship between the university and its faculty.

Government rules of this kind have a broad reach into research practice. Safety regulations require intervention into a whole array of laboratory practices. Everything from clinical drug trials to social science interview studies require Institutional Review Boards made up of faculty members, staff, and often community members. These boards are a government requirement for all projects involving human subjects. In an active medium-sized research university, two such panels (one for medical, one for non-medical) review more than three thousand proposals each year, engaging thirty busy committee members supported by five full-time staff members.

Few would argue that the government is not justified in intervening in the conduct of research to protect public safety or the rights of subjects. But a second, rapidly growing category of federal regulation is both broader and vaguer than process regulation. It employs the rationale that since the government is supplying the funds it can set conditions on the recipient institution. This rationale has resulted in provisions that most would applaud: various equality of opportunity statutes, for example. Other provisions, such as the Drug-Free Workplace and Communities Act, which requires universities to certify that they are policing their campuses to enforce the regulations relating to the use of drugs and alcohol, might provoke more debate. A few provisions apply to matters that had hitherto been thought to lie strictly within institutional discretion. For example, in the late 1970s a bill in Congress for the support of medical education required that any student who applied from an "overseas" medical school to an institution receiving such funds had to be admitted. After strong protests from the academic community, that provision was repealed.[6]

Particularly serious from the viewpoint of the academic research community have been government proposals that restrict the autonomy of investigators with respect to their own data. Among the principles held most dear by scholars are their fundamental proprietorship of their own ideas and data and their right to publish their work freely. In the early 1980s the chief threats to these rights were posed by efforts, mainly on the part of the Department of Defense, to regulate research data using provisions of law that had been designed to restrict the flow of military hardware and performance data. Several visitors to academic laboratories from abroad were denied visas or refused permission to visit particular laboratories or campuses. That problem was eventually solved through the creation of a Department of Defense–Universities Forum in which such issues could be worked out and through an NAS study that strongly recommended against the application of these laws to basic research programs.

More recent incursions have been more ominous. In 1991, the National Heart, Lung, and Blood Institute—one of the National Institutes of Health—attempted to attach disclosure restrictions to a grant for the multicenter clinical trial of a medical device developed by the Stanford cardiologist Philip Oyer. The restrictions were apparently designed to prevent scientists at one center from releasing information on their part of the trial independent of the others. But the terms were unacceptably overbroad, in that they gave the agency the right to put prepublication holds on the researchers supported on its funds. Stanford officials negotiated for months to have the restrictive language removed, but they could not prevail. Eventually, the university decided to take the matter to federal court, where it won on the ground that the agency had violated its own policies.

A new kind of government claim has arisen in the context of academic misconduct. In the course of a multicenter study on breast cancer, a researcher at a Montreal hospital was charged with falsifying data. The matter was referred to the Office of Research Integrity, once a part of the NIH but later relabeled and moved to the Office of the Secretary of Health and Human Services. Representative Dingell, the chairman of the Subcommittee on Oversight and Investigations, House Commerce Committee, as part of a long interest in academic misconduct issues held a hearing in which the director of the National Cancer Institute (NCI)—the sponsor of the study—was called to testify. Perhaps recalling what happens to those who displease the chairman by not giving him what he seeks, the director asserted that his agency clearly confirmed the principle that it can demand, distribute, and disclose a grantee's data in response to a pressing public health need. In other words, investigators have neither ownership nor control of data that they generate in sponsored programs. A government representative may walk into the laboratory, claim a "pressing public health need," walk out with the notebooks, and make the results public. Although it is surely unlikely that this would be a regular occurrence, most scholars would find it an uncomfortable precedent. And it is surely not the state of affairs most researchers foresaw when they first began to accept government funding.

Pressure to restrict research freedom has also come from groups of persons or organizations that have attempted to apply their own moral criteria to the work itself, to its purpose or prospective end-use, or to the source of its funding. During the late 1960s and the 1970s—and more recently in a number of places—groups of faculty and students raised moral objections to the sponsorship or the possible applications of scholarly work, demanding that administrators or faculty committees eliminate projects sponsored by the Department of Defense that were alleged to have military value. The response has usually been that if the research is unclassified and a faculty member wishes to do it, the university should permit it. Otherwise, the institution would be placed in the position of reaching moral judgments on the possible end-uses of all sorts of products. For example, is research on new technologies that are capable of displacing large numbers of workers immoral, as opponents of labor-sparing agricultural projects in land-grant universities have argued? Not surprisingly, support for the principle of academic freedom has kept university decision-makers off that slippery slope.

The conduct of research, as opposed to its output, appears to many to be a more legitimate domain for public challenge. Nowhere has this particular tension been more evident than in the efforts of the animal rights movement to halt biomedical experimentation.

When I became the president of Stanford in 1980, the animal rights movement (which might more properly be called the "mammalian rights movement," given its relative unconcern for creatures more distantly related to ourselves) had become more prominent and more active in the United States. By the middle of the decade, the "liberation" of experimental animals and vandalism of university laboratories had become regular features of academic life. Around that time I received a letter from a promising prospective junior faculty appointee who worked on primates. He said, "I feel a certain insecurity and paranoia, given the climate of the times and the unfortunate experiences of certain colleagues of mine. What is the likely response of Stanford if I, as a faculty member, am targeted by animal rights organizations objecting to my . . . work? . . . The precedents of illegal activities and of incessant harassment are frightening. I have been struck by the range of responses that different institutions have had in . . . standing up in support of their people during such touchy times." In reply, I told him that although the situation was uncertain and difficult, Stanford had been unusually forthright nationally in defense of animal research. I added that we had been successful in preventing break-ins or interference with research, but that I could not guarantee to keep him trouble-free.

The candidate, I'm glad to report, was convinced by Stanford's record that we meant what I said. He came; he got tenure; and his research has been spectacularly successful. But others have been subjected to intense personal and professional harassment, including picketing at their homes in addition to assaults on their laboratories.

What accounts for the persistence of this movement as an effective force? On one level there has been a deepening mistrust of respected, "elite" institutions; it is visible in popular attitudes toward government, medicine, the media, and even organized religions. The animal rights effort has profited from this mistrust of elites as well as from increasingly negative public attitudes toward science. Much of this change dates back to the 1960s and to the "Science for the People" movement, which advocated more public control over scientific agendas and research work. It attracted support from some fairly distinguished practitioners of science as well as from its critics. This version of the Cultural Revolution amounted to a rejection of privileged knowledge and paved the way for a more general erosion of respect for expertise. The consequences are seen in the increased frequency of media reports on science fraud, and in criticisms of research funding. A well-known professor made headlines by calling his fellow scientists "welfare queens in lab coats." This went hand in hand with a growing acceptance of pseudo-science. Half of all Americans say that they believe in astrology; the healing power of pyramids or the virtues of certain crystals also have adherents. It was not difficult for animal rights advocates to argue with some success that animals can be replaced by computers in experiments—a landmark triumph for Virtual Reality.

The problem is not just one of generalized ignorance or the well-documented failures of science and mathematics education at the K-12 level. In the best colleges and universities, we are failing to guarantee a remotely adequate level of scientific literacy. At one of the nation's most prestigious institutions, a student can graduate having taken only 6 percent of a four-year education in the sciences, and that is by no means an exceptional case. Worse still, students with a passing interest in and respect for science are apt to hear nasty things about it in other parts of the university. The courses and the scholarly literature that have emerged from the postmodern deconstruction movement in the humanities are much more profoundly antiscientific than is appreciated by scientists, who for the most part don't bother to read what these scholars write or to hear them talk.

Ultimately, the concern about scholarly work and its sponsorship has to do with how external influences shape the choice and design of research problems. Does the system provide too many temptations for financial opportunism? Are professors picking topics not because they are of the greatest significance, but because they are most likely to be funded? Who will eventually profit most from the work if it succeeds, and how can that benefit be evaluated?

There is no clear or easy answer to these questions. Federal agencies, especially those with a "mission orientation," attempt to move researchers toward their goals by supporting particular lines of work. Some scholars will scan the available opportunities and select one that happens to coincide with their own interests and purposes. A few may well alter their own aims to qualify for unusually attractive programs. None of this is surprising in light of the pressure on faculty today to keep active and productive. The increasing competition for tenure among younger faculty has probably encouraged some adaptation to the requirements of funding sources, whereas older faculty need support to keep large programs afloat. One of the latter refers to this as the "need to keep your grad students alive." Once there is a program, there are people who depend on it. That problem has been severely exacerbated by recent changes in the supply and demand picture for young postdoctoral scholars.

The most rapidly growing pressures in this area come not from the government but from the commercial sector. In the sciences, more and more ideas are seen to have potential value as intellectual property. The growth of entrepreneurial activity in fields such as molecular biology and computer science has proven a powerful attraction to faculty members and graduate students. At one level, this lure poses serious challenges for the institution as it tries to deal with conflicts of commitment and interest. Even before such issues arise, however, we have to ask whether the attractions of prospective financial gain are affecting choices for research or training, and what the implications are for the duty of the university to society.

The discussion of how scholarly work is supported, and how that support may influence its direction, returns us to an issue with which we began. Judgments about quality determine both continued funding, through the process of peer review, and the reputation of the researcher and, indirectly, of his or her institution. For the researcher, a series of positive judgments may bring tangible rewards (a Nobel Prize, membership in one of the national academies, or a Pulitzer Prize) or invitations to speak at important national or international meetings. Less directly, it may bring promotion and salary improvement at the scholar's own institution and contribute a form of psychic income that is even more important than the prizes or the financial rewards.

The quality of these judgments depends on their objectivity. Yet the scholarly enterprise today is an intensely competitive one, most especially in the sciences, but in other disciplines as well. The competition is viewed by many as healthy. Indeed, competition has such high social value these days that it is seldom criticized. Nevertheless, too much competition in research can have negative outcomes. In the most active fields, success is sometimes associated with a degree of self-importance and arrogance that demeans professional stature. When this attitude is publicly revealed, as in James Watson's popularized account of the discovery of the structure of DNA, admiration for the work is mixed with a certain wonder at the intensity with which personal celebrity is being pursued.[7]

Another outcome of competitive scholarship is an unhealthy tendency toward secrecy, which is diametrically opposed to the scholarly ideal of mutual trust and cooperation. Competition and the rewards given to priority of discovery yield unhealthy personal animosities that often hinder progress and prevent collaborations that might improve research productivity. The desire to be first leads to a sense of urgency, and often to the premature publication of results and conclusions that really require a longer incubation period. It may even create the temptation to appropriate the ideas and the methods of others, sometimes under circumstances that stretch the boundaries of professional conduct.

If the context of collegial relationships is primarily competitive, it is possible to avoid mistrust and ultimately animosity only if rules and customs are thoroughly understood, and if the parties take extraordinary pains to promote and sustain an atmosphere of cooperation. Anyone who has functioned in a "hot" field of science has had the opportunity to observe the costs of failure to satisfy these conditions. Rivalries between particular groups have resulted in refusals to share cultures or cell lines, intemperate behavior at scientific meetings, and even charges of plagiarism or the misappropriation of intellectual property. When a leading figure emerges in a discipline, the level of envy among other scholars often rises; and when such a figure encounters difficulty (as, for example, in the celebrated case of David Baltimore, described in Chapter 8), it is sometimes made worse by public gloating on the part of jealous rivals. There is no good English word for this unpleasant phenomenon, but the German term *schadenfreude* captures it exactly.

Research competition, and the impact it has on the sociology of scholarship, have become the focus of serious concern in the scientific community. Indeed, attention is finally being paid to the important influence that competition has on the various forms of academic misconduct. The journal *Science,* for example, devoted part of an issue to the subject of credit and conduct.[8] The issue contained case studies of disputed credit that were full of resentful quotes from those who felt that they had been deprived. Although it gave nearly equal time to accounts of heart-warming generosity, the reader was left with the impression that these latter instances were remarkable in part because of their rarity.

It is important to remember that, in addition to being scholars, academic men and women are moral teachers. By their own style of conduct, they set examples for the next generation of explorers. It thus follows that part of academic duty is the practice of civility in scholarly discourse—through which we may, by example, encourage the kinds of attitudes and behaviors we see among our most generous colleagues.

The university's role in that encouragement is necessarily limited. But institutional leadership can help to create scholarly environments that encourage objectivity and fairness. Most important, it can put scholarship in its proper relationship to other forms of academic duty. As long as research productivity is seen as the dominant criterion of academic distinction, its pursuit will from time to time become excessive. Scholarship is important, but it must be in balance with other obligations. The academic culture in which it takes place needs to provide constant reminders of that balance.

There are specific ways that a university administration can help. It can insist that all the institution's values be preserved in its relationship with the government and with industry, in order to avoid some of the pressures that might direct research or enhance the frenzy to produce. Some of that pressure can be reduced by institutional action to limit the federal role: supplying more private funds to support graduate research. That would reduce the number of graduate students who must be supported by research assistantships and decrease dependence on big projects. The administration can also modify appointment and promotion policies, emphasizing the significant over the spectacular and quality over quantity.

A campus culture in which collegiality and civility are valued is among the most important contributions the university can make. The unfortunate features of too much research competition are behavioral, and, like other behaviors, they are subject to benign environmental influence. Issues of authorship, priority, and credit should be discussed openly and thought-fully, with real leadership from president, provost, and deans. Part of that conversation will turn not only on the scholarship itself, but on the publication process through which it is brought into public view. We now turn to that process.

7

TO PUBLISH

THERE IS AN old story about three baseball umpires in a bar engaged in a tipsy reminiscence about how good they were. "I called 'em as I saw 'em," the first one says. The second, after a brief pause, tops it: "I called 'em as they *were.*" The third umpire reflects for a while, takes another pull on his Scotch, and says firmly, "They weren't nothing 'till I called 'em!"

All the thinking, all the textual analysis, all the experiments and the data-gathering aren't anything until we write them up. In the world of scholarship we are what we write. Publication is the fundamental currency; except for the creative arts and a few disciplines in the applied sciences, research quality is judged by the printed word. In many of the humanities disciplines, publication *is* scholarship; indeed, analysis and the creation of text march in such close order that to separate the one from the other would be artificial. Publication is no less important in the hard sciences, even though much of the work is experimental in character. It is a truism that an experiment is not done until it is published.

Many of the most interesting challenges and problems can be found in the area of scientific publication. The explosive growth of serial literature and the problems associated with multiple authorship, disputes over credit, and even plagiarism are more heavily represented in the sciences than in either the social sciences or the humanities. Both the sheer volume of work product and its tendency to be issued in short bursts, with heavy pressure for prompt appearance, have made the sciences a far more problematic area in this regard than the humanities, where longer incubation times and more extended works are the rule.

Academic societies, universities, and, most important, colleagues evaluate scholars on the basis of work that is not only written but, necessarily, published. The difficulty is that there are no universally agreed-upon criteria for that evaluation. In particular, the relationship between quality and quantity is unclear. In considering candidates for academic promotion, "productivity" is much discussed, but it is uncertain whether that refers to volume or to the importance of individual works.

Important differences also exist among fields with respect to quantity of product. Philosophers and mathematicians often publish sparingly, organic chemists prodigiously. Scholars in the humanities and some of the social sciences, furthermore, tend to produce books rather than articles; production is episodic, and judgments about continuing productivity are therefore hard to make. Scientists, in contrast, usually write papers, in many cases describing experiments that are very lengthy and labor-intensive compared with the length of article it takes to describe them. The article in *Nature* that described the double-helical structure of DNA was less than five pages long.

Most deans and department chairs will say that they are interested in quality, not quantity, but any long dry spell in a scholar's output is surely cause for worry. In the sciences frequency of publication can vary widely; some researchers publish a paper only every few years, whereas those who run large laboratories may produce dozens or, in a few unusual instances, a hundred or more. How any semblance of quality control can be maintained under such circumstances is a mystery, and it is perhaps no accident that these over-producing enterprises, most of which are in the biomedical sciences, are responsible for a disproportionate share of academic misconduct cases.

The most prestigious scholarly academies—the NAS and its sister institutions, the American Academy of Arts and Sciences, and the American Philosophical Society—clearly put the emphasis on quality in the procedures used to elect senior scholars to membership. The NAS's forms for evaluation limit the number of papers listed to ten, and all the academies rely heavily on brief summary descriptions of the candidates' major accomplishments. Several academic leaders have pushed for a similar limitation on the number of publications to be considered in appointments and promotions. That might seem unnecessary, but even in the nation's major research universities, a striking proportion of faculty members believe that they will be evaluated on the quantity as well as the quality of their publications. Cynics in the academic profession have a phrase for it: "Our dean can't read, but he can count." Many of us would much prefer, for ourselves and our colleagues, the epitaph that the medieval historian Helen Waddell gave to the Arch-Poet of the Middle Ages, a wandering troubadour who, despite great fame in his time, left just one poem in writing: "He traveled light, even into immortality."

Of course, even in an ideal world in which only quality counts, there is room for lively debate. What is quality, anyhow? How should we judge it? Are some journals and publishers better than others? Which reviews should one pay attention to? Is the frequency with which an article is cited the best indication of its quality? In the case of books, does popularity matter?

Scholarly publishing is a growth industry. Although this may say something about the robust health of scholarship, the current growth rate threatens the economic health of university library budgets and makes it increasingly difficult for scholars to sort the worthwhile from the valueless. The situation has reached near-crisis status, and it is an outcome of the contemporary fixation on quantity of publication. The explosion of information is not entirely new, but in this century, according to the historian and sociologist of science Derek J. de Solla Price, the number of publications has increased an average of 6 to 7 percent per year. Thus the total information load deposited in the world's libraries has had a doubling time of just over a decade.

This growth rate seems to have accelerated markedly in recent years, most notably in the biomedical sciences. As young investigators have swelled the research population in the United States, there has been heavy pressure from the research community to increase the number of federally funded grants. More scientists and more projects mean that promotion is a more competitive proposition, and that has further augmented the pressure to publish. Not surprisingly, the marketplace has responded to this reality, and the result has been an explosion in the number of serials.

The impact on university libraries, and indeed on the entire domain of scholarly publishing, has been enormous. The pressure generated in the sciences, where the most concentrated activity has been located, is especially intense. Between 1970 and 1990, serial prices for scientific and technical journals increased at an average annual rate of 13.5 percent, whereas the annual rise in book prices was less than 8 percent over that period. At the same time, the fraction of university budgets devoted to libraries was declining. Thus serial prices were absorbing a larger and larger fraction of a shrinking pie.

An especially troubling aspect of the serial growth disease is the increasing dominance of a relatively small number of commercial science publishing firms. In one year in the late 1980s, three European publishers accounted for 43 percent of the total serials expenditure increase at one U.S. university.[1]

The economist Roger Noll has analyzed the economics of this growth.[2] He points out that the "first-copy" investment in a new scientific serial is very high; that is why low-circulation journals are more expensive. Commercial publishers (and the nonprofit society journals, if they are drawn into the same market arena) compete by introducing new journals, which then take circulation away from existing journals at the subject-matter margin. Suppose, for example, that we start with 5 journals covering a fixed field of specialties, each with a circulation of 2,000. Assume that the break-even point for the publishers occurs at a circulation of 500. Now 5 new journals enter the field, each with a specialty domain overlapping that of an existing journal. Each achieves a circulation of 750, of which 250 are "new" subscribers and 500 have been wooed away from the existing journal serving the most closely related field. Now the library must not only carry the additional five journals, but also pay, through increased pass-through prices, for the financial losses experienced by the original 5 journals, each of whose circulation has now been reduced from 2,000 to 1,500. The publishing and vending industry is often blamed for the price inflation in serials, and indeed it has much to apologize for: it has the inefficiencies one would expect from an industry with a large captive market. But, contrary to some assertions, the price increases do not suggest obscene profits. Rather, they result from a peculiar brand of competition that multiplies entities and thereby creates diseconomies of scale.

The new proprietary journals serving relatively narrow biomedical specialties come, in large part, from Europe. What is especially remarkable is that these journals rarely carry the "best" papers in a field. The market niche they often fill is as a publication outlet for papers that are not accepted by *Science, Nature,* or *Proceedings of the National Academy of Sciences*—the fast outlets for "hot" papers of more than ordinary general interest—or the major scientific society journals in which longer specialty papers are published. These European journals publish primarily American work; the proportion may be as high as 90 percent. And their market is primarily the libraries of U.S. universities. So here we have an industry that imports American work-product, adds a minuscule amount of value in the form of editing and printing, and then exports it at a very high price, compared with the value added, to the country from whence the research came. It is the academic equivalent of a *maquiladora*.

University libraries can do little about the situation. I remember that when we began to cut budgets at Stanford and I first came to understand what serial pricing was doing to library finance, I suggested in a large meeting that the research universities ought to get together and refuse to subscribe. My general counsel told me later that he had been sorely tempted to create a diversion by overturning a pitcher of water so that he could then rush me out of the room. Apparently this solution raises certain antitrust problems.

That has not prevented other imaginations from working overtime. Aided by the rapid developments in modern computer technology, new forms of "publishing" are becoming more prominent. Using the device of "anonymous folio transfer protocol," a professor of engineering can scan a preprint of his forthcoming paper into a database that is accessible on the Internet. When he later submits it to a journal, he will assign copyright as requested. If the journal also requires a declaration that any version of the paper be removed from electronic bulletin boards, the professor may sign, and then may or may not remember to effect the removal.

As a further step, some academic authors have chosen to deny journals copyright to their papers. Of course, single authors bring little clout to that negotiation, but some consortia of institutions have considered group efforts of that kind supported by state legislation. The role of quasi-formal electronic communication in supplanting conventional forms of scholarly publishing is bound to pass through some interesting challenges—some of them, no doubt, legal.

The economics of serial publication have been further stressed by the addition of page charges, a fee collected by the scholarly journal from the author for publication of the work. This custom arose, naturally enough, in the sciences, where most work was supported by outside grants and where the scientific societies that published the journals were apt to be under some financial stress. In effect, it was a device whereby the government indirectly subsidized the continued publication of valuable research journals. This is not an irrational policy, but it has now spread to the proprietary sector: NIH and NSF have approved payments from research grant funds to defray page charges levied by commercial journals. It is difficult to justify the allocation of U.S. government grant funds to subsidize for-profit publishers in England and the Netherlands.

Whereas there may be a glut of low-prestige publication outlets in the sciences, there is a real limitation of outlets in other fields. In the social sciences and humanities, getting into print is more difficult—and getting into print without long delay is almost out of the question. This is the case just as the requirements for tenure are stiffening. In fields in which publication is by book or very long article, the time dimension may be critical: the "tenure book," begun in the second year of an assistant professorship and finished in the fifth, barely has time to be reviewed before the critical milestone for the promotion decision is reached in year seven. University presses, the main outlets for book publication in these fields, have not increased much in number or length of list; indeed, they are experiencing great economic pressure as their universities engage in budget reduction. There has been a noticeable trend for these presses to substitute books with promising sales potential for more traditional scholarly works.

At the output end of the publication process are books, papers, and, ultimately, a reception from peers that determines how they and their authors will be valued. Those quality judgments have become more important as the number of scholars in many fields has risen in relation to the number of positions available to them. This mismatch between supply and demand fuels an increasingly desperate struggle to gain access to the better academic posts. And the effect percolates down; those well acquainted with liberal arts colleges know that many of them, once known for a blend of excellent undergraduate teaching with limited scholarship, have now significantly raised the importance of publication as a criterion for appointment. Thus we have, at the source, more bodies and more output per capita. This situation, which poses a challenge for those who seek realistic quality measures for scholarly work, will not change until we revise the incentive structure for training scholars.

One way of seeking measures of quality, common in almost every field, is to examine publication outlets for their "prestige." As the explosive proliferation of lower-quality, mostly proprietary serials has continued, appointment and promotion committees have come to expect that they will contain contributions of lower than average quality. These judgments are, of course, difficult to make objectively and fairly; nevertheless, they are made regularly on the basis of collective experience with the field and its major outlets. If a journal's editorial board is composed of distinguished scholars and if the most prestigious contributors tend to publish there, the journal will have high status. The same general sort of prestige ranking is associated with the (largely) university presses that publish scholarly books, though there the situation is somewhat more complex: a press that is not well known or thought to have a list of uniformly high quality may nonetheless develop very high prestige in a particular field, for example, Western history or Japanese studies.

It is, however, not very satisfactory to evaluate the quality of a published scholarly work by merely guessing at the distinction of the outlet in which it appears. In the end the judgments of peers—often after a substantial lapse of time—will yield the most reliable verdict. But there is an understandable desire for a quicker and more quantitative assessment. It is natural to ask how much a work is used by other scholars, and how those use patterns might be employed to evaluate the degree of influence of an author or a journal on the field.

The availability of computerized citation indexes has made possible a new kind of quantitative analysis of the utility of research papers. Nontechnical publications intended for the scientific community often feature lists of "hot papers" in a particular field, based on their citation frequency. As I write, some publications have even released national rankings of research universities based on averaged citation indexes for a number of disciplines.

The use of citation indexes as a measure of scholarly merit worries many observers, including this one, who doubt the tightness of the correlation between popularity and excellence. There are factors quite extraneous to quality judgments that clearly affect citation frequency. In science, papers describing new methods will be overrated on any such scheme; the paper I cited most often in my own publications, for example, described the composition of the physiological medium for my favorite experimental animal. Moreover, a ranking system based on citation frequency would discriminate unfairly against superb papers in relatively narrow or transiently unpopular fields, and might thereby ignore real breakthroughs.

Nevertheless, there is some correlation between utility and citation. Publications that are never or almost never cited are likely not to be very influential. In this regard, it is surprising to learn how little most papers are cited. Across all fields, recent studies have indicated that more than 75 percent of all papers are never cited at all, and in certain fields the percentage of noncitation is even higher.

Patterns of citation may also be used to assess the degree of influence possessed by different journals in the same field. In an interesting series of analyses, Stephen Stigler of the University of Chicago has compared "exports" and "imports" of citations among journals in the fields of economics and statistics. If papers from Journal A are cited in Journal B four times as often as those from B are cited in A, then A may be thought of as a producer rather than a consumer of information. Of course, being a producer/exporter does not necessarily mean that a journal is of higher quality. There is a strong tendency in Stigler's data for information to flow from theory to application rather than the reverse; and citation patterns can be overly influenced by heavy attention given to a paper in one discipline by consumers outside that discipline. Still, the "export score" methodology developed by Stigler is a potentially powerful tool in evaluating influence in scholarly communication, and it deserves application to fields (for example, biomedical research) in which the journal universe is especially crowded and in which practitioners seem to perceive wide differences in journal quality.[3]

Influence can also be assessed more crudely by measuring journal use in libraries. This is something anyone familiar with a discipline can do easily. For example, an informal comparison of journals in a single subfield of biomedicine, neurobiology, reveals significant differences in rates of use of older, society-sponsored journals (more frequently used) and newer, commercial ones (less frequently used).

Another aspect of overproduction and the serials boom is the increasing frequency of "redundant" publication. Editors of journals, when they gather to discuss the ethical problems they encounter in their work, devote considerable time and space to the problem of repetitive or duplicate publication. This is a problem with many forms. One is "salami publication," in which a single study is presented as a series of short papers instead of a single one of medium length. This is an unfortunate tendency, but little can be done about it. The more serious—and manageable—issue centers on real redundancy, that is, cases in which the same work is offered for publication in different places.[4] The following scenario, taken from a publication of the Council of Biology Editors, illustrates the problem.

A paper describing a small but useful scientific advance is published in a journal. The editor soon discovers that it had already been published in another journal in identical form, except that the authors have rewritten the abstract, introduced a few editorial changes elsewhere, changed the tables and figures to include results in subjects recruited since the first publication (about three times the initial number, but with little change in overall results), and added a sentence with an ambiguous reference to the earlier publication, which is now listed in the bibliography. In response to an inquiry from the editor, the authors say that the large number of new subjects justified publication even with nearly identical text and that the second paper gave adequate notice to the editor and reviewers (as well as to the readers) that it was updating an earlier one. The editor reviews the file and concludes that the correspondence and the ambiguous reference could in fact be interpreted as the authors claim, although the wording of the text seems to be deliberately deceptive.[5]

Of course, all journals specify that the work offered for publication should not have been published or submitted elsewhere. In the sciences, exceptions are often made for papers that follow abstracts of presentations made at society meetings; these usually are very brief, contain incomplete information about methods and even data, and are generally not considered "real" publication.

In the scenario, however, the previous publication was a full paper. What makes the case a difficult one is the addition of a substantial amount of new data. The question is whether that is sufficient to justify a separate publication. In view of the essentially identical outcome and the extensive similarity in all other respects, most scholars and most editors would decide against acceptance of the paper—even without the indication that the authors were trying to put something over on the editor.

Donald S. Coffey, a distinguished editor of long experience, said of the problem in general, "I do not think anyone would claim that duplicate publication is not a serious problem. It affects many of our journals and causes a lot of undue work."[6] It is difficult to imagine how this practice can have become so widespread. Ambiguities are being introduced by the wealth of new devices for semipublication, making it ever more difficult to determine whether or not particular material has actually been published before. But a safe rule is this: if it's been in print, and especially if it's been peer reviewed, it shouldn't be put in print again. For the brave new world of fully electronic journals, of course, that rule may have to be modified.

A special aspect of repeat publication comes into play when a research finding is especially newsworthy. Some peer-reviewed, strictly "research" journals treasure their capacity to make news and have thus imposed strictures on authors that have led to significant controversy. Some years ago the *New England Journal of Medicine* established a policy—called the "Inglefinger rule," after the editor at the time—that it would publish no manuscript whose results had been made public before the issue containing the paper actually appeared. Thus an author with an especially "hot" finding would have to keep it away from the newspapers while the *Journal* was readying it for publication. Though this policy doubtless prevented some forms of mischief, it struck many authors as unduly harsh.[7] It has nevertheless persisted, and has been adopted by other large-circulation scientific journals.

Of all the issues that arise in publication, none is more trying than the assignment of credit (or blame!) between and among multiple authors. It is the source of many if not most of the disputes about credit for research that arise between mentor and student. And it is a source of constant worry to journal editors and to appointments and promotions committees, who ask of any multiauthored work, "Who really did it?"

The answer, of course, is usually the perfectly appropriate one: "We all did." Credit is rightly shared; liability, if there is any—and in the case of alleged research misconduct that may be an issue—should be joint and several, if symmetry of treatment is to prevail.

But there is abundant opportunity for disputes to arise among authors. These tend to cluster around the difficult question of intellectual ownership of the ideas in a published work. If a significant contributor has been left out, that frequently gives rise to complaints. It is especially troublesome when a senior scholar publishes, as part of a review or some other general treatment, the work of a junior colleague without sharing authorship. It is not surprising that failure to allocate credit fairly and properly is the most common problem in this area.

Another fertile source of dispute is authorship sequence. Here custom varies widely by field of study. In some disciplines the senior scholar's name always goes last; in others, it goes first. There are journals in which alphabetical sequence is required, and others in which it is entirely the authors' choice. It is difficult if not impossible to derive much information from authorial sequence. In some disciplines it is usual for the senior scholar's name to be on every paper from the group, based on the assumption that the overall strategy and laboratory "infrastructure" are, after all, that person's contribution. In others, authorship much more directly reflects significant personal involvement. Custom in the humanities and most social sciences tends toward single authorship, and these fields have been the source of much less controversy.

When one or more participants in a project make narrow, technical contributions—for example, perform statistical tests, or undertake a highly special chemical analysis—it is often asked whether they should be listed as authors. The arguments in favor largely rest on the fairness of giving them some recognition; they did, after all, contribute. But if their contributions were marginal and technical, it is acceptable to list them after the authors, following the designation "With the Technical Assistance of . . ." In Big Science, where arrays of specialists congregate around major facilities and the number of authors now occasionally exceeds one hundred, the issue of authorship and credit becomes transcendent; we throw up our hands. In some intermediate cases, it may be possible to define the domain of each author's contribution as part of the list.

Of considerable importance in the issue of authorship is the embedded problem of "complimentary authorship," whereby a person not really meriting a place in the list of authors is given one anyhow. The motives vary; some of them stem from a misguided form of good will—a professor wanting to help a student's career, for example. Whatever the motive, it puts both the included author and the scientific enterprise at risk. The risk for the former is that he or she will be asked about the work and will be found to be ignorant, or, worse, that the work will turn out to be wrong or even fraudulent. For the scientific community as a whole, complimentary authorship amplifies confusion about who is responsible for what work. Misinformation always has costs.

The most common abuse in authorship is the addition of the name of academic supervisors to largely independent work done by students. The fact that this has become a custom in a number of fields does not make it less pernicious. In some institutions coauthored articles are even allowed in a student's Ph.D. thesis. This practice not only confuses later evaluators about the degree of independence involved in the work of a student, but also constitutes a challenge to the very notion of a doctoral dissertation. The idea behind the thesis is that it is a piece of original work, done to demonstrate that the student is ready for an independent scholarly career. But if as part of it there appears a work jointly authored by the student and his or her academic adviser, one of two things is amiss: either the work isn't independent, in which case it should not be part of the dissertation, or it is, in which case it is a plain case of complimentary authorship.

Scholarly publishing, in addition to communicating one's ideas and findings to the worldwide audience of one's colleagues, also establishes ownership of them. By publishing, the author either establishes a claim that converts the work into intellectual property, or disposes of that claim through some contractual arrangement. These issues of intellectual property ownership are important in connection with disputes between faculty members and students; they take on even broader significance when they enter the public domain.

Perhaps the most straightforward form of dissemination begins when a scholar writes an essay or a report of some experimental findings and publishes it herself for distribution to several hundred colleagues. Such publications actually have rather formal status in some fields; the engineering disciplines recognize "technical reports" as a form of publication that, for example, belongs in one's bibliography. By asserting copyright, that is, by attaching a copyright notice reserving all rights to that expression, our scholar owns the work in the sense that she can prevent its distribution by others, or permit it for a fee.

What she owns through copyright is not the ideas but the expression of those ideas. At the moment of their elaboration they become intellectual *property*. Although the mechanism for establishing ownership of a new product, process, or technology is very different, there is an important connection between these two, for it is the process of publication that supports the claim of priority for anything contained in the work that is patentable. Of course, it also puts those ideas firmly into the public domain.

The process of formal publication may entail submission of the paper to a journal of research or some other scholarly periodical. In most cases, publication of an article in this way transfers ownership of the copyright to the journal, which nevertheless may agree that the author's permission will be required—along with the journal's—for any use by others of the material contained in it. The line between informal communication, through such devices as personally circulated manuscripts, technical reports, and entries of material into computerized databases, and formal publication in serial journals has become blurred. It will blur even more as electronic "publishing" becomes more prominent, as it inevitably will.

In many fields, the normal form of scholarly communication is the book. Books, even scholarly ones, have publishers—who have a more or less commercial interest in their success. Normally, a contract between publisher and author places the copyright in the hands of the former, in return for a stream of postpublication royalty payments to the latter. This relationship, trying though it is at times, is straightforward: an author, a publisher, a negotiated contract.

More difficult questions arise in connection with a hybrid form of publishing, increasingly common in academic circles: the multiauthored work in which several scholars contribute portions of the text, which has an overall academic editor. In such cases the author is paid a fee for the work, which then becomes the property of the publisher. In many multiauthored texts or symposium volumes, however, the arrangements are more complex. Drummond Rennie, who has had a long and distinguished career as an editor of medical journals, tells of the case of Professor D, an academic physician who contributed a long chapter to a well-known medical text to form part of a section that had two distinguished academicians as "editors." His chapter was duly published in the fifth edition of the text. When the sixth appeared, the author was astonished to find "his" chapter, virtually unmodified, listed under the names of the two "editors" of the section! He naturally inquired about this, and was told by the publisher— almost without embarrassment—that the two "editors" had in fact been the authors of that section, and that his contribution (for which he had been paid a modest sum) had been a work-for-hire that the publisher now owned. Professor D has a case on grounds of mislabeling, but the ambiguities of "ownership" make it a difficult problem to resolve.

Ownership, in the sense of possession of copyright, does not confer on the copyright holder a license to plagiarize. Suppose, for illustration, that a scholar has arranged part-time employment with a proprietary but "serious" journal in her field, and has been commissioned to write an article on the biology of Amazonian rain forests. The article is a work-for-hire for which she has been compensated by salary payments, and the journal now owns the copyright. That ownership permits the journal to reprint her piece at will, or even to sell it for inclusion in an anthology. But it does not permit the journal to present her article as the work of another.

Scholarly publishing is meant to be useful to the academy, and in that spirit rules about borrowing and distributing have traditionally been rather loose. That has all changed, however, with the advent of modern copying and desktop publishing technology. It is now relatively easy for a professor to assemble a customized set of readings for a class, borrowing material from a number of relevant sources. Of course this is good for teaching, but it may deprive those authors whose works are being used of income to which they are entitled. Thus reproduction, even for class use and even where nothing is being charged for the materials, is limited by the fair-use doctrine, which permits the copying and distribution of limited amounts of material for educational purposes; it would allow the use of up to a thousand words, or a couple of graphs, from some other source, but it would rule out, for example, the copying of a whole chapter. Faculty members who have been using desktop publishing methods to compile multi-source anthologies for use by their students—albeit with the very best of motives—are now being warned by legal counsel for their universities to stay cautiously within the "safe harbor" guidelines for classroom use.

The complexity of this issue has led to a new kind of publishing industry in which the leaders are university bookstores or reproduction companies. For example, a professor who collects a set of readings for a course can supply his campus bookstore with Xerox copies of the items he wants included. The bookstore will then obtain the necessary permissions and do an inexpensive custom publishing job on the collection—making the resulting reader available to students at a price covering (or, perhaps, more than covering) its costs.

Different and even more trying issues are raised by the storage of large amounts of material in computerized databases. It is now possible for an institution to store abstracts of journal articles on a particular subject, or to compile combined bibliographies derived from other sources. The good news is that this gives scholars easier access to a vast and growing store of information. The bad news is that databases can be copied for various purposes, and a fair-use doctrine for such material has not been fully worked out. Some legal challenges may be required before there are have firm guidelines about what is proprietary in this domain and what is not.

✳ The process of publication and review is full of difficult problems, not all of which are "modern." For example, it has always been painful for scholars suddenly to discover that their own unpublished findings have also been made by someone else. When Charles Darwin received the manuscript of Alfred Russel Wallace, in which Wallace had derived the basic principles of evolution by natural selection from biogeographic studies in southeast Asia, he had been working on the *Origin of Species* for most of thirty years. His anguish is reflected in his letters to his friends, the botanist Joseph Hooker and the famous geologist Charles Lyell. In them he begs for help in resolving his moral crises, and afterward asks forgiveness for his "trumpery feelings." Eventually a joint form of publication fair to both was devised—one that recognized Wallace's independence and Darwin's priority.[8] One cannot read Darwin's own account of the incident without wishing that modern scholars could bring the same qualities of fairness and self-understanding to their priority problems that Darwin brought to his. At many points in the history of a particular scholarly publication, they are challenged to do so.

Given the extraordinary informal networks that now link scholars in any active field, it is unlikely that they would receive word of simultaneous findings in much the same way that Darwin did. Instead, Researcher A learns through the grapevine that B has just made a critical methodological breakthrough that, combined with what B has already published, makes it virtually certain that he will soon know what A has just learned. Because B's laboratory is formidable and has a superior line of attack on the problem, A feels under great pressure to publish what she has instead of bringing it to a more finished state. No one knows how often this happens, but it is certainly not a rare event.

Work-in-progress is also brought to the attention of others as an integral part of the publication process. The scholarly enterprise is built on the principle that the work of one person is exposed to the critical judgments of peers through prepublication peer review, a process essentially identical to the one used in evaluating ideas proposed to the government or to some private funding agency for support. In the latter case the proposal is sent to others in the discipline for their evaluation; sometimes it is an established panel or "study section," sometimes an informally chosen set of researchers in the same field. In prepublication review, the editor of the scholarly journal or the university press will ask other scholars to appraise the quality of the work. Plainly, this procedure calls for a great deal of trust, just as does the process of grant review. Outsiders are being made privy to brand-new ideas or experimental results, well before others will have the opportunity to know of them or to evaluate them. It offers significant temptations for reviewers to appropriate ideas or methods presented in the paper before they become part of the public record, or to hold the manuscript in limbo while their own work moves forward toward publication. Because these temptations have all been yielded to on infrequent but widely known occasions, it is troubling to many authors that their valued new works, in which they have substantial emotional investment, are being put at the mercy of rivals.

The problems of prepublication review are sufficiently widespread that they are discussed in some university policies on academic integrity, notably in the policies on the conduct of academic research promulgated by MIT, which are models of thoughtful guidance. The MIT publication "Fostering Academic Integrity" includes a playlet dealing with the kind of ethical challenge that may confront manuscript reviewers. At a Biology Department softball game, a postdoctoral fellow named Jim asks Dan, a young faculty member, whether "there's anything new." The latter responds by reporting a very interesting result from a journal article he has just reviewed; it is by a group of Swedish scientists. This result immediately suggests a way in which Jim's lab can succeed with a stalled project; the trouble is that the project is in competition with the Swedish group's work.

Jim takes the good news back to his own lab, whereupon other members of his research group respond in various ways. One urges that they go ahead and make use of the methodological breakthrough suggested by Dan's report on the Swedish work. A graduate student named Paolo objects, saying that it would be unethical to make use of the result, and pointing out that Dan broke the rules in revealing the finding. He goes on to argue that they should call the Swedish group right away. Jim argues that the Swedish paper will be published first anyway; another postdoc feels that the problem can be solved by giving the Swedish group credit for their contribution. At the end, the professor in charge of the laboratory is asked for his views—but the play ends before he can give them.

The first question posed by the MIT authors is whether Jim is at fault in asking his first question. In discussing the scenario, my own students felt that there was plenty of blame to go around. Jim's first question struck them as probably innocent, but Dan's response was more difficult to defend: the confidentiality provisions respecting manuscript reviews, after all, mean what they say. Those who defended going ahead with the work got little sympathy. Paolo was admired, but his suggestion was recognized as an impulsive leap over the journal editor's head. My students wondered why the boss waited so long to get into the conversation—and they agreed that when he did, he ought to urge a course of action that involved Dan and the editor in a negotiated solution.

Perhaps the problems suggested by this example are peculiar to the sciences; after all, in most other disciplines the incubation time for ideas is longer, and they depend much less on specific bits of valuable data. But even in the social sciences and the humanities there may be significant problems. The scholar whose work is being reviewed may have some worries about the misappropriation of intellectual property, but the real risks are quite different. Will the reviewer, operating (perhaps even unconsciously) from his own professional biases, take an unfairly negative view of the manuscript? Will he punish the manuscript for some past personal or professional difference with its author? Or, worst of all, might he attempt to delay or even prevent its publication in order to obtain priority or exclusivity for some work-in-progress of his own?

Extending or modifying the use of anonymity is frequently offered as one solution to these problems. Before examining this, it would be helpful to know how the present system, which usually entails anonymity on the part of referees but disclosure of the identity of authors, actually works in practice. Anonymity of referees is intended to encourage candor by insulating reviewers from the prospective wrath or disappointment of the authors they may criticize. It is sometimes argued that disclosure of the identity of referees might induce more responsible behavior on their part, and might also invite direct negotiation between referee and author over differences.

In practice, there is less referee anonymity than there is in theory. The concealment of a referee's identity is not at all easy. Most authors in most fields are able to make shrewd guesses from the nature of the review about who wrote it. In my own career, I guess that I penetrated the disguises about half the time.

Scholarly folklore is full of incidents in which referees have deliberately broken anonymity in order to negotiate directly with authors over a difficult point of difference. Wherever there is an abundance of trust, this is actually an admirable solution, with one caution. It is disastrous when it is done over the head of a journal editor. That individual, after all, has the responsibility for the journal's policy regarding anonymity, and he or she will have to deal with any breakage of precedent—as well as clean up the mess if resolution efforts end in a bitter wrangle, as they have been known to do.

The issues are quite different when the question is whether reviewers should know who the authors are. The general practice of leaving the author(s) identified is criticized on two grounds. In the event that the author is a highly respected senior in the field, identification may result in a too-favorable judgment. If the author is a scientific rival, or just not a very nice person, it may have the opposite effect. In an effort to resolve these difficulties, some journals have attempted to maintain author anonymity, but the results suggest that it is even harder to conceal the identity of authors than of referees. The problem is that authors are all too readily identifiable by their work. In scientific papers, where the use of particular methods or techniques provides identifying marks, the policy could not be applied at all. In humanistic scholarship, where the reviewed work is likely to be book-length, specialty and literary style may give reliable clues. At best, this is a solution that, however imaginative and however attractive in theory, is applicable over only a narrow domain.

The relationship between reviewers and authors does not end with publication. A new dimension surfaces once the work is out and falls into other hands for public evaluation. Here it is useful to distinguish between two different modes of review. In the first, a reviewer covers an entire field in a paper that attempts to place recent advances in context; often, such an analysis will be published in a journal explicitly devoted to such reviews.

This is common practice in the natural and social sciences, and somewhat rarer in the humanities. What the readers of such disciplinary reviews expect and need is an objective assessment of the field. In the very best cases that is what they get; but anyone who has read extensively in this review literature will be able to produce a number of discouraging examples of how scholars treat one another's efforts.

In too many cases, authors overcite their own publications. They also tend to be overly critical of the work of others wherever there is a competitive relationship, that is, where the others are working on the same or a similar problem. Scholarly gossip is filled with the legend of rivalry—what senior scholar A has done most recently to competitor B, and what B is plotting by way of revenge. It is in the review literature that these hostilities become public, and they can do real damage to the perception of scholarly work as an objective search.

In the humanities and in those sciences in which publication at book length is the rule, a second kind of review is the most common. The medium is likely to be a nonacademic journal of thought and opinion, such as the *New York Review of Books* or *Commentary,* or even a general-circulation newspaper or periodical. Here the academic scholar is evaluated in a world populated also by "public intellectuals." The tradition of discourse is sharper; some would call it nastier. It is also more public, which makes it somewhat more ambiguous in the academic setting. For example, an academic historian whose biography of a former president gets a favorable first-page review in the Sunday *New York Times* may or may not find that it earns him scholarly acclaim. Nevertheless, he would much rather have a good review than a bad one.

Both reviewing universes settle significant responsibilities on the reviewer. The costs of unfairness can be heavy, even when there is the opportunity to reply to a negative review. The temptation to let political or personal differences influence one's evaluation can be almost irresistible. But when the process of postpublication review turns nasty and the arena is given over to the working out of personal rivalries, it invites further attrition of public confidence in the objectivity and even the maturity of scholars.

Competition in research doubtless produces some good effects. It may make people work harder, and it may spur investment. But in the domain of publication—that is, the formal system for sharing information—there are serious costs. In the sciences in particular, the incentive structure all too often encourages the withholding of information that could make the entire field move ahead more rapidly. This is not usually a problem in the humanities, where scholars tend to draw upon materials that are available to everyone in the field. The exceptions, perhaps because of their rarity, can produce spectacular disagreements, as in the notorious case of disputed access to the Dead Sea Scrolls. Here a heavy price was paid for attempts to assert a monopoly on a scholarly resource. In general, however, there are few secrets to be kept—except in the sciences, where the problem of deliberate nondisclosure presents itself with regularity.

The most fundamental aspect of the nondisclosure problem in the sciences concerns new information. A canonical assumption in the basic scholarly disciplines is that the literature is "open," which means first and foremost that the results of research should be published. That doesn't mean that the scientist must publish everything he knows; some of what he knows isn't ready for critical scrutiny, and a lot else simply isn't worth publishing. But the holding back of newly discovered information that is "ripe" in order to obtain an intellectual monopoly exacts a heavy social cost and violates a fundamental research convention.

Informal communication often enriches a scholarly discipline and aids progress; and indeed, in some fields generosity and openness are the rule. But in others—notably, some of the "hot," highly competitive areas in biomedical research—workers tend to be much more cautious. Informal communication can be an important factor in progress even in these fields, as documented by Patricia Woolf in her analysis of the role of the grapevine in the discovery of cyclic adenosine monophosphate (AMP).[9] Such communication involves not only the rapid exchange of new information, data, and even rumor by the usual media of telephone, fax, and electronic mail, but also the loan of cell lines and other materials. Alas, it is all too often deterred by rivalry and suspicion.

As is so often the case, protective behavior may be encouraged or induced by the fear that others will violate ethical norms. One research group in a major medical school refused to let another group at the same institution have access to a cell line of theirs because they suspected that the second group had made unauthorized use of private information. In a more startling incident, the researcher who published the first paper on "high-temperature" superconducting properties of materials containing the element Yttrium submitted a paper in which the formula Yb, for Ytterbium, was substituted for Y (for Yttrium). The effect was, of course, to divert reviewers from essential knowledge about how this important result was achieved. The author, who described the substitution as a typographical error—an explanation few people in the field are inclined to accept—then corrected the "misprint" in galley proof.

Publication policies adopted by major scientific societies have helped to curb the trend toward secrecy. The American Society for Biochemistry and Molecular Biology and its *Journal of Biological Chemistry* have been leaders. The *Journal* requires as a condition of publication that "unique propagative materials, including, for example, cell lines, hybridomas and DNA clones must be made available by those who develop them to any qualified investigator." This requirement, of course, cannot be invoked before publication, which means that materials may be withheld during that critical period when the work is still developing.

The scholarly venture is surely more damaged by secretiveness than by any of the other impulses that arise from the competitive character of research. The points at which it can be controlled, however, are limited: granting agencies can control it through devices to protect the privacy of the review process, and journals can require full disclosure of methods and postpublication sharing of research materials. But in the end only trust can defeat secrecy, and in many of the scientific disciplines that is in short supply.

Restraints on openness in publication may come from two other, entirely exogenous sources. The first is national security. Even if work under way in a university is not classified, it can be made so by executive order if the government has reason to believe that the information being generated can affect the nation's security. Classification for this reason is rarely imposed; and since most research universities do not accept government contracts under classification, security secrecy has never been a serious problem in academic settings.

That does not mean, however, that it has never been an issue. In the early 1980s, the Department of Defense attempted to apply the terms of arms export control statutes to university research. These laws and their accompanying regulations were intended to apply to weapons technologies and accompanying data, but efforts were made to limit access to U.S.

university laboratories by foreign visitors and to restrict the publication of certain research. We argued that these were inappropriate, and that if the government decided certain projects were of military value it should use its power to classify them—thereby permitting the university to decide whether it wanted to accept the projects along with that burden. That view eventually carried the day.

Many of those who lobbied for restrictions on academic research left no doubt that they thought scholarship needed more such control. Richard Perle, who served as an assistant secretary of defense in the Reagan administration, asked me in a panel discussion before the National Press Club why universities would not step up to their obligations and take on classified research in the national interest. My answer was (and is) that secret work is simply incompatible with the university's joint mission of performing basic work and training the next generation of researchers. If part of a graduate student's thesis research is unavailable for evaluation by all the department's faculty, or if a professor's work cannot be examined by the appointment and promotions committee, then exceptions have been staked out to the most fundamental values of the institution. How a university can exist half free and half secret has never been satisfactorily explained by those who would have it accept classified military research.

The second exogenous restraint on openness in publication has to do with proprietary protection. If work is being done in the hope of commercial development, there may be legitimate reasons for attempting to delay publication in order to establish "ownership" of the idea. For that reason many universities permit publication delays (usually six months or so) when international patent protection is a concern. But there is a more troublesome side to this issue. Stanford has been offered research grants by industrial organizations that would claim exclusive rights (or at least rights of first refusal) on discoveries made in the course of the sponsored project. In other instances, faculty members have been tempted to withhold results deemed important to the success of some commercial development in which they have an outside interest. Needless to say, the first kind of arrangement is, and should be, routinely refused. The second would represent yet another species of conflict of interest. Perhaps the most succinct policy statement on this issue was made by Rear Admiral Bobby Inman, the former deputy director of the Central Intelligence Agency and a thoughtful observer of the research enterprise in the United States. He simply pointed out that universities should not be seen as doing for profit what they are unwilling to do for patriotism.

※ For better or for worse, publication is the medium by which the scholar's work is distributed and judged. Thus much of a scholar's reputation depends upon what, where, and how much he or she publishes, and on how that work is received publicly by others. Unfortunately, competition among scholars often results in many of the problems discussed here, including unfair treatment by peer reviewers and the withholding of important information from colleagues in the field. What would make things better? Surely a less competitive academic universe would help. Indeed, the culture of the academy should favor cooperation and reward those who support colleagues in their discipline when it is merited. As things are, little career headway is made from confirming someone else's result, or supporting someone else's theory with a new line of argument. Because originality and priority hold such high reputational value, it is difficult to see how the situation is going to change very much. Thus the best hope is for a set of standards—cultural norms—that recognize that even in a highly competitive environment departures from fairness simply cannot be tolerated.

Finally, it is surely not too much to ask that research sponsors, especially the government, insist on keeping the venture one in which open communication is the rule. Encouraging the sharing of materials, protecting the fairness of peer review, and above all insisting that its own policies favor prompt and open publication will go far toward limiting the adverse consequences of research competition.

Competition is a good thing in the public mind, especially these days. But the public expects scholarly life to be focused on an objective search for truth, and the searchers disinterested in personal gain. However naive and unrealistic this view may seem, and however much sophisticated observers of the academic scene may deny holding it, it is a meaningful element in the public trust accorded to universities and their faculties.

There is another element as well. As I have argued elsewhere, the central theme of academic duty is a kind of intergenerational responsibility: the duty of faculty members to advance the welfare of their students. Often, disagreements over authorship and academic credit end in disadvantage to junior collaborators. Whenever this happens it looks like exploitation—and it often is.

Society must trust its academic institutions and their faculties. But when they fail to give respectful treatment to the work of others and to tend to the career needs of students, they fail to meet public expectations about their duty.

8

TO TELL THE TRUTH

THE RELATIONSHIP between universities and their public is more dependent on trust than on anything else. For this reason, perhaps, mendacity is viewed as the least forgivable blot on academic duty. In the 1950s Charles van Doren, a faculty member at Columbia University, became an intellectual celebrity when, on a popular television quiz show, he displayed an extraordinary range of knowledge on a variety of subjects. The son of a distinguished academic, he brought both charm and erudition into a medium of exploding popularity. When it was revealed that the quiz show was staged, that is, that van Doren had known many of the answers in advance, a national scandal of extraordinary proportions resulted. Students in my classes at the time seemed bewildered and shocked; they asked how such a thing could have happened. It was a striking reminder of the degree to which truth-telling is the linchpin of academic trust.

Today, alas, the public would react to such a revelation both more calmly and more cynically. The change illustrates just how serious a threat to the public's confidence in the value of scholarship is the belief that its pursuit is marred by personal interest, greed, or dishonesty. Many factors are involved in higher education's fall from grace in the past decade. But surely one of the most troubling, especially for the sciences, is the issue of "research misconduct." Several of the popular books decrying contemporary universities have given it loving attention. It has been the focus of a series of front-page stories even in those newspapers with a reputation for seriousness, like the *New York Times*. At least two congressional committees have made the matter a subject for multiple hearings, generating further publicity.

The list of scientists publicly tainted by charges that either they or their colleagues have published falsified data reads like a Who's Who of biomedical research. It includes a Nobel laureate, the chairs of two distinguished departments of medicine, the director of an NIH laboratory who is credited with what is perhaps the fundamental discovery on the biology of the AIDS virus, a senior researcher who first showed that lead poisoning leads to intellectual deficits in children, and many others. More interesting still is that in many of these well-publicized cases, though by no means all, the initial, headline-producing charges have remained unresolved for years. Some have eventually turned out to be devoid of merit. Thus we are talking about an area of intense public interest, as well as significant controversy—and that raises important questions about where the institutional responsibility for determination and correction of fault should lie.

Academic misconduct has come to be synonymous with research misconduct. Although each covers a wide range of professional sins, as used here (and in most "official" institutional treatments of the problem), both refer to matters that closely involve the world of scholarship. Thus sexual harassment, which could well be the basis for a charge of *professional* misconduct if it occurred in an academic setting, would not fit under this rubric. Nor, even, would some of the more vigorous and controversial efforts to gain credit for one's own work over that of others. Such activities, however distasteful they might be, do not qualify under the generally adopted definition.

There are three important categories of research misconduct. The first concerns issues of authorship and the allocation of academic credit, of the kind that occasionally arise out of the mentoring relationship. A second includes the illegitimate appropriation of the ideas or expressions of another, as sometimes occurs in connection with grant and prepublication review. A third, primarily connected with the sciences, is the deliberate falsification of data or experimental results.

The first two categories are linked in an important way. In scholarship great weight is attached to originality and priority, so authorship is important. Unfair or inaccurate allocation of credit does damage because it confuses the world about who was responsible for what. The improper appropriation of another's ideas creates the same kind of confusion.

Indeed, the ownership of intellectual work product is one of those issues that sounds simple enough: "I had the idea; it's mine." But as we have seen in examining the kinds of disputes that arise between faculty members and their advanced students, identifying ownership of an idea is not always easy. Furthermore, there is the important distinction between the idea and the expression of the idea. To take someone else's idea and use it before it has been placed in the public domain is a form of theft, albeit a difficult one to detect and then to prove. To make further use of someone else's idea after it has been published is scholarship. To borrow not only the idea but the precise form of expression is plagiarism.

Problems may also arise when a scholar is given credit that he or she did not seek. The rapid increase of multiple authorship, especially in the sciences, has given rise to the problem of complimentary authorship, discussed earlier. The following case further illustrates the problem.

An abstract submitted by Professor T includes the name of a graduate student, Mr. K, as second author. Although the abstract journal does not employ peer review, this particular communication contains quite specific data that have been cited in two or three subsequent papers by others, in refereed journals. The authenticity of some of the work on which the abstract was based is challenged. Mr. K, who had moved on to another institution just as the abstract was being published, hears of the problem and is astonished to learn that his name was on the abstract. He immediately telephones Professor T and confronts him, demanding an explanation. T replies that since K had contributed a good idea to the project and had helped with part of the analysis, he had put his name on the paper. "You'd already left by then; since you did make a bit of a contribution, I thought I'd help you out by adding your name to the paper."

Complimentary authorship is one by-product of today's highly competitive academic scene. Jobs are hard to get. Although faculty members often want to help their students for the best of reasons, it is important to remember that they also gain prestige when their students do well. Thus this is a more common transgression than one might suppose, and it is a serious one, not at all mitigated by the elements of good will that sometimes motivate it. Complimentary authorship not only distorts the historical record of who did what, and allocates credit to those who may not deserve any, but also may negatively affect the innocent coauthor if, as in this case, the work turns out to be tainted.

One would not, however, want this argument to be mobilized against the impulse to allocate credit generously. Those who took part in work ought to be included in the list of authors. But because they share responsibility for the quality and truthfulness of the work, they need to have been real—and knowing—participants, and to be fully involved in the decision when and where the work should be published.

Of course, most issues of authorship cut in exactly the opposite direction. The victims in the majority of cases are those who are left out, not those who are involuntarily included. Many of the cases resemble the one in which Professor G publishes the work of graduate student V without the student's prior consent. But there is a larger family of misconduct cases that also involve appropriation. The problem is often seen in clearest form in "review journals," publications that digest advances in some field for the purpose of presenting the reader with an up-to-date summary of that research area. Naturally, it is difficult to review the work of others without borrowing heavily from their thinking. But occasionally, more than the thinking is borrowed, as in the following case.

Professor Z delivers a long article on recent advances in the analysis of homing navigation in birds to the *Quarterly Review of Animal Behavior*. The article deals primarily with a series of papers from two groups of researchers, one in the United States and the other at a German university. Taken together, they indicate that an entire complex of sensory clues—including star maps, Earth's magnetic field, and the sun's position—may be used, depending on circumstances, in directing the homing flights of various species. The reviewer states his reliance on these papers in the first paragraph of the article. After it has been published for several months, a reader notices that the language sounds familiar. He consults the original papers and discovers that the body of Z's review contains lengthy segments of text from several of them, interspersed with summarizing analysis but not set off with quotation marks. He notifies the journal's editor, who, upon repeating the exercise himself, is deeply concerned. The editor contacts Professor Z and tells him what he has found. Z replies that he acknowledged his debt to the U.S. and German work at length at the very beginning of his article and gave complete references. The editor perseveres, reminding Z that the journal's guidelines for authors make it clear that they must indicate when the material of others is being quoted. Z's rejoinder is that he made an appropriate and full disclosure, and that nothing further was required of him.

This is a troublesome case, not so much for the damage inflicted as for what it says about misperceptions, even on the part of the most experienced researchers, regarding the rules of attribution. The prevailing rule is that *all* material borrowed from another source, even when it is one's own previous publication, must be put in quotation marks and referenced. This reinforces the important distinction between an idea and the expression of an idea. A generic acknowledgment of the kind employed by Professor Z is fine for recognizing the origins of an idea. But the particular form of expression of the idea belongs to the original author, even if he or she signed copyright over to the publisher, and cannot be borrowed without a specific declaration that says, in effect, "These words do not belong to me; I copied them from Y."

Failure to respect this tradition is labeled with the ugly word "plagiarism." This sin has a wide range of degrees of severity and occupies a special position in the category of academic misconduct. It involves a plainly illegal act: theft of the expression of another is punishable in the civil courts. But with respect to ideas as opposed to expression the legal situation is murkier. The most brilliant and original idea of a scholar is not "intellectual property" until it has been elaborated—either through publication or by patent protection. Thus the more predominant form of academic misconduct, the appropriation of the unpublished ideas of another, falls under the moral law of scholarship and academe, but not under the civil law.

Plagiarism, in contrast with the wrongful appropriation of ideas, can be dealt with in the courts. But it is nonetheless a form of academic misconduct, and in definitions developed by the Office of Research Integrity (ORI) at the NIH, plagiarism, along with fraud and fabrication, is considered grounds for agency action.[1]

Perhaps the most common form of academic plagiarism consists of the occasional incorporation of short segments from the work of another into a general essay. Many scholars who are guilty of transgressions at this level blame the use of "unmarked notes." Often this explanation sounds hollow, rather like the celebrated student's excuse that "the dog ate my home-work." But in fact the implausible is sometimes true. Conscientious schol-ars may keep extensive notes on file, some of original observations and some of important material taken from the work of others. It is not difficult to see how quotations might metamorphose into evaluative notes in the memory of the scholar who, at a much earlier time, wrote them down. Modern computing has added to this problem by making it much easier to store large amounts of material. More than ever before, plagiarism-by-accident is a serious risk even for the conscientious author.

Almost no area of academic misconduct is so full of lore as this one. What is surprising is how many plagiarists have been forgiven, even when the incidents were highly public. Many years ago the president of a leading university "borrowed" much of the text of his inaugural address from another; the *New Yorker* magazine ran a multiple-page, side-by-side com-parison of his speech and the source document in a department that the magazine used to call "Funny Coincidences." The president nevertheless served out a term of average length, and his university seemed not to suffer visibly.[2] An assistant professor at another institution published as his doc-toral dissertation a piece of contemporary literary criticism. The author of an earlier work on the same subject complained to the university, citing large blocks of identical text. A faculty committee agreed, and the assistant professor was eased out, in the fashion of the times. That story, too, ended less disastrously than one would suppose. The protagonist is now produc-ing favorably reviewed, convincingly original work from a tenured position elsewhere.

In fact, plagiarism is often regarded as a less serious academic sin than other forms of misconduct.[3] Why that should be is mysterious; it involves, after all, the theft of someone else's intellectual property. Perhaps it has something to do with how we are taught to write. The exercise really begins with direct imitation and proceeds from there, through successively more ambitious departures, to independence and originality. "Copying" in school carries less opprobrium than a host of more mortal sins, and we may carry some of that with us into adult life. Other arenas in which truth would seem to be vitally important are also casual about sanctions for plagiarism. A number of the best newspapers, including the *New York Times,* have retained journalists who, in news stories under their own by-lines, have incorporated multiple-paragraph blocks of prose from other sources.[4] It is thus not so surprising that plagiarism is treated more permissively than other forms of academic misconduct.[5]

Nevertheless, these cases are serious ones in academic institutions, where freedom of inquiry and the pursuit of knowledge are treasured values. They are among the most difficult to resolve when formal charges arise. They often present in a form that makes it difficult to decide between unusually sloppy scholarship and intentional appropriation of the writings of another. A well-known biologist once wrote a lengthy review on biolumi-nescence that contained significant amounts of material quoted from the original papers of another author—without benefit of quotation marks. The matter became public because of the distinction of the review's author, who was nominated to be the director of the NSF. He explained that in his notes verbatim material had been mixed with his own commentary, and that he had failed to sort the two out adequately. The forthright character of his admission and the apology he issued in the review journal satisfied most (though not all) observers. He was confirmed in his government post, and later went on to head a major research university.

Disputes over authorship or the origin of ideas are a major source of difficulty for academic institutions and their faculties. Because they often arise in the context of relationships between senior academics and their more junior colleagues (whether graduate students, postdoctoral fellows, or younger faculty members) they raise questions about the abuse of power. Although many of the examples come from the sciences, the humanities have by no means been immune. In recent cases, leading scholars have been attacked for ignoring significant earlier work on the same subjects or even, in the celebrated case of the historian Stephen Oates, charged with appropriating actual phraseology from earlier sources. In the latter case the charges were never substantiated, but the publicity damaged Oates and challenged the public's faith in the objectivity of scholarship.

The last point is clearly central. Universities depend on society's conviction that they are on the up-and-up. This is partly because society needs to trust the knowledge they produce. But there is a deeper level as well. The public sees universities as places to which they have entrusted their young. If the senior scholars responsible for teaching them are seen to lack a sense of duty toward their own work—and in particular if they are seen to prey upon the work and ideas of the young people in their charge—then faith in the entire enterprise is bound to erode. In the public eye professors are supposed to be moral teachers. If they do not practice their craft with rigor, care, and generosity they are bound to lose respect.

❧ Beyond this zone of authorship, credit, and the taking of ideas and expression lies a region of research misconduct that is rarer, more spectacular, and much more controversial. It has fascinated scholars, especially scientists, and those who observe them for more than a century. It is the realm of outright fraud: falsification of results or, in the laboratory vernacular, "cooking data." Because research fraud interests people so much, each incident adds to a folklore that is employed by skeptics to criticize science (the animal rights groups love it) and by critics of higher education to assert the moral decline of our universities.

The research venture is built on trust, and each new venturer needs to know that his or her work rests on solid ground. To ensure that it is solid, we have devised elaborate means for determining whether a given experimental result might have come about by chance rather than as a consequence of the variable we have introduced as part of the design. If, for example, there is a one-in-ten probability that a particular outcome was due to chance, it is conventional to reject it as insignificant; if it is only one in twenty, we consider the result significant. This adoption of the "95 percent confidence limit" as the borderline of reliability is a social policy: it recognizes that scholarship needs to proceed with an extraordinarily high level of assurance about each previous step. In this respect it resembles the standard for proof in criminal trials. In our society, we would much rather let a guilty person go free than wrongly punish an innocent one, so we set the standard high—"beyond reasonable doubt." If in research we cared less about certainty we might have borrowed from the civil standard, taking a 60 percent confidence limit not unlike "preponderance of the evidence." But we didn't.

Because it is impossible to monitor for fraud, we have to trust individual scholars with the academic duty to tell the truth. The spectacular failures—the dramatic cases of well-publicized fraud—are damaging out of all proportion to their frequency. They create a rupture in faith in a realm in which there is no alternative to trust. The early literature on this subject is fascinating. In some cases, the motive for fraud was apparently to engineer a hoax, as in the case of the skull cleverly constructed from parts "discovered" in a British quarry. For about forty years, the so-called Piltdown man was not revealed as a forgery, despite the efforts of skeptics to expose the relatively crude efforts of the perpetrators to make the skull look real. The marvel of the Piltdown episode, in the view of some historians, is that such a transparent fake could have succeeded so well. It reminds us of the degree to which the scholarly enterprise is built on trust; even clumsy fraud can pass undetected when it is widely assumed that no one cheats.

In one of the first famous cases early in this century, the German biologist Paul Kammerer produced a long series of experiments that appeared to demonstrate the inheritance of acquired characteristics, as proposed originally by Jean-Baptiste Lamarck. The most controversial of these involved an amphibian called the midwife toad. This species breeds on land, and the males lack pads on the hands that in related aquatic species are employed to grasp the female in copulation. After a few generations of being forced by Kammerer to breed in water, descendants of the experimental toads allegedly appeared with pads. The results brought Kammerer into conflict with supporters of Darwinian evolution, notably the geneticist William Bateson. Following a long series of disagreements with Bateson about the pads, one of Kammerer's animals was examined by a visiting American biologist, who discovered that the pad had been created by an India ink decoration. Kammerer admitted the fraud, but claimed that it had been committed by someone else. He later died, apparently by his own hand.[6]

Even famous experiments may have involved efforts to make the data look a little better than they really were. The noted British statistician R. A. Fisher reanalyzed the genetic ratios reported by the pioneer geneticist Gregor Mendel and found them too good to be true.[7] The notebooks of R. J. Milliken, the physicist who won the Nobel Prize in physics for the "oil drop" experiments in which he determined the mass of the electron, contain deletions of outlying data points that, to many modern observers, strongly suggest selection intended to make the results look better than they really were.[8]

In a case both more recent and more directly familiar to me, a German biologist named Franz Moewus claimed that the sex of gametes of the alga *Chlamydamonas* was controlled by minute amounts of two related chemicals secreted into the water—a remarkable instance of sex determination by pheromones. His work also laid out an extraordinary set of genetic claims, supported by elaborate statistics. These findings, published just before and just after World War II, received wide international attention from geneticists; indeed, at the time it appeared that Moewus was a pioneer in the use of microorganisms for studies of biochemical genetics. But his results were also widely doubted, particularly after the war, when many scientists in the United States and elsewhere were led to wonder how Moewus could have continued this work under the Nazi regime. But in the manner of the times—it was by now 1954—the matter was handled informally. A leading American geneticist, Tracy Sonneborn of Indiana University, had followed Moewus's work closely and had been a thoughtful defender against the doubts that had already arisen. A confrontation was arranged at the Marine Biological Laboratory in Woods Hole, where Moewus was a visiting investigator. A group of geneticists, algologists, and biochemists questioned Moewus about his work. Not only were his responses unconvincing even to Sonneborn; it became unmistakable that he had even falsified the conditions of his demonstrations. Word spread rapidly, and eventually one of the American investigators who had hosted Moewus published a brief account in *Science* of his failure to repeat the critical experiments. After that, not much was heard about the matter. Informal resolutions of this kind were standard then; indeed, this one was unusually public.[9]

But times have changed. Research misconduct cases now receive intense public scrutiny and are resolved by formal, often highly visible institutional procedures. That is partly because scientific fraud provides a false floor on which others may innocently build. Plagiarism victimizes the person whose expression is stolen and may unduly inflate the reputation of the plagiarist. But the invention of results, if undetected, can have manifold and long-lasting consequences in the form of misallocation of valuable resources. A spurious finding may generate expensive efforts at replication, or persuade other scholars to adopt unwarranted assumptions in their work. The result is that time and money are wasted. And now that government investment in science has grown to be a significant fraction of what are called "discretionary" domestic expenditures, the public and their representatives in

Congress are demanding, in a climate of increasing stringency in the federal budget, a higher level of accountability for the way in which those investments are made.

Thus it is hardly surprising that science fraud issues are now handled in a much more public way. In an influential book published in 1982, Nicholas Wade and William S. Broad, journalists who had worked at *Science* magazine and then at the *New York Times,* drew public attention to the matter. They analyzed several contemporary cases and did an engaging history of much earlier ones. But the main thrust of their book was a claim that the real incidence of fraud was much higher than had been generally believed—indeed, that science is an enterprise much more driven by the desire for financial and reputational gain than most people suppose. At several points in the book, the authors alluded disparagingly to the efforts of scientific leaders to persuade congressional committees and the public that fraud is a rarity and that science is a self-correcting venture.

The view of science that Wade and Broad presented is probably too cynical, just as the previously prevailing view was perhaps too rosy. The actual frequency of fraud in science is very hard to determine precisely. But in the past decade, as the *Times* and other newspapers have paid more attention to the issue, the public has been led to believe that it is prevalent. The impact of highly publicized cases has been magnified, too, by a change in the background against which they are seen. The public has become much more aware of the uncertainties in research. Firm conclusions are regularly overturned, not because they were wrong in their time, but because they are overtaken by new understandings and new methods. Scientists in particular are seen as more fallible individuals, not because of moral failings but because it has become clearer that they don't deal only in "facts." Researchers regularly appear against one another as expert witnesses in tort litigation, and the public sees two reputed "experts" saying exactly opposite things about the same issue. Sociologists of science point out that the views of scientists and even the language they use to describe their work and its outcomes are subject to social influences. In short, the image of scientists (and doctors, and a variety of other "experts" in our society) has already been blurred; they are seen as less infallible, more subject to the same kinds of shaping influences and temptations than affect the rest of us. Laid upon this altered background, examples of actual misconduct—egregious failures of academic duty—have a stronger hold on popular imagination.

The first two cases of research fraud to receive widespread attention were also treated in some detail in the Broad-Wade book. One involved a Harvard researcher in cardiology named John Darsee, who worked in an unusually active laboratory headed by Professor Eugene Braunwald. Even though Darsee was directly observed to create false data for a publication, he was kept on for months, still doing research, while nothing was said by his supervisor or by Harvard. Eventually other irregularities in his work were noted, and an outside committee set up by Harvard finally reached a public determination of his guilt. But it found no fault with Braunwald, even though he had been a coauthor on a number of papers from Darsee's extraordinary list of more than one hundred in two years; and it leveled no criticism at Harvard for having kept the matter under wraps.

There is an interesting and historically significant aftermath to the Darsee story. The matter attracted the attention of two NIH investigators, Walter Stewart and Ned Feder, who were in the process of giving up their work on nervous systems in favor of a new research interest in scientific fraud. They prepared an extensive analysis of the papers coauthored by Darsee during this period, of which eighteen were full research papers and another one hundred were short papers, abstracts, or reviews. This examination, they claimed, revealed a large number of lapses from accepted standards of research and publication; they concluded that such lapses were more common than generally believed, and recommended random audits of the literature to probe the question further.[10]

Stewart and Feder drafted a manuscript based on this analysis. After *Science* rejected it, the authors then sent it around to a number of individuals (I was one) for their comments. I thought the work unworthy of publication on scientific grounds, believing that the involvement of an author known to have committed fraud and two laboratories that were plainly loose about quality control invalidated the conclusions the authors were trying to draw. By correspondence, the authors argued extensively with several of us who criticized it. Eventually the study became so widely circulated that it might as well have been published, as indeed it finally was. But in my view, and in the view of many other scientists, it failed to make the case that lapses from accepted standards were widespread. What

Stewart and Feder showed was only that when fraud occurs, it is likely to happen wherever standards are poorly maintained.

A second highly publicized case involved a very senior Yale faculty member, Philip Felig, and a postdoctoral fellow named Soman. The details are complex, but the case involved a third scientist's detecting that Soman had "borrowed" data and conclusions from her paper, apparently as a result of Soman's having seen it during Felig's review of the manuscript for the *New England Journal of Medicine*. Felig defended the originality of Soman's work, which he and Soman proposed to publish jointly. Several compromises were offered to, and rejected by, the scientist whose paper had been plagiarized; eventually Felig and Soman published, at which point charges were filed and outside audits of the work were requested by Yale. The audits showed that not only plagiarism but also data faking was involved. After a long delay, Felig withdrew a total of a dozen papers and the matter finally became public. Meanwhile, Felig had been offered a senior position at Columbia. When news of the fraud was revealed, the Columbia administration, after review by a faculty committee, withdrew its offer. Yale took Felig back, but at somewhat reduced status.

These two cases involved very distinguished medical schools with responsible, decent deans. But at this milestone in the development of our attitudes about scientific fraud, the first reaction was denial and a retreat to reliance upon "the people one trusts." Revelation was delayed, and opprobrium—when it finally arrived—was focused on the junior researcher who cheated and not on the senior scientist who shared some of the responsibility.

These early incidents underscore a duty of the university, as well as a certain lack of awareness about how to fulfill it. Few institutions at the time had formal procedures for acting on charges of this kind, and they were often overly protective of the senior faculty members who were being charged. A steady growth in their sense of public accountability for federal research funds, partly caused by harsh criticism in the wake of cases like these, has stimulated the development of such rules, which should (and in most cases do) protect the rights of both accusers ("whistleblowers") and faculty members or others who are the subject of research misconduct charges.

In the aftermath of these cases and the Wade-Broad book, a number of additional incidents were reported in the press. By the late 1980s, the popular impression that science fraud was epidemic had become widespread. But in fact the frequency of academic misconduct and its distribution are matters about which abundant speculation and even conviction exist amid a disappointing paucity of hard data. Ever since the issue became a subject of intense public interest, there has been debate about how common science fraud is, with the scientific community arguing that it is (and always has been) rare, and its critics—especially in Congress and the media—declaring that we have seen only the tip of the iceberg.

Much attention was therefore given to a study that the sociologist Judith Swazey and some colleagues published in the *American Scientist* in 1993.[11] This analysis attempted to measure the frequency with which students and faculty members had observed various forms of scientific misconduct, including falsification of data. With respect to this last, 6 percent of faculty respondents said that they knew of another faculty member who had falsified data, and 50 percent reported having been exposed to at least one of the several categories of misconduct listed in the questionnaire, which included use of university resources for personal purposes and sexual harassment. The authors asserted from such numbers that academic misconduct is "not rare," although it is not clear what the normative standard for "rarity" should be.

The study has other difficulties. It drew responses from only 66 percent of those queried, and made no effort to eliminate double reporting of the same case from faculty and students in the same department. It also looked only at *perceptions* of wrongdoing. Those of us who have dealt with numbers of these cases know that most allegations turn out to be without merit. In short, there is good reason to be dubious about the figures cited by Swazey and her colleagues. The study was rejected by *Science* on the basis of peer review before it was published in an outlet not subject to such review.

The treatment of their report in the popular press, however, left little room for reservation. Most accounts referred to the "4,000 persons surveyed," but failed to give the actual response rate or address the possible problem of bias due to self-selection. The general flavor of the press treatment may be gleaned from the headlines of the *New York Times* stories on the subject: "Misconduct in science is not rare, a survey finds"; and, two days later, "Scientific misconduct—study says cheating is not so rare"; and then, in a wrap-up profile a week later, "Her study shattered the myth that fraud in science is a rarity."[12]

We are lacking not only firm data on how much scientific fraud there is, but also a basis for normative judgments about what level might be acceptable. Suppose that one in a hundred researchers has, at one time or another, engaged in some form of scholarly falsification. One view might hold this to be unacceptable; after all, if the researcher held his or her proportionate share of the federal research budget, a congressional critic would very likely say, "Do you realize that we are actually giving more than fifty million dollars a year to cheaters?" That point might well be a political winner. But the same Congress tolerates, year after year, a much costlier ethical defect level in the student loan program. There is, in short, no particular incidence of transgression at which we are tempted to say, "This is too much; we must root out sin at all costs."[13]

The only proper test, I suggest, is whether the cost to the entire research enterprise of a certain level of misconduct is greater than that of the regulatory interventions needed to eliminate it. Before we can approach that issue in a sensible way, we need to know something about the distribution and the character of research fraud, as well as about the history of efforts to control it.

Of the fewer than fifty well-known cases of academic fraud, the overwhelming majority are in the biomedical sciences. The reasons for this are not clear, but a few general properties of the field may suggest some explanations. Biomedical research laboratories tend to be large and relatively well supported; postdoctoral fellows and graduate students tend to work independently, with relaxed supervision. The experiments often depend on personal skill and "technique," the replication of which may present difficulties. True team efforts that involve construction of large apparatus and group analysis are rare in comparison with, say, experimental physics. The field is highly competitive, and because it often involves well-known and even life-threatening diseases, major advances are given significant public attention. It could be argued that opportunity and incentive to falsify results are both maximized in biomedicine.

Within that field, Patricia Woolf has undertaken a careful analysis of the distribution of academic misconduct.[14] She examined twenty-six cases that took place between 1950 and 1987, twenty-two of which were in biomedicine. A large proportion of the institutions involved were prestigious by national ranking, and many of the individuals charged were graduates of highly regarded institutions. Most were senior scientists, not graduate students or fellows. There was a heavy preponderance of "busy" research groups in the sample. To one who has looked at this problem from all sides, the most interesting fact about research misconduct is that it tends to occur in places where the pace of activity, the size of the group, and the scope of work make personal accountability difficult. A terse but perhaps not terribly useful conclusion would be that fraud occurs when the right people aren't paying enough attention.

When charges of research fraud surface, the next question is, Who should take responsibility for doing something about it? The natural answer is the institution in which it takes place, usually though not always a university. But there are other possibilities. For example, the work under suspicion of fraud has usually been published, and the journal in which it appeared has subjected it to peer review; perhaps the journal is the right party to deal with the problem. Two difficulties stand in the way of this solution. The first is that peer review is entirely unprepared to deal with the kind of misconduct that entails the invention or "cooking" of data. Journals don't ask for data books and challenge entries in them; they couldn't possibly afford to devote the time or financial resources to the task. Second, even if they devised mechanisms for examining papers for fraud, they would have only limited power to impose sanctions. They could close their pages to future contributions from guilty authors, but in a world full of journals that would be a weak punishment. They could publicly expose the authors of rejected papers, but that would invite a level of legal counterattack that few journals (or their attorneys) would care to risk. In short, journals have a very low capacity to detect fraud, and even less to pursue and punish it.

If not the journals, why not the research community itself? Scholarly work is done through an elaborate social structure involving societies, their annual meetings, and their journals. In principle that system would have the power to exclude from further activity anyone violating basic standards of academic conduct. This solution would appeal to many researchers because it would keep the matter within the scientific community, subject— like other aspects of research—to peer judgment.

As the subject began to attract public attention in the late 1980s, the three chartered national academies—the NAS, the National Academy of Engineering, and the Institute of Medicine—began to play a useful if largely hortatory role in dealing with research misconduct. A Panel on Scientific Responsibility and the Conduct of Research was established under the chairmanship of Edward David, a former science adviser to the president. The panel's report summarized the state of knowledge about academic misconduct and made a number of recommendations about educating scientists, establishing definitions and guidelines, and designing government and university procedures for dealing with the problem.[15] It also recommended the formation of an independent Scientific Integrity Advisory Board to address ethical issues in research, frame model policies, and collect and share data.

Those functions are indeed important responsibilities of the scientific community. A giant further step, however, would be for the scientific community to contemplate a direct role in particular cases. The scientific system is loosely structured and lacks any mechanism for making findings of fact or reaching judgments in adversary situations. And the historical record is curiously mixed. On the one hand, scientists have often been tolerant even of reasonably well known instances of academic fraud, preferring to remain silent rather than endure a public blot on the escutcheon of scholarship. On the other hand, recent committees and panels of scientists have sometimes been careless in their analysis of particular cases, or lax in their efforts to preserve due process for those charged.

In 1993, following escalating concerns about the failure of institutions to pursue academic misconduct cases, the presidents of the three academies issued a statement approved by the governing bodies of each. It expressed disappointment that the recommendations (directed at both universities and the government) of the previous reports had not been adopted, and it restated several major concerns, including confusion over the definition of intent (see below), inconsistencies in the definitions of misconduct adopted by different agencies, and slowness on the part of universities and other research institutions to put in place clear policies. Perplexingly, though, the statement said nothing about the difficulties of due process encountered in the then-recent spate of prosecutions undertaken in the NIH—or the mixed record of scientific review panels, including the academy's own. Instead, it emphasized the responsibilities of universities and government for ensuring that fraud does not occur.

Thus the institution left with the primary responsibility for monitoring research misconduct, evaluating charges, and delivering sanctions is the university itself. This is certainly not an inappropriate outcome; the university is, after all, the employer. But the role is not an easy one for the university to undertake. A long and powerful tradition of academic freedom controls and limits the role of institution as prosecutor. This tradition, developed to protect faculty ideas and expression from the interference of political orthodoxy, imposes heavy (and appropriate) burdens of due process on the employing institution. It is small wonder that few universities had formal procedures in place for dealing with allegations of academic misconduct in the early 1980s. Now virtually all have them.

Typically, these policies provide for complaints to be lodged with the dean or provost, who then appoints a preliminary inquiry committee. The committee recommends whether a formal investigation is warranted; if so, the dean or provost reveals the identity of the complainant, notifies all parties, and appoints a formal investigation committee. That committee reports to the provost anything encountered in the course of its inquiry that might affect funding of the respondent's research, and the provost then conveys that information to the funding agencies. No provision is made for the respondent to question the complainant or other witnesses; respondent and complainant may be represented by an "adviser," who may be an attorney but may not participate in the proceedings. A final report of the committee is due within ninety days, and there is an opportunity for the respondent to reply in writing. If the charges are substantiated, the provost may then invoke the institution's normal procedures for faculty discipline, which in most cases do afford the opportunity of a formal hearing.

The above procedure is that used at the University of Pennsylvania, but it is fairly typical of those in force at most research universities.[16] Such rules have been challenged frequently. Faculty groups have sometimes argued that they offer inadequate protection for those charged. Members of Congress, by contrast, often charge that universities do not go far enough in monitoring conduct and dealing with transgressions.

The question of who does the investigating within the university can prove troublesome. Faculty members generally feel more comfortable if their colleagues are involved. Sometimes, however, the matter involves financial issues (as, for example, the management of federal grant or contract funds) or raises sensitive legal issues for the institution. Under such circumstances it may be appropriate for the administration, upon receiving the complaint, to assign an auditor or an attorney to perform an initial investigation. In some cases that has resulted in faculty complaints, on the ground that academic freedom principles grant faculty the right to be investigated only by other academic appointees. Such a "right," whatever its perceived merits, does not exist in most places.

Ultimately, in this still-unsettled area, the initial investigation and sanctioning of research misconduct will become part of the university's portfolio of academic duties to society. In my view, the procedures will have to evolve if the university is to fulfill its duty fairly. At present, too much depends on processes that have been made private and nonadversarial, thus permitting the university to err in two directions: to be overly protective of its own faculty, as in the Darsee and Felig cases, or to be overly responsive to external cries for a scalp. The appropriate legal protections include representation by participating legal counsel and the opportunity for those charged to cross-examine witnesses against them—and also firm provisions for the protection of those bringing charges.

It is not surprising, given the difficulty of university prosecution and the early reluctance of university administrators to initiate it, that the government has stepped into the breach, using the authority it possesses by virtue of providing much of the funding for basic research. Several different agencies have formulated regulations, and these badly need coordination and standardization. Most of the action in the government's management of academic misconduct cases, except in the special instance of clinical trials conducted for regulatory purposes, where misconduct is handled—more aggressively—by the Food and Drug Administration (FDA), has been concentrated in the NIH, the supporter of the vast majority of basic biomedical research. The first agency created for this purpose was located within the NIH itself and was called the Office of Scientific Integrity (OSI).[17] Established in 1989, it undertook a number of celebrated cases. The handling of these drew widespread criticism on grounds of due process: researchers often had little opportunity to question accusers or provide rebuttal evidence. In 1992 the office was renamed the Office of Research Integrity and moved, first to the office of the assistant secretary for health, and then to that of the secretary of health and human services.

The history is important primarily because of a special relationship among academic misconduct, NIH, and the Subcommittee on Oversight and Investigations, House Commerce Committee. As the chairman of the subcommittee until 1995, Representative Dingell took a special interest in academic misconduct cases. His subcommittee held well-publicized hearings about the charges against Thereza Imanishi-Kari, a collaborator with the Nobel laureate David Baltimore; Robert Gallo of NIH, a pioneer worker on the AIDS virus; his colleague Mikulas Popovic; the Cleveland Clinic researcher Rameshwar Sharma; and others. Pressure generated by the hearings, and, in their aftermath, by subcommittee staff members, was said to be an important factor in persuading OSI to prosecute these cases. Suzanne Hadley, a former deputy director of OSI who left under pressure from the director of NIH, Dr. Bernadine Healy, went to work for the subcommittee in 1992. So did Walter Stewart, an NIH scientist who had become a full-time fraud investigator after his analysis of the Darsee case.

It was at Chairman Dingell's insistence that ORI was removed from NIH and installed downtown, in the headquarters of the Department of Health and Human Services (HHS). The new office has grown in size since its transplantation: by 1993 it had more than fifty employees, including six full-time attorneys, and a budget of four million dollars a year. But in the efforts to expose academic fraud that have been of greatest interest to the subcommittee, prosecutions following the initial hearings have not been successful. A key disappointment came in the case of Popovic, Gallo's collaborator, who had been charged with including misleading statements in his scientific papers.

These charges originated from work by an investigative reporter, John Crewdson of the *Chicago Tribune,* and from the continuing interest of the subcommittee and its staff. They related to an important series of papers published in 1984, in which Gallo, Popovic, and collaborators showed that a retrovirus (HIV) was the cause of acquired immune deficiency syndrome (AIDS). The OSI's inquiry began early in 1990. OSI asked the NAS to provide a list of scientists who could advise the director of NIH on the process and on the quality of the final written report. That report was completed in July 1992; it reached the conclusion that Popovic was guilty of scientific misconduct, and was harshly critical of Gallo. The consultant group, in responding, supported the report's conclusions in the main but criticized it in several respects for not reaching stronger conclusions regarding Gallo. The final report from ORI was released in March 1992, although various interim versions had been leaked to the press at earlier times.

The HHS has a Departmental Appeals Board, which appoints Research Integrity Adjudication Panels, composed of experienced attorneys and sometimes scientists, to hear appeals on such cases. Popovic's appeal before the panel offered, for the first time, an opportunity for the respondent to challenge the evidence and to cross-examine witnesses. The panel's reexamination of the charges against Popovic produced a reversal as remarkable for its sense of outrage as for the result itself. "One might anticipate that from all this evidence, after all the sound and fury, there would be at least a residue of palpable wrongdoing. That is not the case," the report said in its summary decision. And it concluded, "ORI did not prove that the *Science* paper contains untrue statements or data, much less that it contains intentional falsifications."[18]

Shortly afterward, ORI abandoned its prosecution in the Gallo case. An important controversy then arose, and it says much about how such allegations should be handled. In dropping the Gallo matter the director of ORI, Lyle Bivens, claimed that a new standard of proof had been established by the Adjudication Panel in the Popovic case—one that made it impossible to proceed. What the panel actually said was that scientific misconduct cannot be found unless the preponderance of the evidence supports a finding that the respondent had intentionally made statements that were false and thus intended to mislead. The claim that this is a new standard seems odd, in view of the history of regulatory development in this area. HHS drafted misconduct guidelines through notice-and-comment rule making in the late 1980s. Researchers criticized the first proposals on the grounds that the definition of academic misconduct was vague and overbroad. A revised version defined academic misconduct as "fabrication, falsification, plagiarism, or other practices that seriously deviate from those that are commonly accepted within the scientific community." The regulations went on to exclude "honest error or honest differences in interpretation or judgments of data." The exclusion plainly covers the kinds of inadvertent mistakes and judgmental errors that researchers occasionally make, and that are normally worked out through the scientific process of repetition and review. The issue of intent badly needs further clarification.[19]

It is difficult to imagine instances of fabrication or falsification in which intent to deceive is not implicit. Every once in a rare while, a scientist does manage to publish a "joke" paper, with invented methods, data, and conclusions on a silly subject. Here, plainly, there is falsification, but it is with intent to amuse rather than to deceive. (There is even a rather funny quasi-scientific periodical called the *Journal of Irreproducible Results.*) Perhaps this category would be excluded under the new, putatively "higher" standard, but it is hard to think of any other; a requirement to find intent actually seems entirely consistent with the old standard. Indeed, one could argue for an even higher one (for example, a "beyond reasonable doubt" standard) as a deterrent against careless or overzealous prosecution. The real problem is the lack of *any* consistent standard, as well as a failure to exercise sensible prosecutorial discretion. ORI's overall record through 1994 showed that of forty-five cases, only sixteen resulted either in admissions of guilt or in a final judgment against the researcher charged, though there has been some recent improvement.

The Gallo and Popovic cases contain several lessons that should be pondered by those concerned about research conduct and its regulation—indeed, by anyone considering engaging in government-sponsored research. The first is obvious: definitions, even carefully crafted ones, leave much to argue about, especially in the difficult area of intent. Second, prosecutorial discretion is subject in this area as in all others to political pressure. Congressional hearings and media pressure can bring about decisions, whether by the government or universities, that are based more on a perceived need to respond than on the merits of the case. Finally, researchers who feel friendly to the concept of peer review in other contexts may be tempted to say, and often do say, that if only such matters could be left to scholarly peers (who really understand the content) and kept out of the hands of the lawyers, all would be well. The record suggests otherwise. In Gallo-Popovic and other cases as well, scientists have shown unexpected prosecutorial zeal as well as a tendency to deal carelessly with the details of content. Feelings of professional jealousy and resentment may have played a role; Gallo was personally disliked by many of his colleagues and thought to be greedy about taking credit.

That might help to explain the zeal, but it does not explain the carelessness with respect to content displayed in the report of those the NAS designated to review the case. The group named by the academy to review the ORI findings in Gallo-Popovic did not produce a formal report, perhaps because NIH did not want it to fall under the provisions of the Advisory Committee Act. The group met for two days, and subsequently the chairman filed and signed an informal report.[20] It was not made a part of the docket examined by the Appeals Board and hence remains unpublished. But it was leaked to the press and became the subject of several stories adverse to Gallo and Popovic. Gallo's counsel, after reading the stories and obtaining a copy, wrote a line-by-line refutation of the report, identifying numerous errors in it. These are of an interesting sort. Although the subject matter is rather arcane virology, the mistakes have to do not with the subject matter but with the sequencing of historical events, the order of manuscript drafts, and the details of records. They are exactly the kinds of things that a scientist absorbed in the technical content might miss, but a litigation attorney would find every time. In view of this record, a scientist on the wrong end of such a charge might do well to select lawyers rather than fellow scientists to hear the facts and make the judgment.

Unfortunately, the universities themselves have a mixed record in pursuing allegations of academic misconduct. In the cases of Felig and Darsee, highly prestigious institutions were reluctant to proceed vigorously on charges brought against senior faculty members or their protdegdes. That was early in the development of university procedures for dealing with such cases. Since then, a number of recommendations and guidelines have been developed, and responses are prompter and more standardized; but now some instances of university overzealousness are emerging. Neither is the government's apparatus working very well, as the Imanishi-Kari case demonstrates. Indeed, the Gallo and Imanishi-Kari cases—each in some sense unfinished—are a good way of summarizing the present situation. They demonstrate that we still don't have in place clear policies for dealing with academic misconduct that work effectively and fairly.

Of all the contemporary instances of academic misconduct, the Imanishi-Kari case has drawn the most publicity and had the most drastic consequences. In large part that is because of the involvement of one of the most celebrated scientists of the day, David Baltimore, a Nobel laureate, codiscoverer of the enzyme reverse transcriptase, director of the Whitehead Institute at MIT, and then president of Rockefeller University in New York. Indeed, for much of its tortuous, nine-year course in the public eye this case was referred to as the "Baltimore case," even though no one has ever suggested that Baltimore himself was guilty of misconduct.

The affair begins with the 1986 publication in the journal *Cell* of a paper

on alterations in the expression of immunoglobulin genes in transgenic
mice. It is a complex, highly technical paper on a very arcane subject.
Thereza Imanishi-Kari, then a postdoctoral researcher at MIT, was an author, and there were five others, including David Baltimore. Margot
O'Toole, a postdoctoral fellow in the laboratory of Imanishi-Kari, became
convinced that there was something wrong with the data, on the basis of
seventeen pages of past laboratory records. She communicated her concerns to her former mentor at Tufts University, who was in the same
department to which she had just agreed to move, and spoke to a senior
faculty member at MIT. She also talked with the MIT ombudsman and
prepared a memo for MIT. In none of this was there any claim that fraud
or misrepresentation was involved, and O'Toole declined to make any
official complaint about the matter. Informal reviews at both Tufts and
MIT were inconclusive as to whether the scientific objections raised by
O'Toole were correct, but misconduct had not been made an issue at this
stage.

It soon became one, however. A former graduate student at MIT, not
himself involved in the work, brought the matter to Walter Stewart and
Ned Feder, the two NIH scientists who had become, following their role
in the Darsee case, full-time, self-appointed investigators of scientific fraud.
They examined the seventeen pages that O'Toole had found and prepared
an analysis that was widely circulated in the scientific community. In it,
Feder and Stewart alleged that the data had been presented "in a grossly
misleading and inaccurate way in the *Cell* paper."[21] That claim, though it
falls well short of alleging fraud, soon metamorphosed into a claim of
academic misconduct. Stewart and Feder roused the interest of the Subcommittee on Oversight and Investigations of the House Energy and Commerce Committee and its chairman, John Dingell. Dingell promised to
hold hearings on the matter, and soon did. His staff began to use the term
"fraud" in discussing the case with the press.

At the first Dingell hearing, O'Toole, Stewart, and Feder testified, but
Baltimore and Imanishi-Kari were uninvited. The NIH, in response to the
continuing criticism, appointed a three-person expert panel to evaluate the
scientific issues. It produced a draft report that was widely circulated, but
in which no finding of misconduct was reached. Dingell nonetheless
planned a new hearing, this one to involve both sides in the growing controversy; it took place after much fanfare in May 1989. At the center was
a new analysis, done by a Secret Service laboratory, of the age of inks and

other features of the seventeen notebook pages. The conclusion offered was that some of the critical entries were made after the fact, and thus must have been fraudulent efforts to establish the validity of the original findings. Baltimore vigorously contested the Secret Service results, and, in a dramatic closing statement, criticized the conduct of the entire investigation and the hearing itself.

Some scientific observers thought that the data in the seventeen pages were "bad data" (that is, not convincing) but hardly fraudulent. In the view of others, they could support a misconduct charge. The "dating" work by the Secret Service thus appeared likely to be dispositive. Efforts by the NIH review committee and others to obtain details of the Secret Service laboratory analysis, however, were repeatedly frustrated by claims of secrecy on the part of Dingell and his staff.

The report by an augmented OSI committee was finally leaked to the press in 1991. It charged misconduct, praised O'Toole, and criticized Baltimore for not being more responsive in the early going. Baltimore responded with an apologetic statement in which he joined in praise of O'Toole and conceded that he himself had erred in "failing to heed the warnings." But yet another shift in the wind was in store. Imanishi-Kari's lawyers submitted the Secret Service analysis to an independent forensic scientist, who criticized them in an affidavit to the U.S. Attorney. The latter, having been invited by Dingell to consider criminal prosecution in the matter, decided in mid-1992 not to proceed. At this point Baltimore announced that, having retracted the *Cell* paper because of the evidence of fraud, he now proposed to unretract it. In the meantime, Baltimore had accepted the presidency of Rockefeller University. At the very time of his apology, faculty controversy over the appointment was growing, and reports of internal dissension were being transmitted regularly to the *New York Times*. Eventually Baltimore resigned the presidency, under pressure of heavy anonymous criticism from his new faculty.[22]

With the removal of OSI (now relabeled ORI) to the office of the secretary in the Department of Health and Human Services, the report on the case—still in draft—began a new life. The new director of the office assigned three staff scientists to the project, and reported that they did "substantial amounts of additional work." Their final report was sent to Imanishi-Kari in August 1994, and she was given ninety days to respond. Her attorneys protested but were refused additional time. The report was issued in November 1994; it found her guilty of misconduct on nineteen counts and proposed that for ten years she be ineligible for federal research support.

The appeals board of HHS, officially termed the Research Integrity Adjudication Panel, the same entity that had reversed ORI with respect to Popovic, then heard the case. This time the panel consisted of two lawyers and a distinguished senior scientist. For the first time, Imanishi-Kari and her attorneys had an opportunity to challenge the evidence of the Secret Service tests, to cross-examine witnesses, and to make their case in a judicial venue in which standard rules applied. The final report of the panel was issued on June 21, 1996. It cleared Imanishi-Kari of all charges and removed the penalty. In a number of respects, the report is a remarkable document. It is bluntly critical of the ORI and its procedures, stating that they "raised fundamental questions of fairness," and that "frequently ORI interpreted the same or similar results one way for one purpose and another way for another purpose." It says of much of the ORI case that it was "internally inconsistent, lacked reliability or foundation, was not credible or not corroborated, or was based on unwarranted assumptions." By implication, the appellate result is also an indictment of the process itself.

The damage done by that process was heavy and quite unwarranted. During the lengthy investigation, various versions of the interim findings were selectively leaked to the press. Imanishi-Kari was being considered for tenure at Tufts, and of course she was denied. David Baltimore's reputation suffered severe damage, and he lost the presidency of Rockefeller University. Even if the appeal had not produced the result it did—indeed, even if Imanishi-Kari had committed real research fraud—it would be difficult to justify a conviction based on such a procedure. Had a criminal prosecution involved as many violations of a defendant's rights as this, it would have been dismissed with a torrent of judicial disapproval.

Of special concern is the relationship among the federal agency involved, the congressional investigators, and the media. Members of the Dingell subcommittee have made no secret of the fact that they selectively "leak" material to the press as part of their investigative strategy. In this instance, preliminary information damaging to Imanishi-Kari (and thus to Baltimore) was regularly made public as the case developed.[23] Material in draft was treated, outside ORI, as if it were the final disposition of the matter; the press, the public, the scientific community, and the institutions involved were permitted—indeed, invited—to take action on the basis of this material.

Some have argued that the principal actors in this case, Baltimore and Imanishi-Kari, contributed to their own difficulties by the way they personally handled the situation. They have been asked frequently in the aftermath, by reporters and others, whether a different approach would have ameliorated the personal consequences they suffered. Having been asked that question about the not-dissimilar situation in which I found myself in the indirect cost controversy at Stanford, I think it's a difficult one to answer. Undeniably, Baltimore offered a strong defense of his colleague, leading some to call him arrogant, and to speculate that a more humble approach to the subcommittee and his media critics would have changed the outcome. I doubt it very much. Chairman Dingell has sometimes praised humility in his "targets," but he has seldom turned them loose. And the combination of forces in this case—a powerful congressional subcommittee, a frightened federal agency, and media eager to print leaks—add up to a formidable problem.[24]

The appeals decision in the Imanishi-Kari case launched a flood of new media attention, and much of it focused on the role of the subcommittee and its chairman. Anthony Lewis wrote a scathing column on Dingell in the *New York Times* with the title "Tale of a Bully." The same newspaper issued a mild *mea culpa*, in which it referred to its earlier editorial assault on Baltimore as perhaps a "rush to judgment." To my astonishment, I found myself quoted approvingly on the editorial page of the *Wall Street Journal* to the effect that "a lot of people owe David Baltimore an apology."[25]

Indeed they do. But the second look comes a little late. Baltimore's personal courage and determination allowed him to stay brilliantly productive in science during his travail, but science policy lost an important voice. So did higher education: his truncated presidency of Rockefeller University lasted just long enough to show what promise we were denied. His postvindication appointment as the president of CalTech has, fortunately, reclaimed much of it.

The original, Orwellian title of the Office of Scientific Integrity was, ironically, first suggested by a lawyer for a defendant in an academic misconduct case. It was apparently made in jest, but adopted in earnest. It would be in keeping with the theme if HHS also had an Office of Reputational Restoration. Of course, it does not. And if there were such an office, its task would be far more formidable than the reassembly of Humpty-Dumpty; in cases like this, the losses tend to be irreversible. That is why justice deferred is justice denied.

A conflict of interest of a very different kind—and perhaps a more pernicious one—is involved in the case of Herbert Needleman. Needleman, then at Harvard Medical School, published a remarkable study in 1979 in the *New England Journal of Medicine* on the effects of lead on the intellectual development of children. I was paying close attention to lead at the time; as the commissioner of the FDA, I had been engaged (with other federal regulatory agencies) in an effort to rewrite the standard for lead in blood. Lead is one of the oldest and most severe toxicants known, but at that time its effects were thought not to be serious at very low concentrations. Evidence for lower-dose effects was accumulating, and the FDA and the Environmental Protection Agency (EPA) together were proposing to limit lead exposure due to lead use as a fuel additive and as a component of the solder in food-containing tin cans.

The 1979 Needleman paper was a bombshell. By using the lead in dentine from the deciduous teeth of children as an indicator of average exposure, he showed effects on intellectual development (including psychometric IQ) at levels far below the previously established "safe" levels. These data were reanalyzed by the EPA's Clean Air Act Scientific Advisory Committee after objections were raised to some of the methodology; that reanalysis and subsequent work has fully confirmed Needleman's findings, which have since been widely repeated in other laboratories and are no longer controversial.[26]

Not so the work itself. Objections to it on methodological grounds were first raised by Dr. Claire Ernhart, a psychologist who during the 1980s appeared as a witness for the Lead Industry Associates and other metal industries groups, and had received research funding from those sources. Along with Dr. Sandra Scarr, another psychologist, she represented the lead industry in a 1990 suit brought by the Department of Justice against three firms charged with causing lead pollution under the Superfund Act. In the course of pretrial discovery, the two psychologists examined Needleman's raw data. After the court had returned a verdict in favor of the Department of Justice and fined the firms more than sixty million dollars, Scarr and Ernhart—as a result of their examinations of the discovered research notebooks—submitted a document to the OSI accusing Needleman of scientific misconduct and of unscientific behavior. OSI instructed the University of Pittsburgh, by then Needleman's home campus, to conduct an investigation.

A Preliminary Inquiry Panel did so; it found no evidence of fraud or falsification but said, strangely, that it could not exclude the possibility that "misrepresentation" had occurred. The university then passed the case to a Hearing Board. There followed a series of efforts by Needleman to persuade his administration to include scientific experts on the board and to open the hearings to the public. The university administration at first refused these requests; much later, following a unanimous vote of the Faculty Senate and petitions from the external scientific community, it reversed its position. When the hearing was finally held, Ernhart and Scarr retreated under cross-examination by Needleman, saying only that they had reasons for "suspicion" but no specific charges of misconduct.

The concerns that the two psychologists raised had in fact all been dealt with as scientific issues in the EPA hearing eight years earlier, referred to above. Since the fundamental findings had been confirmed, the only possibility remaining was that Needleman had been guilty of needless bias— that is, selecting his subjects or failing to control for particular subject variables with the intent of making the results more convincing. These aspects were, as far as can be told, fully resolved in the public hearing. The Hearing Board concluded unanimously that it found no academic misconduct. ORI examined its final report and agreed. But a cloud still hovered over Needleman's work, and it was attributable in large part to the University of Pittsburgh's failure to handle the case expeditiously and fairly. This sad episode also demonstrated the power of economics: increasingly, industries threatened by impending government regulations have sought to obtain data from research that has been used to support those regulations, in order to challenge the conduct of the work.[27]

As is often the case with procedures of this sort, there are delicate issues of fairness. Powerful academic traditions provide protection for researchers charged with misconduct, and it is perhaps not surprising that these predominated in the earlier history of science fraud in universities. More recent fairness concerns, not only in the academic sector, but in others (especially government), have tended to focus on those who bring charges. "Whistleblower" protections are now offered as a matter of law to government employees and the employees of government contractors. Federal rules also prohibit universities from retributive actions against those who make charges of academic misconduct. The Commission on Research Integrity, formed by Congress in 1993, held several hearings on the subject in which it was told of university efforts to cover up misconduct or to punish whistleblowers. One of the witnesses before the commission was Margot O'Toole, the postdoctoral fellow who first charged that Thereza Imanishi-Kari's data were faulty. Her claim that Tufts University and MIT treated her badly may well be true. Suppose, however, that it could be proven conclusively not only that Imanishi-Kari didn't cheat, but that the work was sound in all respects. Would that change our view? And—regardless of the outcome—does the procedural history in this case suggest that the whistleblower or the defendant lost more in the way of due process? The commission praised the initiative and courage of whistleblowers, and went further to provide a detailed "Whistleblower's Bill of Rights." It provided little, however, by way of a balancing set of rights for accused scientists. We'd do well to remember that however courageous they may be, whistleblowers are often wrong.

The record of universities themselves is certainly replete with instances of inappropriate self-protection, especially in the early 1980s. As the Needleman case shows, however, universities can also lean too far in the other direction, by failing to protect the rights of their faculty members when they believe that their own interests are threatened. The University of Pittsburgh was in a difficult position in that case. ORI had thrown it an issue that was especially uncomfortable for an institution located in a city unusually dependent on the heavy-metals industry. The results of its preliminary inquiry, though exculpatory, were expressed in an unusually wishywashy fashion, and its reluctance to accord Needleman the benefits of an open hearing and the right to examine witnesses were striking failures of due process.

Indeed, economic interests are not the only ones that can lead to spurious prosecutions. In several academic grievances in which the author has been asked to become involved, professional rivalries or personal hostilities have been at the root of claims of academic misconduct. The leverage that ORI exerts over universities, and the cloud that can be placed over a scholar merely because a charge has been filed, make it a tempting venue for working out personal agendas.

From end to end, academic misconduct is a vexing problem, and it has visited serious damage on the credibility of science and of universities. The competitiveness of research, the importance of reputation, the size and scale of certain scientific fields, the difficulty of obtaining tenure—all probably contribute to the occasional incidence of misconduct. How common it is will be difficult to determine without a social cost to the scientific enterprise that most would regard as much too high. For example, some have proposed random "integrity audits" of one kind or another. But these would be so intrusive, not to say administratively expensive, that they would be likely to yield more damage than enlightenment.

The question of how to treat accusations of academic misconduct fairly and consistently has thus baffled both the government and the universities. But it is a subject now of immense media and public interest, and it must be dealt with. We are only beginning to learn how; and the growing complexity of the whole area is making the learning more difficult. Of course, if all scholars observed their duty to truth, the problem would disappear. But that is too much to hope for, and the university is therefore left with a fundamental academic duty, indeed, the core duty of a community of scholars: the certification of the work of its own members. That is a challenging task, but the public credibility of academic scholarship ultimately depends on its convincing pursuit.

9

TO REACH BEYOND
THE WALLS

TECHNOLOGY TRANSFER is the newest addendum to the roster of academic duties. In a time when basic knowledge is seen as an important driving force behind product development, and therefore behind growth, the public has come to expect that the university, as knowledge producer, will share what it discovers. Indeed, there is a deepening conviction on the part of society that basic knowledge should be put into human service wherever it can be, and as soon as possible.

Technology transfer is accomplished most effectively by the movement of people, and many university faculty members devote a significant fraction of their time to activities off the campus, with the approval, tacit or otherwise, of their institutions. Some of their efforts, for example, consulting for a proprietary company, are financially compensated. Others, such as reviewing books or advising the government, are uncompensated or earn honoraria so modest that they are hardly more than symbolic. Some of these outside activities are directly related to the faculty member's main intellectual pursuit at the university, whereas others are not. And an increasing number of these "offshore" commitments raise important and challenging policy questions—for the faculty member and for the institution alike.

The university quite properly has first claim on the primary scholarly and teaching activity of its faculty. Although that claim is hard to argue with, at the margin there are some troublesome ambiguities. One concerns the relationship between the institution's claim on a faculty member's time and effort and the rules it makes with respect to intellectual property. Another has to do with how limits on outside engagement can be fairly drawn—in particular, whether they should be based on time, on income, on the nature of the activity, or on all three. A final challenge is how the institution can deal with problems that arise when outside activities infringe not on the faculty member's time commitment to the university but on some other interest of the institution, such as its reputation for objective scholarly work. Off-campus engagement is a confusing and poorly mapped terrain of loyalty, commitment, and interest.

Conflicts of commitment arise whenever outside activities interfere with the devotion of a faculty member's full professional energies to the university. These are sometimes carelessly lumped with conflicts of interest, but they are quite different; the latter involve actions pursued to benefit the faculty member personally in ways (often but not always financial) that may be damaging to the institution, whereas the former usually arise because faculty members simply give too much time to outside enterprises, diminishing the quality of their research and teaching activity on behalf of the institution.

At the most fundamental level, of course, the university's expectations do not differ from those of any other employer. In a typical workplace in the profit sector, the boss is entitled to expect that employees will show up from nine to five (or whatever time span has been specified) on a regular basis. The university is a special employer, however, in at least two ways. Faculty work is by nature creative, opportunistic, and therefore somewhat irregular. Accordingly, a tradition of flexible time accounting has developed in academic settings; as was pointed out earlier, the academic "work week" is very poorly defined. In practice, it is therefore difficult to determine whether *any* particular outside commitment—from recreation and the fulfillment of family responsibilities to the various forms of externally directed economic activity—is actually interfering with the faculty member's primary commitment to the university.

Another difference is that the university has a special and legitimate interest in the nature of what is done outside. In most employment settings, workers are free to "moonlight" in whatever domain they choose. Holding down two jobs is right in line with the traditional American respect for ambition and upward mobility. This is often true even when the two jobs are similar. The sous-chef who works days for the Cafe d'Elegance and nights for Frandcois's Bistro is admired and thought to be hard-working.

But the university cares very much about the night job if the outside work relates to the faculty member's scholarly specialty. In this respect its policies reflect those obtaining in other technical areas, in which an employee would not be permitted to work for a competing entity. The university assumes that by employing faculty members on a full-time basis, it has, in effect, purchased exclusive rights to their activities in the particular area of their academic knowledge, with certain generally understood exceptions. This notion is closely tied, for obvious reasons, to the institution's policies regarding intellectual property, the essence of which can be summarized briefly.

A few universities give faculty members primary ownership of the intellectual property resulting from their work, even if it is done in university facilities on university time. The vast majority, however, lay a limited claim to it—limited in the sense that they frequently share royalties or other intellectual property revenues with faculty innovators. In other areas, however, the university makes no claim at all. Books, articles, works of art, and other creative products of scholarly effort are exempted by custom from the institutional control.

Consulting is another domain in which faculty members are partially released from the commitment to full-time university employment. Professors in most institutions are allowed and even encouraged to consult for private commercial organizations, that is, to provide them with professional advice and guidance, and to receive compensation at "market" rates. The rationale supporting this practice is straightforward: faculty members may benefit from contact with researchers in the for-profit sector, may gain access to data that are proprietary and thus might otherwise be unavailable, and may make valuable contributions to the transfer of new technology from the university to the public domain. In adopting this policy, universities have pursued an enlightened self-interest, fulfilling an obligation to society while making employment more attractive to faculty members.

At the same time, they have recognized that the practice of consulting for money can get out of hand. Accordingly, nearly all institutions limit outside consulting to about one day per week, and many retain the right to audit the nature, purpose, and extent of the consulting relationship in order to be certain that it stays within the time limit. Exempted from the one-day-a-week limit are several kinds of off-campus professional work that may superficially resemble "consulting": providing editorial advice to professional journals, counseling governments, reviewing grant proposals for foundations or federal funding agencies, and the like. These are excluded not because they aren't compensated (some are, albeit modestly) or because the efforts are in behalf of nonprofit organizations (some aren't). Rather, it is because they are held to be good for the discipline—and perhaps also because they would be impossible to regulate anyhow.

There is, understandably, much confusion about the rationale underlying the rules in this domain, which is full of arcane and special histories. Consider, for example, the university that employs a sculptor and a surgeon on its faculty. Each has learned extraordinary skills in a demanding course of graduate study; each does campus-based work that is hailed as pioneering; each teaches in credit-bearing courses for advanced students. Which one of them is allowed to practice for financial return outside the institution?

The answer, which surprises many people outside the academy, is the sculptor, who is given free rein to produce and sell his work, even though it may be produced inside the institution with the help of its facilities and with the support of a full-time academic salary. The surgeon (in nearly all institutions) must limit her activity to a "faculty practice program," a medical group practice composed of the clinical faculty and organized by the university, which collects all professional fees.[1] The surgeon cannot perform operations outside the practice except for limited charitable purposes. The difference between the treatment of the sculptor and the treatment of the surgeon reflects, on the one hand, some long-standing traditions about artistic freedom, and, on the other, a history of increasing dependence on clinical income to support instruction and research in American medical schools.

University policies that attempt to control conflicts of commitment have important limits. The time rules apply only to work done in the area of one's expertise. The university might pay little attention, for example, if a faculty member decided to open and run the aforementioned Cafe d'Elegance on weekends, or to teach skiing at a nearby resort, as long as the work plainly had no impact on his time commitment to the institution. It may appear that this work is exempt because it is done on Saturday and

Sunday, outside the normal work week and thus beyond the institution's reach. But if that were the reason, then it would be within the rules for the same faculty member to consult for a pharmaceutical company on the weekend. In fact it would not. For a professor, 100 percent time is not forty hours a week nor seven days a week, but whatever time he or she spends doing professorial work. The limitation on weekend consulting comes about if (and only if) it takes the faculty member's time commitment over the one-day-per-week limit. If our pharmaceutical consultant is doing outside work two days a week—even if the days are Saturday and Sunday—that is one day too many.

Consulting rules limit time but not compensation. In earlier times, there was seldom any need to raise that issue, because the income yielded from consulting work usually represented relatively modest increments to the typical faculty salary. But more recently, consultantships, especially those for the small, start-up companies that typify academic spin-offs, have often been compensated through equity participation. If the young company succeeds, faculty members can receive large, well-publicized windfalls, and these in turn have led to public concern that something indecent and possibly corrupt is afoot. It is difficult, however, to see how a workable limit could be placed on consulting payments. The university has a clear right to protect the faculty member's time commitment, but it is not so clear that it has a right to monopolize his or her compensation.[2]

More serious challenges may arise from the character of the consultation. In the past, most consulting arrangements were between faculty members and well-established business concerns or clients. A professor of finance in the business school might spend a day a week advising Goldman Sachs on asset allocation problems; a pharmacologist would work on an occasional basis with Upjohn on the development of new therapies for cardiac arrhythmias; a civil engineer would help out with the design of a dam for Bechtel. Now, because of the increasing role of faculty members in start-up companies that they may have helped form, and in which they may have substantial equity, there is strengthened incentive for a deeper involvement, one that may actually entail line management.

That proposition is quite different from conventional consulting, and it is difficult to believe that such engagement does not make a call upon time and energy that goes beyond the one-day-a-week limit. Writing on this subject in 1982, the late president of Yale, A. Bartlett Giamatti, stated the concerns of many university leaders: "I believe that if a faculty member becomes a manager of a company pursuing commercial application of his or her university-based research; or acquires, through gift or purchase, stock shares in this kind of company in such proportion to the total number of shares that he or she can have a significant effect on the decision-making of that company . . . there should be a review of the relationship, the possible consequence being that the faculty member might well have to decide to leave the faculty for a limited period of time, perhaps one year, by taking an unpaid leave of absence to pursue these outside interests."[3]

At about the same time, a group of university presidents and business leaders met at Pajaro Dunes, California, to establish some guidelines for these new relationships. Most of the guidelines dealt with conflict-of-interest situations, but the commitment issue was taken on as well in the statement agreed to by the participants: "Professors' relationships with commercial firms should not be allowed to interfere with their overriding obligation to the university to fulfill their primary responsibilities of teaching and research. In recent years, the problems of achieving this goal have assumed greater urgency by virtue of the growing tendency, especially in the biotechnology field, for professors to own significant blocks of stock in commercial enterprises, to assist in the formation of such enterprises, or even to assume substantial executive responsibilities. These developments underscore the need for universities to consider the rules and procedures needed to ensure that faculty members fulfill their responsibilities to teaching and research." Many universities have since established firm rules prohibiting faculty members from holding management positions in outside entities.

Some of the concerns about the deflection of faculty time and attention away from the campus have nothing to do with excessive corporate involvement. Many of the most respected *pro bono* activities that professors undertake outside the institution—indeed, commitments that traditionally are part of the workload of a successful and professionally engaged faculty member—have grown significantly in their time demands. Fellowship boards, grant review, journal editorships, advice to foundations and government, lecturing elsewhere, and a host of related activities now engage more of the average faculty member's attention than ever before.

Visiting lectureships, for example, have multiplied dramatically. The trend is especially noticeable in the nation's medical schools, where basic science courses increasingly make use of guest lectures; in some places, the typical course in the basic sciences will feature as many visitors as professors from the home campus. Under such conditions, students are unlikely to receive a well-integrated education. The practice results, moreover, in a steadily increasing disengagement between members of the medical school professoriate and their own institutions.

The allocation of faculty time to the primary tasks of teaching and research is increasingly regulated only by the conscience of the individual faculty member. In his farewell report to the Faculty of Arts and Sciences at Harvard, quoted earlier, Henry Rosovsky laid some of the blame for the decline in that faculty's "civic consciousness" on the allure of outside activities.[4] In many universities there are rules about permitted absences from campus, but these are often unaccompanied by any mechanisms for monitoring and compliance. Some years ago a faculty member was able to draw simultaneous full-time salaries from Yale and the State University of New York, and fulfill whatever requirements were imposed on him by each. This lasted for more than a year before a problem was detected. Annual leaves without salary are permissible in most universities; Harvard places a limit of one year on such leaves, but will extend it to two whenever public service is involved. The university received considerable publicity for enforcing that limit on Henry Kissinger during his term as secretary of state. One suspects that the attention given to this action was due less to Kissinger's celebrity status than to public amazement that a university would actually carry out the sanction implicit in such a rule!

Even those faculty members who stay at their institutions most of the time, and it is surely the majority, find their schedules relentlessly fragmented by activities that are related to, but not a central part of, their responsibilities to the institution. Reviewing and refereeing chores, responsibility to scholarly societies, and extra lectures that benefit the community all make increased demands on busy lives.

Not surprisingly, there is some movement toward formalization of rules regarding outside engagement. Most of the attention has been given to the problems of conflict of interest, to be discussed below. But concern has also been directed at the division of primary allegiance that can result from extensive outside commitments. Thus the policy at Stanford states, "Faculty members owe their primary professional allegiance to the University, and their primary commitment of time and intellectual energy should be to the education, research, and scholarship programs of the institution." But the reinforcing provision is carefully vague. It states, "A full-time appointment conveys an obligation for a faculty member to have a significant presence on campus ... to be accessible to students and staff, and to be available to interact with Stanford colleagues throughout every quarter during which he or she is on active duty." With respect to outside commitments, it adds, "Outside professional activities are a privilege and not a right, and must not detract from a faculty member's full-time obligation to his or her university duties."[5] In particular, a faculty member on full-time active duty must not have significant outside managerial responsibilities and may not act as a principal investigator on sponsored projects submitted and managed through another institution.

These additional provisions do rule out some of the more demanding forms of external commitment. But otherwise they are largely hortatory, amounting to a faint cry against a background of deafening silence regarding the exact nature of faculty obligations to the university. Indeed, the signals sent to the faculty—particularly by the major research universities—have strengthened the notion that as long as adequate amounts of prestige can be generated on behalf of the employing institution, presence isn't very important. The problem is not just one of vagueness of rules. The fact is that most universities know very little about how their faculty members spend their time. Information about actual teaching loads, how much of the teaching is shared, how many advisees there are, and so on is said to be available, but it is hard to dig out, and it often depends on very distant (and often friendly) estimates. Against such a sparse background of data, accountability is very difficult to achieve.

Very few institutions have, and still fewer enforce, rules regarding the duration of term-time campus absences. On the contrary, many encourage them by appointing scholars to highly visible chairs that require the incumbents to be present only part of the time. In a case that came to enjoy a prominent place in academic lore, Duke University in 1989 appointed Professor Henry Gates to a chair that appeared to leave him free to be away from campus one semester out of every two. Because Gates is a remarkable scholar—one of the most prominent "public intellectuals" of his day—the arrangement attracted a lot of attention. In fact, Duke had agreed only to give him, during his first year, the semester of sabbatical leave that he had already earned at his previous institution. The message, however, which unfairly damaged both Gates and Duke, was that if you're famous enough you don't need to stay at home and endure the drudgery of teaching students. Gates soon left Duke for Harvard, but that kind of message is difficult to erase.

The administration's treatment of teaching loads, discussed earlier, delivers a similar message. Indeed, the duties of formal classroom instruction are loosely codified. The university also lacks clearly expressed expectations with regard to office hours, advising obligations, and the times at which faculty members should be available on campus. Of course, it can be argued that this arrangement is well-suited to an activity in which personal creativity, flexibility, and intellectual opportunism are highly valued attributes. Whatever the justification, the result is a thinly upholstered regulatory framework that leaves largely in the hands of the faculty the determination of its own allocation of time and effort. Though conflict of commitment is a simple enough concept, it is thus surprisingly difficult to identify.

Conflict of interest, which refers to any clash between the self-interest of an individual (whether it arises from monetary gain, career advancement, or commitment to some personal agenda or ideology) and the interest of the institution that individual serves, is quite different. Nothing is inherently wrong with conflicts of interest; they are frequently unavoidable in contemporary life. Universities are no less plagued by them than most other institutions, and most conflicts, when acknowledged, do not present difficulties for the institution or its faculty members. The real problems arise when such conflicts are resolved in the individual's favor, and against the interest of the institution.

In recent years, the subject of conflict of interest in the academy has surfaced in a very public way; the focus has been on university scientists who are involved with private, profit-making enterprises during the period of their full-time faculty employment. The emergence of a few biotechnology millionaires has captured much of the public attention. So have a small number of spectacular scandals: drug trials conducted by researchers with a financial interest in the outcome, or the use of university facilities for research on and promotion of commercial products by faculty entrepreneurs. Such occurrences have, fortunately, been rare. Nonetheless, the public has become concerned because in a number of fields—computer science and electrical engineering, in addition to the biomedical sciences—

the degree of industry involvement on the part of faculty at the major research universities has become both more intense and more visible.

These relationships pose significant challenges for the university, which must often consider its own investment or licensing policies in light of outside involvements by its faculty. They generate similar challenges for faculty members, since their work on outside ventures may adversely affect some broader interest of the institution, or of faculty colleagues or students.

As the primary employer, the university is entitled to assume that all the *professional* activity of the faculty member is directed toward its benefit, or at least not against it. Professional activity means all work done in the domain of the faculty member's academic and scholarly interest. The definition is the same as that used earlier in connection with consulting. Suppose that it is a professor of statistics, Professor Badger, who happens to be an accomplished gourmet chef and opens the Cafe d'Elegance as a weekend business. Badger's venture would not present a conflict of interest, even if it occasionally competed with an equivalent service run by the institution, because cuisine has nothing to do with statistics. His weekend work is unrelated to his academic profession; thus his moonlighting activity does not present a conflict-of-interest problem, just as it would not count as "consulting" under the university's rules.

It is important to note that in regulating in this area, universities—like the government and many other institutions—are concerned not only with actual conflicts of interest but with the perception that they may exist. Thus the definition in Stanford's policy reads as follows: "A conflict of interest occurs when there is a divergence between an individual's private interests and his or her professional obligations to the university such that an independent observer might reasonably question whether the individual's professional actions or decisions are determined by considerations of personal gain, financial or otherwise."[6]

The best-known conflict-of-interest problems involve personal financial gain, in situations for which the term of art is "self-dealing." If, for example, a faculty member were to employ university resources to support a private business venture, he would clearly be violating the terms of his employment. But in some instances the conflict-of-interest problem arises within the university itself. Suppose now that Professor Badger, finding himself in great demand for a new set of ideas that he has developed about actuarial tables, opens a small consulting service for the insurance industry. His business cards for this purpose list both his academic affiliation and Actuarial Consulting Services, the name he has selected for his corporate entity. A telephone number is given for the latter; it is a private line in his university office for which he pays, and it is answered by a secretary whom he employs.

Badger, when queried about the possibility that there may be a conflict here, replies as follows: "I am entirely within the rules. In the first place, there isn't any conflict of commitment; I carefully limit my work for Actuarial Consulting to one day a week, the limit under the university's own consulting policy. Nor is there a conflict of interest. I pay for the phone and the secretarial support, and use no other university services."

His defense ignores several realities. The activity is taking place in university space, consuming resources intended for teaching and research. That our statistician is conscientious about meeting the direct costs of his private operation does not relieve him of responsibility for some of the less obvious external costs of his venture. For example, his employee adds to the load on general university services (including parking—a chronic invitation to community dissatisfaction if ever there was one!). Yet no staff benefits are being paid to the institution to defray these external costs.

More important than these financial matters, however, is the likely prospect that two entities, the consulting firm and the university, will become confused and quite possibly merged in the minds of those who consider using Actuarial Consulting Services. It is almost certain that the university address, and the linking of the statistician's identity as a consultant with his identity as a distinguished academic, serve to lend prestige to his commercial venture. In that sense the university's reputation is being used for private financial advantage. There is a potential for institutional damage here, because the expectation is that the university exists *pro bono publico* and not for the purpose of creating personal profit for its members.

The conflict of interest in this case is actually one form of self-dealing. The corporate officer who directs business to his company from a contractor in which he has a personal financial interest is doing a similar if somewhat more obvious thing. So, though less directly, is the university treasurer who makes use of the institution's financial analysis to make "side-by-side" investments of his own. The case of the statistician is parallel in this respect: an institutional asset (in Badger's case, reflected prestige) is being used to create personal financial gain, in ways that might reflect adversely on the institution.

The faculty member who is involved with a company located away from the university has a different set of potential conflicts. With the rise of small, academically connected industries such as software and biotechnology, these conflicts have become much more visible, and they have raised policy challenges for the university and its faculty members alike.

Some of the new problems will be illustrated by the hypothetical case of Professor Eunice M, a distinguished molecular biologist at C. University who has made pioneering discoveries in immunology. A tenured full professor, she was persuaded by a group of venture capitalists to participate in the founding of a company called Clotech. Clotech is pursuing the commercialization of several of M's discoveries, which may make possible the development of monoclonal antibodies against several autoimmune diseases.

The circumstances of this case are not unusual. In many universities like C., with large medical schools and successful research programs in the biomedical sciences, several dozen faculty members may simultaneously be involved in outside start-up ventures. Generally they hold substantial "founder stock" in these companies; and the companies themselves work on the development of ideas that originated in the faculty members' own university laboratories. In developing the story of Professor M, I will add features that would not be common to all such cases but that occur frequently enough to challenge university rules and policies—to say nothing of the faculty member's sense of what is acceptable behavior and what is not.

Professor M's fundamental discovery, if it were to be commercialized, would have to be protected by a process patent. When it became obvious that her idea had commercial (indeed, life-saving) potential, she sought advice through lengthy discussions with the dean of the medical school and the provost at C.U. She learned that the university would patent her discovery through its Office of Technology Licensing, and that if companies obtained licenses in order to commercialize it, some of the resulting royalty income would flow to her department and her own research program. Professor M was surprised to learn that the NIH support of her work did not affect the university's ownership. The provost explained that since the Bayh-Dole legislation in 1980, the government had followed the university's own rules regarding the disposition of intellectual property.

Expressing her surprise, M asked the provost, "How can it be that research done with public funds can be turned to private gain?" "I understand the point," replied the provost, "and in fact a number of public interest groups have objected to that policy. But the justification for public investment in research has always been that the work will produce ideas or technologies that will benefit people. Unless these are commercialized, nothing useful will emerge; so it is intended that risk capital, with the expectation of reasonable returns on investment, will take care of the 'development' phase of the innovation cycle." For that reason, the provost went on to explain, the university had established its own office for patenting faculty innovations and marketing the licenses.

Professor M was delighted when the patent was eventually secured. At about the same time, she met with members of an interested venture capital firm called Chardonnay Partners. They persuaded her that a strong commercial venture could be built around her work, and they offered to work with her to obtain financing and set up the company. The initial round of financing—about ten million dollars—was quickly secured, and the young company rented low-cost generic laboratory space a few miles from the C.U. campus. A chief executive officer was hired, and two Ph.D. molecular biologists came on board to begin experiments on producing the monoclonal antibodies at larger scale and testing them in animal models.

In the most successful ventures of this kind, and the subject of this case study is one of them, new developments are likely to raise new questions, both about institutional policy and about the proper role of the faculty member. Some of these will be explored as we follow the subsequent history of Clotech.

Phase I. When the first "offshore" experiments at an expanded scale began to look promising, Clotech asked C.U. for an exclusive license on the patent. As a member of the board and the owner of a large amount of founder stock, Professor M felt it inappropriate to approach the university directly. Instead, she and her Chardonnay Partners colleagues prevailed on a long-time friend and former trustee of the university, attorney L, to begin these discussions. L, who had helped set up the financing and was a member of the Clotech board, made an appointment with the provost. He argued that nonexclusive licensing was unlikely to attract any interest; only

Clotech, after all, had the know-how to develop the technology further. After some consultation the provost approved the granting of the license, and the first year's work in the corporate laboratory was looking very promising.

Phase II. A second round of private financing was soon required, and attorney L made another call, this time to encourage the treasurer's office at C.U. to participate through a direct investment of the university's endowment fund. There was promise, he argued, of a substantial return; in his view, the university had not just the right but the responsibility to retrieve some of the value associated with its own innovations. The treasurer promised to take the proposal before the next meeting of the Investments Committee of the C.U. Board of Trustees.

Phase III. Clotech was in need of new ideas about how to exploit this expanding opportunity. One of Professor M's new colleagues, Assistant Professor F, had just arrived at the university. He had valuable experience working on a related immunological problem, and M was eager to engage him as a consultant. But so was a more established firm, and she knew her bid would have to be persuasive. She invited F to have lunch with her at the Faculty Club. When he arrived at the appointed hour, he was surprised to find not only M but attorney L, along with a senior member in M's department who had already signed on as a consultant for Clotech. The three gave F a warm welcome, and during lunch they made a strong case that his participation would be of great benefit not only to Clotech but to C.U. as well.

Phase IV. A, a graduate student in Professor M's laboratory, had nearly completed his dissertation research when M realized that his work could be of great benefit to the second-generation experiments now under way at Clotech. She offered him summer employment at the firm, at a salary substantially higher than the research assistantship he held on her NIH grant. A, worried about finishing his thesis and getting on with a postdoctoral appointment, demurred at first. M pointed out that he could have access to better facilities for pursuing some of his own experiments, and offered to let him work part-time on them during the course of his Clotech employment.

Phase V. Growth is not always easy to accommodate, and it turned out that the chief executive officer who had led Clotech from the beginning was much better at designing innovative research programs and hiring excellent scientists than at managing a firm with nearly fifty employees. The board reluctantly reached a separation agreement with him, and brought in a new president from another firm. The transition promised to be difficult, however, and the board asked Professor M to take a line management position for six months to help the new chief executive learn the ropes. She was convinced that the job could be done on a one-day-a-week basis, thus staying within the C.U. consulting limitation, so she accepted. Soon afterward she reported her appointment to the provost, as the university's rules required.

Phase VI. Professor M's NIH grant became inadequate to cover her program at C.U. The research was exciting and offered expanding opportunity, and her proposal for a renewal year received an excellent priority score from the study section's reviewers. Unfortunately, NIH had required her study section to reduce the budgets of all "noncompetitive renewal grants" by a fixed percentage, in order to help meet the NIH target of 6,000 new grants annually. At the same time, the needs of M's program were growing. To help keep things running, Clotech offered the university a gift of $150,000 annually for support of Professor M's laboratory. In return, Clotech asked for rights of first licensing refusal on any patentable work that emerged from their support. The gift was not restricted in any way other than its designation for use in her program.

Phase VII. The new company made rapid progress in developing its first product, and a Phase II clinical trial of unusual scope was completed. The results met the outcome criteria that had been established in discussions with the FDA, and the biotechnology trade press reported the news prominently. This was so encouraging, and the research in the Clotech pipeline so promising, that Gigantic Pharmaceuticals offered to buy a 51 percent share in the company at a very favorable stock transfer price. Because Gigantic promised to leave the company's management intact and independent (save the two seats on the board reserved for their own senior management), the directors of Clotech quickly agreed to the deal. Professor M's paper profit, had she sold her Gigantic stock immediately, would have amounted to about forty million dollars. A profile in the *New York Times Magazine* described her as "the richest of the young molecule mavens."

✳ In each of these phases, challenges arise both for Professor M and for the university. Before attempting to analyze them in turn, I should emphasize that although this scenario is hypothetical, it does come from the real world—that is, each of the phases replicates a situation that has arisen at one major research university or another during the past decade.

The issue for the university in Phase I is whether exclusive licensing constitutes a form of favoritism to Professor M and her company that might set a troublesome precedent. In the end, the decision will hinge on what policy will transfer the technology most effectively. In the early 1980s, under circumstances like these, universities approached exclusive licensing with great caution, perhaps because it seemed perilously close to a form of self-dealing. But many argued that the university's first obligation is to get useful innovations into human service as quickly as possible. There has thus been a general shift of institutional policy toward the view that if exclusive licensing is plainly the best way to transfer the technology (and that is at least a plausible conclusion in this case), then the university is justified in doing it, as long as adequate provision exists for the university to march in and repossess the rights if the project stalls.

The problem of direct investment by a university in a venture in which one of its own faculty members is a principal—the situation encountered in Phase II—raises serious questions. This issue received national attention in 1981, when the *New York Times* reported that Harvard was considering substantial investments in a company of which Professor Mark Ptashne was the scientific founder. The report was actually premature; Harvard's president at the time, Derek Bok, looked at the proposal and eventually decided against it.

On what grounds? The group of university presidents, trustees, and leaders from the high-technology business community that examined emerging problems in university-industry relationships at Pajaro Dunes, California, in 1982 published a set of guiding principles that, though deliberately left rather unspecific, have covered the development of actual practice quite closely. The Pajaro principles discouraged co-investment, largely on the grounds that it places the university in the position of potentially benefiting from certain faculty research but not from other work. If the university were to invest, it was argued, how could it be seen as an even-handed allocator of resources to different scholars and their work?

The Harvard case added another concern. Professor Walter Gilbert, a colleague of Professor Ptashne's who had started a company of his own at an earlier time, complained about the proposal. Was it fair, he asked, for Harvard to invest in a prospective rival company and not his own? It's difficult to respond to this argument with more than a wry shrug, but it nevertheless illuminates the problem of perceived favoritism that the university faces.

On the other hand, it is not easy simply to say that the university should never invest in such companies. That would amount to a university prohibition against *any* gift of founder stock in a company in which there is faculty involvement. In fact, there is always the possibility of co-investment when faculty members and the university's treasurer are each independently trying to pick stocks. Surely accidental cases shouldn't be penalized; they would be impossible to avoid anyhow. To avoid serious conflict-of-interest problems, many universities have adopted policies that contain *de minimus* exceptions: co-investment is permitted as long as neither the faculty member nor the institution owns more than a certain percentage of the stock, say, 5 percent.

The propriety of co-investment also has to be evaluated in terms of what else is going on. If a company with a faculty founder also has an exclusive license from the university—and even more, if it supports research done there by that faculty member—there is a more compelling case for conflict of interest.

Finally, a word needs to be said about the behavior of Mr. L, the helpful and ubiquitous attorney in the case. He clearly has the institution's best interests at heart, but he also stands to profit personally from the company. His position as a former trustee gives him special access and unusual power; if he were a current board member his actions would clearly be labeled self-dealing. As it is, most would view his involvement as at least unwise, and perhaps ethically questionable.

In Phase III, it is difficult not to conclude that M has gotten off base in the Faculty Club luncheon scene. As a senior faculty member, she—along with the tenured colleague who is already consulting for Clotech—has substantial power over Assistant Professor F's future in the department, including his eventual promotion to tenure. The appearance of a former trustee at the luncheon adds to the pressure, which is present no matter how delicately the recruitment is handled. There is, in short, an unacceptably high level of coercion in this situation.

The same issue arises in Phase IV. Is A really able to make a free decision, or is there an implied personal penalty for declining his professor's invitation? The answer is that the mentor of a Ph.D. student has enormous power over that student's career, and graduate students all know this. To fail to respond to one's mentor's wishes is quite likely to compromise one's future, unless one has an unusually permissive or understanding mentor. The very putting of the invitation, some would argue, suggests that that is not the case here. In fact, the proposal is a form of self-dealing—one that has grown to troublesome proportions in some applied departments of research universities. The Committee on Research at Stanford considered this problem in 1988 and decided to make an explicit rule against the employment of graduate students or postdoctoral fellows by faculty members in their own companies. The rule applies not only to the students in a given professor's own laboratory, but to all the students in the department.

A difficult problem surfaces in Phase V. On the face of it, perhaps C.U. shouldn't be concerned that Professor M is consulting as a decision-maker rather than as an adviser. The consulting policy is designed to protect against conflicts of commitment—and the time spent, it can be argued, ought to be the only thing that matters.

But management and advice clearly are different. The former is much more engaging, and might well take a much larger share of the faculty member's "thinking time."[7] Especially if the university is involved in other ways with Clotech (as co-investor, or licenser), the opportunity for genuine or perceived conflict of interest may be magnified. In recognition of these difficulties, many universities have barred faculty members from taking line management positions in outside companies.

Professor M could, of course, be given a six-months' leave without pay, provided that the dean and the department had enough notice to fill her teaching role. In most institutions, that decision would be made on a case-by-case basis, but usually such leave requests are granted.

One more complexity is added in Phase VI by the prospect of a gift from Clotech to support M's laboratory. Given the entanglements already suggested in earlier phases of this scenario, such a gift might multiply the risk of public misinterpretation. Could the grant be interpreted as a quiet, deferred way of meeting a condition for the licensing arrangement? Were other commitments made in advance, in return for the award? And is the firm's insistence on rights to any intellectual property emerging from the research an appropriate limitation for the university to accept? One at a time, these questions might not be so difficult to answer, but taken together, the features of this grant would invite mistrust both within the institution and outside it. Once the relationships become sufficiently elaborate, it is very difficult for any observer to have confidence that things are on the up and up.

In short, at the margin—and if there were no other history—this might be a reasonable proposal. But meeting its conditions might produce difficulty with faculty colleagues less favored than the beneficiary. And even if the repercussions on campus turned out not to be serious, revelation of the arrangement could carry a heavy penalty in lost public confidence.

When very large financial gains are realized by faculty members who form companies, as in Phase VII, the entire character of the issue changes. Something about the outcome seems wrong to people; much as Americans admire entrepreneurship and financial success, they react negatively to the professor who secures a windfall—even if it came about through a brilliant discovery that will save many human lives. And there is also a serious risk of dissonance within the institution. Professors are not a wealthy lot, and it is probably unreasonable to expect that collegial regard will triumph over a certain amount of fiscal envy. The university is, after all, a community of scholars, many of them in fields where there is no possibility of financial reward. Dramatic departures from equity are thus likely to create trouble.

At Stanford, a well-publicized case of this kind developed in 1992–93. Professor Irving Weissman and a postdoctoral collaborator, Michael McCune, made an extraordinary series of discoveries about the formation of the blood elements and the immune system in mammals. In an earlier study, Weissman and another collaborator were able to isolate a small population of cells in mice that were capable of differentiating into all of the formed elements of the blood. These were called hematopoietic stem cells. McCune and Weissman then found that they could transplant the embryonic tissues from humans that nurture stem cells so as to reconstitute, in an immunologically suppressed strain of mice, an entire immune system of genetically different origin.

Their discovery, of course, raised the possibility that the human immune system could be created in a mouse. Soon McCune and Weissman had achieved partial success; complete success would require the isolation of human hematopoietic stem cells using methods analogous to those previously used in the mouse. Various tests would then have to be performed to see whether the resulting mouse—called SCID-hu—would be a suitable animal model for the human immune system.

A number of factors suggested that these experiments would be more suited to a commercial than to an academic setting. The work was not novel; the basic methodology for isolating hematopoietic stem cells had already been worked out. The scale required was much larger than could readily be accommodated in Weissman's crowded campus laboratory. Finally, there was real commercial potential in some of the possible applications. Accordingly, Weissman did two things. He turned his idea over to Stanford, and the Office of Technology Licensing applied for a patent on the isolation of the hematopoietic stem cells in mammals. He also decided to help organize a company to pursue commercialization of the technology.

In order to avoid some of the pitfalls that others had encountered along the same route, Professor Weissman consulted Stanford about the formation of his company; these consultations included a long conversation with me, since I was Stanford's president at the time. He was very careful in defining which work he thought it was appropriate to keep in his academic laboratory, and which to put into the young company, to be called SyStemix. I agreed with his plan, and the company was formed—with no financial participation from Stanford. Care was also taken to eliminate possible conflicts of interest: Weissman took no management position, and no scientific work moved back and forth across the barrier we constructed in the original agreements.

SyStemix research went well, and the young company prospered and expanded. A patent on the human hematopoietic stem cell was duly applied for by the company and granted. So bright did SyStemix's prospects seem that soon afterward, in 1992, the large pharmaceutical firm Sandoz purchased a major interest. The stock swap was negotiated on very favorable terms to the SyStemix shareholders, and as a result the founders, including Weissman, made a great deal of money. This was quickly noted by the *Wall Street Journal*, a newspaper that likes money a lot but academia a good deal less.

As one might expect, the reaction was prompt and not particularly positive. Most scientific colleagues who knew Weissman were happy for him;

the reaction of some others appeared to contain equal parts resentment and envy. At the time SyStemix was formed (but not during the time when most of the fundamental research that made it possible was going on) Weissman had held an appointment as an investigator of the Howard Hughes Medical Institute (HHMI). This large operating foundation has units at many leading centers of biomedical research. It leases its own space and supports the research of its investigators, including their salaries; but HHMI investigators are also regular faculty members of their academic institutions.

When the *Wall Street Journal* article appeared, the HHMI leadership expressed deep concern over Weissman's financial gain. In an extended series of negotiations with Weissman and Stanford, HHMI took the position that the level of equity held by Weissman was inappropriate, and demanded that he undertake divestiture—this despite the nonexistence of any equity limitations in the agreements made by HHMI with Stanford or with Weissman. We had a long meeting with the senior officers of HHMI at Stanford, in the course of which it became clear that HHMI considered Weissman an embarrassment because of the publicity that followed his commercial success. Eventually we concluded that the relationship was so badly infected that we had to amputate it. So we did, and Weissman went back to being a regular member of the Stanford faculty without HHMI support.

As this case illustrates, even the best-intentioned policies sometimes generate a result that people have difficulty accepting. The vision of a professor's getting rich—really rich—just gets under people's skin. Teaching and scholarship are supposed to be activities that bring their own psychic rewards and don't require financial ones. I don't happen to think that this is a particularly fair attitude, but all my experience tells me that it represents political reality and that universities and their faculties need to recognize it and live with it.

Weissman's story brings to the surface a number of the problems faced by the research university as it develops rules for faculty conduct and its own licensing and investment policies. But of course faculty members should make, and often do make, their own decisions about their activities—independent of limitations set by their universities. The decisions they make span a broad range of possibilities.

At one extreme is the position taken by Carl Djerassi, a professor of chemistry at Stanford. Djerassi had a long personal history of research discoveries that turned into commercial successes—notably, those that made possible modern pharmaceutical birth control and helped build Syntex Corporation. His interest later turned to insect endocrinology and the design of "biologically rational" chemical pest control. To pursue these drug-development interests, Djerassi formed and led a new company called Zoecon. He then reduced his Stanford professorship to half time so that he could devote the other half to Zoecon. He maintained a rigorous separation between the work done at Stanford and the work done at Zoecon; indeed, he did nothing whatever on insect biochemistry or endocrinology at the university.

A very different approach was attempted, and maintained for some time, by Professor Walter Gilbert at Harvard. He helped to found a company called Biogen, which proposed to employ the then-new techniques of recombinant DNA to the microbial production of prospective anticancer agents like interferon. He maintained active laboratories in both places. In a press conference that prominently featured both of Gilbert's affiliations, he announced a new Biogen success in the synthesis of what was claimed to be biologically active interferon. Newspaper accounts based on the press conference trumpeted Biogen's success in a race with another pharmaceutical firm, Roche, and the stock market rewarded the announcement with a substantial increase in the price of Biogen stock. Gilbert's failure to provide an adequate separation in this case may have put Harvard in the awkward position of helping to hype a stock—a situation that was later resolved when Gilbert resigned his Harvard position to join Biogen full time.

An especially damaging aspect of conflict of interest is the real or perceived loss of objectivity that may affect scholars when they have a direct financial interest in the outcome of their work. Before turning to that subject—one that has attracted much attention from the media and from government—it is important to note that not all temptations to depart from objectivity are financial in nature. Like everyone else, scholars have political and intellectual commitments that run deep. None run deeper than the commitment to one's own pet theory or favorite finding, and that attachment can make it very difficult to evaluate the work of others fairly. It may even prove an irresistible temptation to misinterpret or even to alter one's own findings.

But the financial motive is the one that touches most directly on our sense of propriety, and it has received most of the public attention. I remember very well when I first encountered a practical problem of this kind. I had just arrived in Washington in 1977 to serve as the commissioner of the FDA; shortly before I got there, the agency had been plunged into a major controversy over the artificial sweetener saccharin. A well-conducted animal study had demonstrated a weak but clear and dose-dependent association between saccharin and bladder cancer. As a result, the FDA had announced that, under the law, it would have to remove the compound from the marketplace. There was an enormous outcry, partly stimulated by the soft-drink industry, which had about 17 percent of its sales and a substantially larger portion of its profit tied up in diet soda. Coca-Cola and Pepsi, with other producers, formed one of those industry organizations with a consumer-friendly, innocuous name—the Calorie Control Council—to protect the continued availability of saccharin.

As required by law, the FDA published a notice in the Federal Register stating its intentions and asking for public comments. They arrived in huge numbers; the Calorie Control Council had placed full-page ads in major metropolitan newspapers asking readers to clip comments and send them to the FDA. In the meantime, an epidemiological study had been published that suggested a direct association between saccharin consumption and bladder cancer. This was plainly an important finding, and a researcher at a leading university quickly conducted a reanalysis of the epidemiological data. It was submitted as a formal comment as part of the FDA's rule making, but was quickly picked out of the blizzard of coupons as something significant. The author had identified himself only by institutional affiliation, but it turned out that his research had been funded by the Calorie Control Council. We asked him if the source of funds didn't raise questions about the objectivity of his study—questions that at least warranted disclosure of the source of his support. His response was that he didn't think so. (He was, as it turned out, probably right on the science. Saccharin is carcinogenic in rats all right, but almost certainly not in people.)

Much has changed since 1977, and I think that heightened public sensitivity to this issue would make disclosure an absolutely minimal requirement. Indeed, new government regulations severely restrict participation by scientists in various roles if their objectivity is open to doubt on account of financial interests. For example, researchers may not participate in clinical trials of a new drug if they have any financial interest in the company manufacturing that drug.

Few would argue that these limitations are inappropriate. But government efforts to manage conflict of interest have not stopped there, and some have wondered whether the zeal to solve this problem has not led the regulators overboard. To university researchers who hold grants from the NIH or the NSF, it seemed for some time that they were far overboard. Regulations first proposed in 1989 by the U.S. Public Health Service (the parent of the NIH) would have barred university investigators receiving NIH support from any stock ownership in companies that might ultimately benefit from their research. That proposal generated heavy complaints from the university community, and was eventually withdrawn. The replacement, finally adopted in 1995, requires scientists to disclose payments of all kinds, including equity interest, from or in any company that is related to their research, if the total of such payments or holdings amounts to ten thousand dollars or 5 percent of the value of the enterprise. The determination whether a conflict of interest exists is left to the university, which can decide to deal with it by disclosure requirements, by independent monitoring, or by requiring divestiture or disqualification from participation.

There are, of course, bound to be cases in which some financial interest exercises an undue influence over a researcher. It seems likely that such cases will continue to be rare, because most scholars have values that make them avoid such conflicts like the plague. Well-publicized abuses have, as is often the case, prompted Congress to spur the research agencies to undertake fairly heavy-handed intervention. The social cost of such intervention—in paperwork, in the decisions of scientists that they simply don't want to be involved in anything that's so much trouble—is apt to be greater than the benefits we gain in discouraging the occasional misdeed.

In any event, the more subtle kind of conflict, the kind that depends on loyalty to one's own ideas and positions, will remain; and it lies well beyond the reach of external regulation, whether by the government or by the university. It can be dealt with only by the scholars themselves, whose responsibility it is to challenge the propriety of their own conduct. The cost of failure is high. If this form of academic duty cannot be managed cleanly, then society will lose many of the benefits of university research.

10

TO CHANGE

Universities are in a dynamic equilibrium with society. On the one hand, they appear to lag behind it, acting as conservators of its history and archivists of its highest cultural attainments. On the other hand, they are seen as leaders, adventuring into new knowledge domains, developing transforming technologies, and serving as the seedbed for novel and often disturbing ideas.

Both these roles are part of the university's academic duty. Institutions of higher education reflect society to itself, and at the same time challenge that self-image by asking difficult questions: What have we become? Why don't we do things differently? Not surprisingly, the university thus sometimes finds itself seemingly at odds with society, especially during periods of rapid social change. The pace of technological change, the transient character of employment, calls for the political reformulation of everything from welfare to health and safety regulation, and the increasingly critical character of public discourse all create a climate in which traditional institutions, perhaps especially universities, feel besieged. The one thing that the university's critics agree on is that academic institutions have to change along with the rest of society—or fail to fulfill their duty. Change will not be easy. But neither is the requirement for it unique in recent history.

The shape of higher education in America has been repeatedly refigured in episodes of dramatic, even wrenching change. The contemporary form of the modern research university was set at the end of the nineteenth century, as the notion of the German graduate school took hold. This revolution helped set the course for the developing land-grant institutions that had been established through the Morrill Act, and it changed forever the future even of those liberal arts colleges that did not become universities, because it put in place the system that would soon supply the nation's professoriate.

After World War II came another revolution, the "endless frontier," which transformed the leading universities into engines for achieving world preeminence in the sciences. If the first revolution was scholarly, this one was surely utilitarian. Its accomplishment was the enlistment of universities as instruments of national economic purpose.

To many who see the contemporary university at the edge of a dynamic but troubled society, it seems probable that the end of the twentieth century will usher in a wave of change as dramatic and far-reaching as the two that preceded it. Others, familiar with the innate conservatism of academic institutions and the enormous size to which the enterprise has grown, doubt that any revolutionary (that is, nonincremental) change is possible. I am among the former, but I recognize that predictions of this kind are full of risk. How can we judge the prospects for change? To begin with, what driving forces are at work?

One force is surely public disaffection with higher education, evident not only in the media attention given to all forms of academic scandal, from research misconduct to athletic recruiting violations, but also in the more thoughtful and private criticism of employers, government leaders, and parents. The public attention given to colleges and universities shows just how much they mean to Americans. But our ambivalence about learning—respect for its invitation to self-improvement, suspicion over its potential for creating elites—helps to explain why the American public is prepared to turn hostile when the news is bad. There has been no shortage of bad news, and the attention lavished on it by the media has put academic leaders on the defensive.

A second force is the impending transformation of education by economic and technological changes taking place all around it. The life-cycle of nearly everything in the United States has shortened—of useful information, of technologies, and of special skills. In the new corporate lexicon, "buy don't make" and "outsource where possible" have become watchwords. Organizations that once invested heavily in human development and rewarded loyalty in order to reduce turnover now engage in extensive job-shopping. Consulting firms are growing in number and influence, and organizations that supply temporary employees are prospering as never before. The most admired executives are those who can engineer corporate "turnarounds" by "downsizing," and if they are especially successful they may gain a coveted place among America's Toughest Bosses in *Business Week.*

The result has been a new occupational obsolescence in which large numbers of employees are being cast aside before they reach what was once called normal retirement age. Their transient replacements in the specialty job shops will follow them out of the workforce, because their special knowledge is so vulnerable to technological displacement. In many parts of this country, prematurely retired forty-five and fifty-year-olds with expert knowledge and good educations are becoming commonplace.

Spot employment has become a way of life. New kinds of placement firms specialize in finding executives for one- or two-year appointments, to repair a company or serve in an interim capacity in a unit put into receivership or scheduled for rebuilding. Displaced workers will be pressed to specialize in whatever new technological niche is going at the moment—thus becoming the architects of their own premature retirement once that specialty has been superseded. It is ironic that just as we are eliminating mandatory retirement on the basis of age, we are substituting involuntary retirement on the basis of disutility.

In effect, we are stretching the envelope of retirement as we have known it. At the far end, it has been extended by increased longevity and by the uncapping of mandatory retirement. And at the near end, it is expanding to include the new wave of involuntary retirees. There will be important consequences for society, both positive and negative. Spot employment may bring new opportunities for part-time or home work through tele-commuting. By contrast, finding creative and challenging occupations will be very difficult for unemployed people of high ability. The resulting problem will be exacerbated by the present demographic structure of the U.S. population. The baby-boom generation, with its peak about twenty years from the traditional retirement age, is the largest in our history. Following it, and being counted on to provide the kind of support retirees have traditionally received from our society, is an unusually thin generation. If the baby-boomers retire prematurely in significant numbers, an already heavy prospective burden will become heavier still.

These changes have significant implications for higher education. They suggest the importance of educating young people for flexibility and adapt-ability. Particular skills will lose their utility fast; the ability to think, reason, and analyze well will be much more durable. Knowledge about our na-tional culture and its historical antecedents will be an increasingly impor-tant asset, as the need to learn about and penetrate new occupational en-vironments grows. We will need to wean ourselves from the idea that education is something that happens at a particular, early phase of the life-cycle and then stops. Instead, higher education will have to create abun-dant, accessible opportunities for relearning—including taking advantage of unusually accomplished but prematurely retired people as teachers as well as learners. In short, the new demography of employment suggests that the universities will be forced to think more imaginatively about how to provide education throughout life. Academic duty may expand from its present single-generation focus to encompass "students" at a number of different phases of their careers, becoming, in effect, "multicohort" edu-cation.

Institutions and individuals will also have to adapt to the revolution being brought about by computer technology, which has radically revised the way in which data and information are stored, retrieved, and com-municated. Scientific communication, including publication, has been transformed by the Internet. Educational software is proliferating, and it now plays a significant role in instruction. The traditional tasks of editorial criticism and evaluation of problem sets can now take place electronically, in ways that—at their best—link professor and students more closely for more of the work than ever before. Yet despite these important and prom-ising changes, we will be wise to look with some caution on the potential of computer technology for transforming higher education. A quarter of a century ago, it was freely predicted that television would make then-current university teaching methods obsolete. A tour of the typical "mod-ern" classroom built in the early 1970s will almost always reveal expensive installations for videotaping and for display on television monitors. Yet no one can remember when the TV facilities were last used. At best, TV turned out to be a useful adjunct.

Still, there are reasons to believe that academic computing can engage students with their own learning in new and powerful ways. The best examples of effective academic software involve "manipulables": programs that invite students to plan and undertake their own inquiry. Although the best-known cases are in the sciences, there is a wealth of opportunity in other fields; indeed, stimulating courseware exists in which the student can plot, through a series of decisions, his or her own rise through eighteenth-century French society, or arrange the stage sets and actors for a Shakespeare play. Perhaps the most potent idea in the growing literature of educational reform, whether at K–12 or in the university, is that students learn best by active engagement with a subject, through decisions they make themselves. Computers may not reshape the teaching function in the university, but this idea may well do so.

Meanwhile, the Internet and the World Wide Web are vastly expanding students' access to information. The more entrepreneurial and computer-literate undergraduates now routinely probe a depth of bibliographic material heretofore available only to sophisticated doctoral candidates. Recently I suggested to a junior that she consult the Government Documents Library to get a particular Federal Register notice. She responded, "Oh, I picked it off the Web last night . . . It was quite helpful." Indeed, the level of familiarity and comfort that the best students now have with this extraordinarily rich source of information represents the opportunity for an increased emphasis on analysis as opposed to information acquisition—on working with facts instead of accumulating them.

But that opportunity comes attached to some challenges. For example, there is now an awkward and growing generation gap between computer-literate young people and their professorial elders. Differential access to the technology is widening another gap, between adolescent and post-adolescent "haves" and "have-nots." In many institutions, computing has increased the access that ambitious students have to their professors, thus creating new pressures on workload. Perhaps most troublesome of all is the danger of too much "research information" available on the Internet and the World Wide Web and too little quality control. Students need to develop the intellectual taste that will make them discriminating customers in what is rapidly becoming an information flea market.

The international character of the problems most Americans consider important will be another force for change in higher education. International competitiveness; arms control and disarmament; linkage of world financial markets; "sustainable development"; global environmental change; terrorism and the refugee problem—these are but a few examples of the kinds of issues that are rapidly spawning new centers of interdisciplinary activity in U.S. universities. At the same time, postgraduate (and, increasingly, undergraduate) students from abroad are seeking educational opportunity in this country. Our system of higher education has become a magnet for students from all over the world. Almost no sector of the U.S. economy enjoys such a favorable balance of international trade, and surely none is as important in spreading understanding of (and sympathy for) U.S. aims and institutions around the world. The increasingly international nature of our concerns will challenge us to create innovations in curriculum and the organization of scholarly work.

Finally, there is growing concern that the public and private financial resources that have been placed at the disposal of higher education are becoming more constrained, and that the constraints will tighten further, at least until the end of this century. Since the late 1980s, that concern has claimed a major share of the attention of college and university administrators, who worry that resource scarcity will increasingly limit what they can do. When resource constraints increase, institutions tend to examine their programs and make hard choices. Sometimes, in fact, they make changes that lead to dramatic improvement—changes that they invariably fail to make in good times.[1] Hardship, in short, often lowers institutional resistance to change.

It also tends to diminish self-confidence. Sometimes that, too, can be an agent for restructuring: turnover increases, the roots of established habits and ideas are loosened, and new ones find it easier to become established. But it can also build resistance, causing institutions and their leaders to hunker down and hope they can ride out the storm.

In the hierarchical structure found in typical corporate or governmental settings, changes in direction are achieved by the capacity to enforce accountability to some central authority, and to bring in new people to replace others. But in the university, long-standing traditions of delegation (as well as of academic freedom and peer review) locate the power of appointment with departmental faculties; tenure imposes strong limits on replacement, and accountability to the center is minimal. Strong academic leadership from deans and department chairs could overcome these influences. But, in fact, the trend is toward weaker and not stronger leadership at these levels in the research universities, where the traditions of peripheral (that is, faculty) control are strongest. Departments and schools within the university are accorded the dominant voice in selecting their own leaders. These positions are becoming both less desirable and more transitory as constraints increase. It is rare for a department chair to serve more than a three-year term. Deans—once relatively permanent fixtures—move in and out almost as quickly. The current group of deans at Stanford have been in office for an average of only about four years. The frequency of rotation makes it likely that leadership at these levels reflects consensus below rather than any call for change from above.

The dominant patterns of departmental-level choice of chairs and deans favor cautious incrementalism over broad-scale change. The practical requirement that new faculty appointments be supported by a super-majority leads to a form of log-rolling, in which subdisciplines enter into unspoken agreements that act to retain their current representation. Faculty members are heavily invested in their own special fields; each belongs to an invisible transinstitutional academy that commands its loyalty, and each knows that if the discipline prospers, he or she prospers too.

Presidents and governing boards, however influential they may appear, have sharply limited powers. Although the university is sometimes seen from the outside as a relatively apolitical institution, it is in fact intensely political. Without faculty support, leadership from the administration building simply does not work. Proper respect for the faculty's prerogatives in the academic domain restricts the zone of possible intervention. For example, administrations sometimes seek to intervene at the school or department level by the use of visiting committees, from whom they solicit objective evaluations about the quality and effectiveness of academic programs. But those programs and their parent disciplines have strong advocates and effective mechanisms for injecting their views into the decision-making process. Program alumni are often vociferously loyal to the educational units in which they were trained. The visiting evaluations as a result are often less objective than their appointing agencies hoped. In forty years of serving on, or being advised by, dozens of these bodies, I never heard one propose significant reductions in the department it visited.

Instead, the committee members usually become advocates for their area—one of unique potential—or, in the words of one overly enthusiastic colleague, "a virgin field, pregnant with possibilities."

At every hand, universities display their devotion to programs and physical plants that endure. Most buildings are constructed as monuments for the ages, not as flexible, inexpensive, modular facilities that invite changes in function. Appointments are made at senior levels in preference to junior ones whenever the opportunity presents itself. Programs are designed and launched with elaborate care, and longevity is often cited as the primary criterion on which their success is to be judged. Perhaps as cause and perhaps as consequence, universities seek to endow nearly everything. Endowment is an attractive form of fund-raising, because it can attach a program or a building to a donor's name and because it has such a reassuring ring of permanence. But it inevitably builds in longevity, often causing programs to outlive their usefulness and to resist change.

In short, nearly every aspect of the university has a long product lifecycle and is associated with a high "regret function." The immediate consequence is that it is difficult to envision a new or radically altered condition, and the eventual result is a set of policies and practices that favor the present state of affairs over any possible future. It is a portrait of conservatism, perhaps even of senescence.

This description does not apply to all institutions. The comprehensive public institutions, in which most U.S. undergraduates are enrolled, are driven more by student enrollment levels and the perceived needs of the communities they serve; the same is true of community colleges. Administrative decision making, sometimes following negotiation with unionized faculties and always more responsive to external governance, is more the rule in such places. Independent liberal arts colleges are more communitarian and faculty-led, but much more attention is given to institutional as opposed to sectional interests. Church-related colleges have their own rules and customs, often more hierarchical in character. There is less endowment in these sectors, and therefore less in the way of lingering obligation. But in every sector, there is a powerful attachment to the status quo.

This notable resistance of universities can hardly preclude change entirely. The task is to evaluate what new directions seem probable, which ones we prefer, and what patterns of institutional response are most likely to deliver the best outcome.

One trend in higher education that has already demonstrated limited effectiveness is the implementation of policies and devices that have proven successful in the for-profit sector. The professionalization of administrative staffs, the adoption of more carefully considered and managed human resources policies, and the design of better benefits programs are all examples of good corporate practices that have been adopted by universities after what has seemed an unconscionably long delay.

But corporatization must be viewed with some caution. It is a little alarming to hear admissions officers (now sometimes called directors of enrollment management) talk authoritatively about marketing and the business managers speak of total quality management. These notions are not without value, but their adoption increases the estrangement between the administrative and academic cultures—already a serious problem in the university. Academic culture strongly favors individual initiative and a pioneering kind of creativity, whereas those of the administrative culture stress accountability, team loyalty, and discipline. Wherever there is interaction at the boundary, these values are often in conflict.

The newer "business values" run counter to the traditional image of the university and its people as less self-interested and more devoted to noncommercial values than other institutions. When outsiders hear university people talking about productivity enhancement, or learn of deals with industry that involve research agreements, they wonder whether higher education is really free of the values that motivate for-profit companies. While this trend is neither all bad nor all good, it bears careful watching. Many trustees press for the adoption of such corporate values, which they bring with them into the boardroom.

Another trend is the enhancement of American higher education's pluralism. In most industrial nations large, publicly supported institutions dominate the scene; but in the United States a wide range of choice is possible—from small, intensely focused liberal arts colleges, through medium-sized public or private institutions and comprehensive state universities, to a rich and heterogeneous array of research universities. Competition is brisk among similar entities; in the view of some it may be too brisk, acting to forestall the sharing of resources and thus forgoing savings. But others would argue that the competitive character of the enterprise is one that encourages high achievement.

Because heterogeneity is regarded as a virtue, because competition is much admired, and because "freedom of choice" among a broad range of possibilities is an American hallmark, the differentiation of higher education in the United States is very likely to increase. The better liberal arts colleges across the country are flourishing. Formerly "lesser" campuses in big state university systems, such as the University of California at San Diego, and earlier UCLA, have grown to rival the flagships; and in the same state, the comprehensive California State University system is improving and adding campuses. The predicted demise of "women's colleges" has been reversed by new evidence that they offer special opportunities not available to women in other settings. Never has it been clearer that there is an extraordinary incentive to quality in our diverse system. The Harvards, Stanfords, and MITs may deserve praise as centers of innovation, but remarkable things are happening at many institutions that receive less attention: Bowdoin, Portland State, Alverno College, Miami-Dade Community College, and Carnegie-Mellon—to take a sampling across the entire spectrum.

Another positive trend is the increasing awareness of our duty to undergraduate students, especially in the research universities. A lively source of controversy in such places is the question of how much attention ought to be paid to the education of undergraduates. Even though these institutions are responsible for only a small fraction of the baccalaureate degrees awarded annually in the United States, it is in them that the tension between the research and the teaching commitments of faculty members is at its highest. Because they are prestigious and highly visible, they are often seen as models. They are also the places in which future faculty are trained—and thus they are the incubators of the academic culture for the next generation.

The improvement of undergraduate education has become a national movement, visible on many fronts. The NAS, the most prestigious organization of research scientists, instituted in the last century to advise the government on scientific and technical matters, has expanded a center devoted to the improvement of science teaching for undergraduates. Calls for revision of the requirements for promotion to tenure so as to place greater emphasis on teaching are heard in many places, and even heeded in a few. Thoughtful observers like the late Ernest Boyer have called for redefining scholarship to include original efforts in the instructional sphere. In short, educational reform is again at the center of concerned conversation in colleges and universities.

That said, it must be admitted that the results are still meager. At Stanford a highly visible faculty commission completed a review of undergraduate instruction in 1994. Its recommendations were thoughtful—including, for example, a clear call for peer review of teaching effectiveness—and occasionally bold; the commission mandated a first-year interdisciplinary science course to be developed and required of all students. But the course is still being tested, and the new evaluation system is not fully installed. Here as in many places, we have what looks like a lit fuse, but no explosion yet.

Reform in undergraduate education has a deeper and more philosophical side. Particularly in the most selective and rigorous undergraduate programs, the academic "atmosphere" is intensely competitive. Though it has softened somewhat in the past two decades, the practices of grading large courses on a curve, of making seminar discussions a form of debate competition, and of discouraging group projects are still quite common. To describe a course as "rigorous" is to give it high praise, and often the test of its rigor is how many students fail to make the grade.

The larger society invites and encourages this view of education through its insistence that colleges and universities serve a credentialing function— telling employers and others that John is a better bet than Julie. The national anger and frustration over the problem of grade inflation are manifestations of the perceived importance of that function.

Yet the larger society also complains that it doesn't like the results of all this competition. Organizations, whether government agencies, companies, or nonprofits, get things done by grouping people with different skills and telling them to solve problems. The effective employee in such a setting is the one who can apply skills constructively through cooperation with others, and if necessary recruit those others through the exercise of personal leadership. Why, employers are asking, are we being sent young men and women who know how to compete but find it difficult to harmonize their efforts with others?

This concern is finding resonance with several movements in higher education. One is toward public and community service organizations, which are becoming more visible on campus, and the commitment of undergraduate students to them. Such organizations have been accompanied by an emphasis on service learning—academic experiences coupled closely with national or community work toward particular objectives. The experiences themselves most often entail group projects, and the academic venues for follow-up courses are especially promising opportunities for cooperative efforts. Campus Compact, a consortium founded by several university presidents in the early 1980s and now including more than five hundred institutions, has been a leading force for examining and extending service learning, a distinctively new and promising approach to higher learning.[2]

In another movement, many faculty members are finding opportunities in their own teaching to assign cooperative work and deliver group rewards for outstanding performance. In writing courses, reciprocal peer review is being used effectively. In schools of engineering, teams of students compete in design competitions in which the outcome is a device and success is determined by, say, its duration of flight rather than the percentage of correct answers. Frequently, the most important lesson of a group project is only loosely connected to its primary academic purpose: students have to deal with the skilled colleague who has a difficult personality, or solve the "free-rider" problem.

There are real but usually unspoken disagreements among faculty as to whether a university education ought to focus entirely on intellectual development or entail some efforts to direct and encourage personal maturation as well. Advocates of the latter are often associated with a "student-affairs mentality" and seen as intellectually soft by many faculty members. Advocates of the former may come across as "hard-nosed" or inflexible to those in the other camp. This philosophical split is vital to the institution's purpose, but unfortunately the contest is now being waged in the dark. We need to recognize that there are substantive choices to be made, and that they ought to be the subject of careful and public deliberation. The change to a more holistic view of our educational responsibility is well under way, but until it becomes the active subject of policy debate we can only guess at whether change is forthcoming.

A very different force is to be found in the growing demand, on the part of students as well as external critics, for policy studies and other work relevant to real-world problems. This is not a new problem for universities; indeed, they have always wavered between "academic" detachment and worldly engagement. The university's reluctance to be "relevant," a lingering after-effect of the painful 1960s, is being eroded by an increasing realization that the great problems confronting the world are too interesting and important to be ignored—and that they do not come in disciplinary packages. The list of challenges is endlessly fascinating and thoroughly "academic" in the sense of being analytically demanding and intellectually exciting. Arms control and disarmament; ethical issues in genetic testing and counseling; contemporary extinction rates and their implications for conservation policy; utilization incentives in health-care systems; the influence of education and economic status of women on fertility rates— this is only a partial list of issues on the academic agenda of one institute in one university in one month. Students find these problems gripping; they insist on learning about them. And increasingly, faculty members want to work on them. Reluctance to do so comes partly from the traditional academic suspicion of "applied" work, and partly from the considerable difficulty of being an interdisciplinary scholar.

Most "interdisciplinary" work should properly be called multidisciplinary; it harnesses different specialties toward some common objective, but without asking students to master them all. Some programs, however, actually try to train students to gain competence in several disciplines. This approach is open to the criticism that it involves "watered-down" biology or "soft" economics. Critics are right to insist on rigorous disciplinary review; indeed, that is probably necessary to keep interdisciplinary work honest. But to insist that the combination of disciplines inevitably involves weakening each of them is merely stubborn and perhaps fearful adherence to traditional approaches.

Members of Congress, foundation executives, the most experienced journalists, and other thoughtful observers of the American scene are all asking the same question—"Can the universities really make a difference with respect to the Big Problems facing us?" The question stems from real concern about the seriousness of the problems, and equally from a mistrust of the ability of the academic sector to mobilize in a way likely to produce solutions. It is not that there is a lack of respect for the intellectual firepower of the universities, or even for their capacity to make major contributions of a practical sort. The success of university research in biomedicine and the physical and engineering sciences has been spectacular, and it is widely appreciated. The skepticism is about the universities' ability to reorganize, to marshal the diverse talents necessary to approach complex problems of large scale. Whether the academy can overcome the resistance of departmental structure and long tradition to "re-engineer" itself in the face of these challenges is an open question.

In the first two-thirds of the twentieth century, university faculty members played a dominant role among the nation's "public intellectuals." Today there is growing doubt that academic scholars enjoy that level of prominence or have that much influence in the shaping of public awareness. This is partly the result of an admirable growth of intellectual resources in other sectors. The emergence of more reflective and critical journalism, the increasing role of foundations and think tanks in public life, and the expanded capacity of government and the for-profit sector have all enriched the quality of national thought. But it is difficult to avoid the conclusion that the role of universities has been diminished in part by their own failure to exercise intellectual leadership in the areas that a thoughtful public believes to be important. Critics point to the faddish and often incomprehensible preoccupations of the humanities, to the absorption of the social sciences with the detailed quantification of not very important problems, and to the resistance of various diseases to the ambitious claims of molecular biologists. They wonder at the time and energy expended on internal discussions of whether this or that is politically correct.

It is perhaps neither necessary nor possible for the universities to exert the dominant influence they once had; the nation is a more complicated and pluralistic place, and it has lots of thinkers in lots of areas. But an important role will be reserved for the university and its faculty if, and only if, they can reconnect to the society that nurtures them. The question is how to do that.

One way is through strong leadership from the top. Yet to many critics of the university, presidential leadership has become an oxymoron, like amateur athletics. Where are the Nicholas Murray Butlers and the William Rainey Harpers? Or, to take a somewhat more recent example, could a James Bryant Conant exist now? The "great presidents" of yesteryear are actually more admired for their visibility and influence in national affairs than for what they did within their own institutions. Conant as ambassador to Germany was better understood than Conant as president of Harvard. The much-admired president of Notre Dame, Father Theodore Hesburgh, is better known for his splendid service on various presidential commissions or the wisdom of his observations about American society than for his service to Notre Dame.

It is doubtful whether university presidents can, in this day and age, gain the kind of celebrity status enjoyed by their most noted predecessors. Mass media, visibility, and shifting cultural ideals tend to give the spotlight to athletes, rockers, politicians, and even computer giants. The most noted academic death of 1996, to judge by the front page of the *New York Times,* was that of Timothy Leary, a Harvard professor noted chiefly for having persuaded his students (and many others) to break the law and put their central nervous systems at risk with various recreational drugs. At bottom, perhaps managing, which is what presidents do most of the time, simply lacks glamour.

Managing a university is harder and more consuming work than it once was. Institutions of higher education are more complicated places, with more constituencies, more government involvement, and more stress. There are often too few hours in the day to deal with every constituency and every emergency. That reality received national attention when Harvard's president, Neil Rudenstine, took a prolonged leave for what was described as exhaustion. The national press treated this with uncharacteristic but deserved compassion, but for many it raised the question, "Are these jobs too tough?" The answer obviously depends on who is doing them, and how much dedication the president insists on bringing to each aspect of the task. But it is clear that escalating obligations and the expanded scale of the university have imposed more stringent limits on the kind of public visibility and outreach that presidents can achieve.

Within the university itself, administrative responsibility is a key ingredient in the design of the institution's objectives. Although presidents don't make curriculum decisions, vital choices about what should be taught and how are arenas for the assertion of presidential leadership. The proposed revisions of the Western Culture course at Stanford brought one such arena to the surface. Others loom. What should be done to improve the scientific "literacy" of college graduates? What should be done about the prevalence of postmodern teaching in some humanities departments, through which students learn that all of the objective reality claimed by scientists is entirely constructed from their system of values? When academic legitimacy is asserted for propositions of this kind, departments and committees can do little. Strong persuasion and mediation from the top are necessary to fulfill the institution's responsibility to its students. And when interdisciplinary approaches to such vital subjects as environmental policy or arms control cannot break departmental monopolies on the budget or the curriculum, presidential initiative should be brought to bear.

Questions arise not only about what we should teach but about whom and how many. At the undergraduate level, particularly for those colleges and universities that admit selectively, the question almost no one asks is, "Are we concerned with value, or with value added?" Admissions officers in such places compete avidly for the "best" applicants, by which they usually mean those who are most likely to graduate with the highest probability of subsequent success. A strong case, at least in some institutions, could be made for accepting those students for whom the institution is likely to make the greatest difference. Such a choice, which would seem heretical in most places, would clearly have to be made at the top.

There is hardly a subject more prominent in the national conversation about higher education than "affirmative action" and its role in admissions decisions. With hefty political leadership from the governor, the Board of Regents of the University of California resolved to abolish racial preference (while, of course, saying nothing about other, much steeper preferences, such as those regularly exercised on behalf of athletes and the children of influential persons). The president of Stanford, Gerhard Casper, issued a strong and thoughtful explanation of why his university would continue to pursue an admissions policy that employed preferences to assure diversity in its student population. It was a splendid example of presidential leadership at the right moment, emphasizing a strong academic consensus that a diverse student body confers educational advantages on all students.[3]

Financial aid, so closely related to admissions in the policy context, raises questions all its own. It is the primary device for determining access: poor and minority students simply cannot come to the more selective institutions without substantial help. Financially favored selective private colleges and universities have maintained policies of "need-blind" admissions; by doing so, they guarantee that no student will be denied admission on the grounds of inability to pay. Unfortunately, this policy is fading fast as budget constraints tighten. The capacity of private colleges and universities to assemble diverse and highly selected student bodies depends on how they arrange financial aid packages. This capacity is limited, of course, by available funds—the vast majority of which, following a long spell of reduction in federal student aid, come from private sources.

In the best of all possible worlds, a student with a given amount of financial need would be offered a standard amount of financial aid, which would vary from institution to institution, since tuition and other charges also vary. The student would then be able to choose according to the suitability of the academic program, not the price. To most of us in higher education, this seems the best possible outcome. Price competition—offering fat scholarship assistance to especially desired admittees—merely wastes scarce resources that could be applied to other students with need. It pits institutions against one another in a kind of "tragedy of the commons," in which the victims are qualified students who don't get helped.

In 1991 the Department of Justice served more than fifty institutions with Civil Investigative Demands, requiring them to submit reams of documents on the history of tuition-setting and financial aid policy. The theory was that the similarity of financial aid packages and of tuition charges at the selective private institutions amounted to an antitrust violation. Eventually the government narrowed the case to the eight Ivy League institutions and MIT, which had met annually in a so-called overlap group to compare awards and deal with differences in the institutional estimates of financial need by joint applicants. In staff time, institutions the size of Harvard and MIT had to spend between half a million and a million dollars each to satisfy the federal investigative demand. The government eventually sued, and the eight Ivies settled before the case came to trial—agreeing to abandon the practice of overlap analysis. In a courageous exercise of presidential leadership, Charles Vest of MIT decided to stay in the fight. MIT lost at the district court level; the attorney general, Richard Thornburgh, had decided to try the case in Pennsylvania, where he was then running for the U.S. Senate. MIT persevered and won at appeal. Although its victory may not have made much difference in financial aid policy in the long run, it put an emphatic punctuation mark at the end of an overbroad and unreasonable exercise of harassment on the part of the U.S. government. Vest's determination in this matter boldly underscores the value of institutional leadership: sometimes university presidents must protect their institutions against powerful outside forces.

Perhaps the most visible and influential presidential role is that of spokesperson. The president of any well-known institution has a "bully pulpit," and there is no shortage of temptation to use it. Students want support from the top on any issue that is deeply felt at the moment. Outside organizations hope for the same. And the presidents themselves, as human beings, have strong convictions that they sometimes want to express in the most public and forceful way. Others, of course, feel differently. Trustees generally hope that their presidents, like nineteenth-century children, will be often seen and seldom heard. They know that any strong view expressed publicly is remembered far longer by those who differ with it than by those who agree. They regularly hear from their friends—in another boardroom, or at the club—whenever "their man" or "their woman" says something controversial. Furthermore, they understand, quite correctly, that when their president tries to take positions as a private individual, members of the public will not make the distinction between person and institution. Most presidents therefore heed these warnings, temper their impulses with judgment, and avoid taking public positions.

When the matter entails a challenge to their own universities or is highly relevant to some institutional interest, academic leaders should be heard. With respect to issues or controversies outside the university, there is more room for doubt. If a matter relates to a specific interest of the institution or of higher education generally, then it is a proper subject for the president to take on in a public way. But if the issue does not matter to the institution itself or to one of its constituencies, then it does not warrant depleting a valuable resource (the public's attention). For example, the institution might not have a direct interest in a particular federal provision regarding student aid if it doesn't affect the university's finances; but if it adversely affects the welfare of its students, the president would certainly be justified in speaking out on their behalf.

It was not difficult to apply these criteria to two of the issues on which I spent the most time during my years as the president of Stanford. One of them was students' engagement in public and community service. It seemed clear to me that it was in the interest of our students, and of our sense of institutional self-worth, to encourage them to seek outlets for helping, both on the campus and in the community outside. With other presidents, I tried to make this a national effort through the founding of Campus Compact. The second was to move universities toward a recognition of their responsibilities for the quality of elementary and secondary public education. The interest of higher education in that subject seems to me self-evident, and I think our neglect of the rest of the educational system contributed to the erosion of public esteem for all our institutions.

On some other important issues, the case for engagement was not so clear. In the mid-1980s, apartheid in South Africa was a hot topic on many campuses, including ours. Students in large numbers demanded that we divest our stock in corporations doing business in that country, to protest human rights violations there. At Stanford we insisted on a case-by-case review, divesting only companies with poor performances under the principles devised by Reverend Leon Sullivan to evaluate corporate citizenship in South Africa. Even then, we divested only after some jawboning to persuade them to improve. Of course this policy did not satisfy many of the students. At the same time, the Congress was considering trade sanctions, and I was urged to comment publicly on those proposals. I did so in the belief that the issue had become so linked to our own institutional policy that it was impossible to separate them.

Finally, there are issues that, even though they do not directly concern the university and fail to meet the criteria I have just suggested, seem of such transcendent importance that the consciences of many people are deeply stirred. A widespread outburst of racial violence, or an episode of unjust and unlawful government action, might justify a presidential statement. If the matter is highly controversial, as it is likely to be, taking a position will entail considerable cost. But the purpose of a self-denying policy, after all, is not absolute constraint. Rather, it serves to remind one of those costs, and to permit only the most carefully considered exceptions.

The vital activity of Ph.D. training is a domain in which the faculty, not the institution's leadership, plays the key role. In the early years of this century, the Ph.D. degree, newly imported from Europe, was represented as a highly advanced scholarly credential. But it soon evolved into a required credential for teaching at the college or university level, across the board. Now lower-tier institutions regularly advertise the proportion of their faculty members who hold Ph.D.s, as though that fact alone were a reliable indicator of the quality of instruction. In fact, it is anything but that: doctoral study has always trained people to do research first. Thus intent and reality drew further apart. William James recognized the problem early on; he talked of the "Ph.D. octopus," and indeed it was, reaching out from the research universities to wrap its tentacles around the entire system of higher education.

To modify higher education in America it is necessary to change the ways in which doctoral students are trained. That is not easy; doctoral training is hand work, and the workers have always done it in a certain way. But there are promising indicators of movement. A new program entitled Preparing Future Faculty, sponsored by the Pew Trusts and the Association of Graduate Schools, is centered on several research university campuses; each institution is part of a consortium that includes a liberal arts college, a community college, a comprehensive public institution, and (often) one or more others. The doctoral candidates at the research university do supervised teaching in the other places, and have the opportunity not only to develop their skills but to absorb and perhaps appreciate the norms in different kinds of settings.

The attitudes of researchers trained in the usual way may be changing. There is an annual convocation of Presidential Young Investigators, recipients of highly prestigious postdoctoral awards from the National Science Board. The fellows choose their own topic, and at a recent meeting they selected undergraduate science education. This decision, somewhat unexpected given that the group is selected on the basis of research accomplishment, led eventually to a serious set of recommendations about how to improve the teaching function.[4]

Indeed, there is real ferment about undergraduate education in the sciences, and about the way we are preparing future faculty for the teaching profession. A major convocation at the NAS in April of 1995 led off a "year of national dialog," during which regional symposia on the subject were held across the country.[5] The NSF has sponsored additional meetings, with participation from other government agencies that support research.

In the humanities, where graduate life is often more isolating than in the sciences, and may lead to a more unrealistic view of the future, a major ten-year study of doctoral education is under way with the support of the Andrew W. Mellon Foundation. That two of the nation's major private foundations and its leading academies are engaged with the problem of how we train Ph.D. candidates is important news. It tells us that there is a problem, but it also suggests that we may be on our way to a solution.

When I was a graduate student, close to finishing a doctorate, some of us would entertain one another with visions of a place we would all like to work. With only the slightest blush, I confess that we called it Good Guy U. Its central feature was the nearly complete collapse of most of the hierarchical traditions that had rubbed us raw in our lowly status as graduate students. The professoriate at GGU consisted of sympathetic people who spent lots of time with students and shared credit generously, not only with students but with their colleagues. At GGU many of the competitive features that characterize research environments were replaced by widespread sharing of ideas, equipment, and space. Interdisciplinary scorn was notably absent, and respect and resources were doled out even-handedly by a supportive administration. Faculty roles in institutional governance were strong, but departmental decision making had much less influence over academic appointments. Students were given a larger role in institutional affairs, which led to a greater sense of belonging to the institution. Junior members of the various student affairs staffs were recognized as real members of the academic profession. GGU's athletic teams, naturally, won regularly—with bona fide students who displayed relentless good sportsmanship.

In this bit of 1950s fantasy, there are a few hints of what a reinvented university ought to be like; and indeed, much has happened since then to convert some of our youthful imagination into institutional reality. Students and their views are much more thoroughly integrated into evaluation and even policy determination. Faculty participation in university governance is both more extensive and more meaningful. Course planning and thinking about curriculum are done more thoroughly, too; indeed, anyone comparing the quality of higher education in the United States, then and now, has to agree that it is better now.

But in some respects the changes have been meager, and in others they have moved in the wrong direction. Departments are still the focus of academic development in the university, but their leadership has tended to narrow its vision and interests, thereby losing its public voice and regard. A kind of pessimism has set in, both about the future of scholarship and about the capacity of universities to be part of the solution to the problems that beset society.

The central force in institutional change, the faculty, has experienced severe crises of morale and status. Feeling pressed from the bottom by students and parents and from the top by administrators, they often feel like scapegoats for everyone's complaints. Yet they remain the heart and mind of the university. Their commitment is essential for university health. Wherever creative energy and institutional loyalty abound, the faculty is willing to experiment and to engage actively with the needs of students. Wherever they are lacking, things seem to stay where they are. Visiting many other institutions and watching the history of my own has convinced me that faculty engagement can be reliably summoned under the right circumstances.

Innovation and commitment are most evident in colleges and universities below the top rung of the prestige ladder. Elites find it difficult to modify a winning formula in this arena, as in many others. The "transforming institutions" are often those that perceive a special mission—for example, to a particular urban center, as is the case with Portland State or Indiana University/Purdue University at Indianapolis. Or they may be founded on the idea of a particular kind of experiment, like Hampshire College or Evergreen State. In such cases a number of faculty members are either gathered to, or convinced by, an explicit vision of institutional goals. Sometimes a college or university is empowered by circumstances or competitive zeal to raise its rank, and the momentum of improvement builds faculty enthusiasm and carries it along. Stanford in the 1960s was described by David Riesman as "a meteor in our business," and those of us on the faculty, exhilarated by the sense of moving up fast, invested heavily in the institution.

In more stable situations, faculty engagement does not come so naturally. Loyalty is often fragmented, and morale is low. Institutional commitment can be summoned, but it will require new ways of making faculty members feel responsible for the institution and for its students. A big part of the task is to develop a more centralized sense of direction, yet maintain a shared governance structure in which faculty members (and, to a degree, students as well) feel more like stakeholders. It is also important to make the institution more flexible and responsive to newly arising needs and opportunities, by deliberately retaining funds for new initiatives and by cultivating the spirit of innovation.

University leadership is critical here. The faculty's confidence in the institution depends on a sense that its role is accepted, appreciated, and protected. Faculty work and faculty service are often poorly understood and rarely congratulated. The university administration needs to be a more active advocate for its own faculty and for a public understanding of its role. If presidents and Boards of Regents, trustees, deans, and administrators would express pride in, and understanding of, them, the work of teaching and scholarship, faculty morale, and faculty responsibility would benefit greatly.

These are the dimensions along which institutional redesign must proceed. It can happen if boards and presidents and faculties come together on the need for change and set out to accomplish it together. It will *not* happen by *obiter dicta,* from boards or the administration; the traditions of academic governance are too strong for that. Reconstruction of the relationship between the legal owners of the university and its academic proprietors is an essential condition. It will be met in a few especially enterprising and imaginative places, and from there it will spread to the rest.

The commanding feature of this process of redesigning the university will be the reclamation of its central mission. It is, after all, society's agent for cultural transmission and cultural change. It works by the thoughtful, participatory transfer of knowledge and excitement from one generation to the next. Accordingly, its improvement must entail putting students and their needs first. Once that is done, the rest falls into place: the complex challenges posed by intellectual property disputes, the tension between teaching and research, the ethical problems in faculty-student relationships, professional misconduct issues, the need for creative thinking about undergraduate education reform—indeed, all the manifold difficulties so prominent in the growing public mistrust of our academic institutions. Placing students first is a simple design principle, but it has great power.

None of this will happen, of course, without some attitudinal change. That is why, in the vast and pluralistic landscape of American higher education, the research universities must be the agents of change. They are the nurturers of the ambitions and the values of the next academic generation. The difficulty is that they are both successful and prestigious, and they lack the natural appetite for renovation and reform that characterizes the striving, transforming institutions. But unless they change, little else will.

It is perhaps not too hopeful to foresee a new understanding of academic duty emerging from that change. For the university, the essential task will be to maintain its special role with respect to the larger society: independent, provocative, but dutiful in its attention to the successor generation. From the faculty, one can hope for a shift in loyalty: more scrupulous attention to the needs of the institution and its students, and a passionate commitment to new ways of knowing and of teaching. And those who manage and lead the institution will need to summon both a readier willingness to assert vigorously, and if necessary defend, the university's values to the public, and the capacity to envision opportunity and welcome change.

NOTES

1. Academic Freedom, Academic Duty

1. D. Charles Whitney and Ellen Wartella, "Media Coverage of the 'Political Correctness' Debate," *Journal of Communication* 42 (1992): 83–94.

2. This story proved irresistible to critics of the Stanford curricular revision. But it is untrue. Although some student demonstrators did use such a slogan within Jackson's hearing, he neither led nor joined them. In fact, he admonished them, saying, "Of course you have to study the West. You're *from* the West." The mythic version is recited in, for example, Roger Kimball, *Tenured Radicals: How Politics Has Corrupted Our Higher Education* (New York: Harper and Row, 1990), p. 28.

3. B. Lewis, "Western Culture Must Go," *Wall Street Journal,* May 2, 1988, p. 24.

4. Derek J. de Solla Price, *Little Science, Big Science . . . and Beyond* (New York: Columbia University Press, 1986, enlarged ed.).

5. Kenneth Prewitt, "America's Research Universities under Public Scrutiny," *Daedalus* 122 (1993): 85–99.

6. Leon Lederman, "Science: The End of the Frontier?" (Report to the Board of Directors, American Association for the Advancement of Science, Washington, 1992.)

2. Preparing

1. This pattern of delegation in the area of educational policy is characteristic of the research universities and the most selective liberal arts colleges. It is apt to be less firm in other kinds of places.

2. Lawrence Veysey, in *The Emergence of the American University* (Chicago: University of Chicago Press, 1965), describes this passage in the development of graduate education at Harvard as "an earthly moment during which all the academic potentialities seemed to be realized" (p. 233).

3. Robert M. Rosenzweig, with Barbara Turlington, *The Research Universities and their Patrons* (Berkeley: University of California Press, 1982), p. 1. This short book is a very useful account of problems and opportunities facing the research universities at the beginning of the 1980s.

4. This history is given in more detail in D. Kennedy, "Making Choices in the Research University," *Daedalus* 122 (1993): 127–156. This volume of *Daedalus (The American Research University)* contains a number of useful papers about the status of the research universities. For additional statistics about government research support, see Office of Technology Assessment, *Federally Funded Research: Decisions for a Decade* (Washington: U.S. Congress, Office of Technology Assessment, 1991).

5. For a summary of these and related studies see D. E. Drew, *Strengthening Academic Science* (New York: Praeger, 1985).

6. In fact, many university administrators and department chairs now find that the most crucial element in most faculty recruitments is employment—often academic employment—for the spouse. This has led to real internal tensions, as members of Department A lobby colleagues in Department B for a slot for the husband of high-powered Professor X, whom they desperately wish to attract.

7. There have been several systematic analyses by social scientists of the factors that determine salaries, promotion, and other career indicia. These are valuable sources of quantitative information; see, for example, L. S. Lewis, *Scaling the Ivory Tower* (Baltimore: Johns Hopkins University Press, 1975), and M. J. Finkelstein, *The American Academic Profession: A Synthesis of Social Scientific Inquiry since World War II* (Columbus: Ohio State University Press, 1984).

8. H. P. Tuckerman, *Publication, Teaching, and the Academic Reward Structure* (Lexington, Mass.: Lexington Books, 1976).

9. I once reported on this subject to a group of Stanford faculty. Rather grimly, I told them the startling fact that in only a little more than a decade, they had aged five years! They feigned great delight at this news.

10. For a useful summary of these data, see A. Rees and S. P. Smith, *Faculty Retirement in the Arts and Sciences* (Princeton: Princeton University Press, 1991), especially Chapter 4.

11. Edward Shils, *The Academic Ethic* (Chicago: University of Chicago Press, 1983).

12. Until the late 1980s, TIAA-CREF had a virtual monopoly on private university benefit plans, which it maintained by refusing to permit fund transfers to other vehicles. That monopoly was broken in the late 1980s through the efforts of a leading retirement expert, Oscar Ruebhausen, and a small coalition of universities. Now most institutions offer a number of retirement investment products from which faculty members may choose. All, however, are of the "defined-contribution" type.

13. The life expectancy of a sixty-five-year-old male in the United States is about fifteen years, of a seventy-year-old male, about eleven years. If insurers used these average figures in their actuarial calculations, the seventy-year-old retiree would have an annual income 15/11 larger than the sixty-five-year-old. Of course, insurers try to use actuarial data for particular regional and occupational groups in order to make their predictions more accurate.

14. Rees and Smith, *Faculty Retirement*, Table 2–5.

15. Ibid., p. 90.

16. O. Ashenfelter and D. Card, "Faculty Retirement in the Post-Mandatory Era:

Early Findings from the Princeton Retirement Survey," Princeton Conference on Higher Education, March 1996.

17. Dale E. Johnson, acting dean of the Graduate School, University of Washington. Personal communication.

18. William G. Bowen and J. A. Sosa, *Prospects for Faculty in the Arts and Sciences* (Princeton: Princeton University Press, 1989). Chapter 6 contains a thorough analysis of doctoral production by fields.

19. National Academy of Sciences, Summary Report, 1993, *Doctorate Recipients from United States Universities* (Washington: National Academy Press, 1995).

20. The extent of the increase is difficult to measure precisely. If one measures by looking backward, at all Ph.D. students who finish in a given year, the average time to the degree is overestimated; a better measure is to look forward, starting with an entering cohort. Even with this more conservative measure, the increase for 1968–1993 is more than one year.

21. A lively exposition of this view is found in D. L. Goodstein, "After the Big Crunch," *Wilson Quarterly* (Summer 1995), pp. 53–60.

22. See, for example, "Congress: Was the Shortfall Phony?" *Science* 256 (1992): 172.

23. R. C. Atkinson, "Supply and Demand for Scientists and Engineers: A National Crisis in the Making," *Science* 248 (1992): 432.

24. Bowen and Sosa, *Prospects for Faculty.*

25. The cost comparison is tilting in favor of postdoctoral fellows for several reasons. Graduate research assistantships entail "tuition remission" payments that reimburse the university for half-time study, whereas postdoctorals are paid straight salaries. Tuition costs have risen faster than salaries, on average; in addition, in some universities these must now be charged directly on research grants instead of being charged to the staff benefits pool.

26. A poignant and thoughtful analysis of the para-faculty is found in J. M. Gappa and D. W. Leslie, *The Invisible Faculty* (San Francisco: Jossey-Bass, 1993).

27. For an exploration of these tensions see P. Gumport, "Graduate Education and Organized Research in the United States," in B. Clark, ed., *The Research Foundations of Graduate Education: Germany, Britain, France, United States, Japan* (Berkeley: University of California Press, 1993), pp. 225–293.

28. W. F. Massy and C. A. Goldman, "The Production and Utilization of Science and Engineering Doctorates in the United States" (Discussion Paper, Stanford Institute for Higher Education Research, 1995). Other difficulties with this analysis include an arithmetic error in reporting foreign retention that inflates the "gap," and two tenuous assumptions: that postdoctoral appointments last only a year, and that all academics who leave positions before retirement fill other academic slots.

29. National Research Council, *Meeting the Nation's Needs for Biomedical and Behavioral Scientists* (Washington: National Academy Press, 1994).

3. To Teach

1. H. Rosovsky, "Report of the Dean of the Faculty of Arts and Sciences, Harvard University," 1990–91.

2. E. Boyer, *Scholarship Reconsidered: Priorities of the Professoriate* (Princeton: Carnegie Foundation for the Advancement of Teaching, 1990).

3. David Kennedy, McLachlan Professor of History at Stanford, writes, "Several of the most valuable and widely read books on recent American history have come not from the pens of academic historians, but from journalists or independent scholars. One thinks, for example, of David McCullough on Truman, Walter Isaacson and Evan Thomas on the early Cold War, Richard Rhodes on the atomic and hydrogen bomb projects, Doris Kearns Goodwin on the World War II home front, or Richard Kluger, Taylor Branch and J. Anthone Lukas on civil rights and race relations. There is something to ponder here about the structure of university-based historical scholarship, and especially about the capacity of academic historians to speak to a general reading public beyond the captive audience of their own guild." Personal communication.

4. Edward Shils, *The Academic Ethic* (Chicago: University of Chicago Press, 1983).

5. F. M. Cornford, *Microcosmographica Academica: Being a Guide for the Young Academic Politician* (London: Bowes and Bowes, 1908; sixth edition, 1964). This delicious little volume is required reading for anyone interested in academics or politics, the fusion of which was famously described in this way: "Academic politics is so vicious because so little is at stake." Often misattributed to Henry Kissinger, this was apparently first said by the Columbia social scientist William Sayre.

6. K. G. Skeff, A. Stratos, J. Berman, and M. R. Bergen, "Improving Clinical Teaching: Evaluation of a National Dissemination Program," *Archives of Internal Medicine* 152 (1992): 1156–1161.

7. There are a few exceptions. Especially notable was the use by Swarthmore's honors program of visiting examiners!

8. The Center for Academic Integrity, a coalition of colleges and universities, is proving a useful forum for analysis of these issues. See, for example, D. L. McCabe and S. Cole, "Student Collaboration: Not Always What the Instructor Wants," *AAHE Bulletin* 48 (1995): 3–6, for some valuable analysis.

9. D. L. McCabe and L. K. Trevino, "Academic Dishonesty: Honor Codes and Other Contextual Influences," Journal of Higher Education, forthcoming.

10. Henry Rosovsky, personal communication.

11. H. Shapiro, Chapter 9 in *A Higher Education Map for the 1990s*, G. Budig, ed. (New York: ACE/Macmillan, 1993), pp. 55–63.

4. To Mentor

1. Carl Djerassi, "Mentoring: A Cure for Science-Bashing?" *Chem. Eng. News*, Nov. 15, 1991.

2. D. Kennedy, "Academic Authorship," Stanford University, 1985; distributed by Council of Learned Societies.

3. Henry Rosovsky, *The University: An Owner's Manual* (New York: Norton, 1990), pp. 293–294.

4. Stanford's statement on "consensual relationships" applies only to "those who supervise or evaluate the work of others," and remains silent on the more difficult question of whether a coercive element is present even when direct supervision or evaluation is absent.

5. As institutional attention to this situation intensified, it only came to look more complicated. The situation in medical institutions is special in that there is a work hierarchy in which a traditionally male-dominated profession (doctors) ranks above

and supervises a traditionally female-dominated one (nurses). As medicine achieves a more equitable gender balance, dissatisfactions are amplified.

6. For a detailed and fascinating account of these and related problems in the sciences, see E. Seymour and N. M. Hewitt, *Talking About Leaving* (Boulder: Westview Press, 1997).

5. To Serve the University

1. One might suppose that professional pride would make professors hesitate to reach for that definition. Such unionization efforts on the part of faculty members have in fact been relatively rare in the more prestigious research universities, where individual professors may have high mobility and relatively favorable conditions of employment. Attempts to form unions are more common in state or community colleges and the less affluent independent institutions.

2. *National Labor Relations Board v. Yeshiva University,* 100 S.Ct. 856 (1980).

3. These principles, originally established by the Reverend Leon Sullivan, required companies active in South Africa to meet standards of affirmative action in employment as well as to avoid activities that would benefit government or police entities, that is, would assist the institution of apartheid. A later addition was the requirement that firms actively intercede with the government of South Africa in attempting to abolish specific provisions supporting apartheid, for example, the "Pass Laws." Adherence to the Sullivan Principles was monitored by a group of nonprofit investor entities, including churches, pension funds, and universities, called the IRRC (Investors Responsibility Research Consortium).

4. There is, of course, another problem with the "investment responsibility" movement. The movement originated at a time when institutional investments were relatively stable, and shareholders could be held responsible for the corporations in which they held equity. With the advent of computerized trading, the average lifetime of an investment dropped dramatically, so that many institutions found themselves surprised by the stocks they had on any given day. Not only was the very notion of "investor responsibility" altered; it became technically difficult to divest, and to guarantee that the divested stock (or an even less "responsible" one) wouldn't unexpectedly reappear.

5. This problem, known as "Baumol's cost disease," was identified and applied to higher education in W. Baumol and W. Bowen, *Performing Arts: The Economy Dilemma* (New York: Twentieth-Century Fund, 1966).

6. For this correction I am indebted to Howard Bromberg, Stanford Law School (see H. Bromberg, "Revising History," *Stanford Magazine* (March–April 1996: 116). Bromberg shows that—strangely—a number of "authoritative" American academic histories have the reasons for Ross's dismissal wrong, among them L. R. Veysey's *The Emergence of the American University* (Chicago: University of Chicago, 1965) and (more recently) G. Marsden, *The Soul of the American University* (New York: Oxford University Press, 1993). Marsden even says, quite inaccurately, of Jane Stanford: "Her expectation for professors was that they would be Republican. That could be taken for granted of most professors almost as much as that they would be Protestant."

7. The ability of the parking issue to stir vivid academic controversy is legendary. The most notable indication of its role in campus affairs was given by Clark Kerr, the distinguished former president of the University of California. He promised the in-

coming president of another institution, at his inauguration ceremony, that he would be a success in his job if he could solve the three central problems of the university: football for the alumni, sex for the undergraduates, and parking for the faculty.

8. An excellent recent summary of the issue and the relevant literature is found in B. Brooks, "Adequate Cause for Dismissal: The Missing Element in Academic Freedom," *Journal of College and University Law* 22 (1995): 331–358.

9. I have consulted several Stanford provosts in an effort to confirm this. Albert Hastorf, who was provost for much of the relevant period, does not recall the event—but confirms that the story was circulating widely.

10. It is by no means clear that this decision is the right one for all seasons. Indeed, some thoughtful observers have advised private universities *never* to waive that special status. In this case we felt that the special values associated with speech on a campus justified abandoning a position we probably would have been able to sustain only at a high political cost.

11. At Stanford, following the extension of mandatory retirement from age 65 to 70, the average age at retirement rose from 64.5 to around 68.

12. There once was a fairly common rank below assistant professor but still on the tenure line. At almost every research university there were some instructor appointments, usually of persons who had just (or had not quite) completed the Ph.D. In the humanities they might do much of their teaching in sectioned courses; in the sciences—where they were somewhat more numerous—they would run laboratories and do some advanced teaching. This rank has virtually vanished, to be replaced by an array of categories (lecturer, and so on) that are more plainly *off* the tenure line.

13. David Helfand, "Tenure: Thanks But No Thanks," *Chronicle of Higher Education* XLIII: 16 (1995), p. B-1.

14. H. Rosovsky, "Report of the Dean of the Faculty of Arts and Sciences."

15. The result, two years later, was a significant drop in premiums of all Stanford's participating health plans—the first in decades.

6. To Discover

1. Robert M. Rosenzweig, Testimony before the President's Council of Advisers on Science and Technology, July 24, 1992.

2. An excellent account of this issue in general, as well as of the development of SLAC, is to be found in P. Galison and B. Hevly, *Big Science: The Growth of Large-Scale Research* (Stanford: Stanford University Press, 1992).

3. This statement applies not only to research support payments from all government agencies to Stanford for the 1980s, but also to extramural funding supplied by the NIH to all universities for approximately the same period.

4. An extraordinary account of the behavior of the Dingell staff in another academic investigation is found in an article by Jock Friedly on the David Baltimore case, "How Congressional Pressure Shaped the 'Baltimore Case,'" *Science* 273 (1966): 873–875.

5. A. Lewis, "Tale of a Bully," *New York Times*, June 24, 1996, A11.

6. This category refers not to "foreign" medical schools, but to a special class set up by Americans in various overseas locations, largely to serve students unable to gain admission to regular "onshore" U.S. institutions. Some readers will remember that there was one in Granada at the time of the U.S. invasion of that island kingdom. The

parents of such students lobbied heavily in support of the special provision in the capitation bill.

7. J. D. Watson, *The Double Helix* (Boston: Athenaeum Press, 1968). A "Critical Edition," including commentary by contemporaries and rivals, was edited by Gunther Stent and published under the original title by Weidenfeld and Nicolson, London, 1981. For a tolerant view of Watson and insight into a very different kind of scientific temperament, see E. O. Wilson's charming autobiography, *Naturalist* (Washington, D.C.: Island Press, 1994).

8. J. Cohen et al., "Conduct," *Science* 268 (1995): 1705–1708.

7. To Publish

1. N. Cummings et al., "University Libraries and Scholarly Communication," Mellon Foundation Report, 1992.

2. Roger Noll, personal communication.

3. See S. M. Stigler, "Citation Patterns in the Journals of Statistics and Probability," *Statistical Science* 9 (1994): 94–108; and G. J. Stigler, S. M. Stigler, and C. Friedland, "The Journals of Economics," *Journal of Political Economy* 103 (1995): 331–359.

4. An intriguing special case of this is described in D. S. Coffey, "When Is Repetitive Publication Justified?" in *Ethics and Policy in Scientific Publication* (Bethesda, Md.: Council of Biology Editors, 1990). Coffey reports having received identical manuscripts from two different authors in the same university for publication in a journal he edited! He then sent each manuscript to the other author for review. Needless to say, the problem disappeared.

5. This scenario is taken from *Ethics and Policy in Scientific Publication.*

6. D. S. Coffey, "When Is Repetitive Publication Justified?" p. 219.

7. Strenuous debate has also arisen over certain ethical aspects of such rules. Suppose the embargoed paper contains information that might affect the welfare of patients with a life-threatening disease who are enrolled in a clinical trial of a highly promising therapy. In such cases, news organizations have argued, the requirement for prepublication secrecy is against the public interest.

8. Darwin's correspondence on this subject is poignant. The letter to Lyell, supposedly written on the day he received the Wallace manuscript, is anguished: "Your words have come true with a vengeance that I should be forestalled." Darwin says he plans to send the manuscript off to be published anyhow, even though Wallace had not asked him to. Later, after Lyell and Hooker had interceded, uninvited, on his behalf he writes that he would be glad to publish a sketch of his own views but "I cannot persuade myself that I can do so honourably... I would far rather burn my whole book than he or any man should think that I had behaved in a paltry spirit." See F. Burkhardt et al., eds., *The Correspondence of Charles Darwin* (Cambridge, England: Cambridge University Press, 1985), vol. 7, pp. 107, 117–718, 121ff. A revisionist version insists that Darwin's behavior was far less praiseworthy; it rests on evidence suggesting that the Wallace manuscript actually arrived much earlier than Darwin claimed, and that he held onto it while nurturing less admirable motives. For a credulous review of this claim see D. Quamman, *The Song of the Dodo* (New York: Prentice-Hall, 1995).

9. P. Woolf, "The Second Messenger: Informal Communication in Cyclic AMP Research," *Minerva* XII (1975): 3.

8. To Tell the Truth

1. In the recommendations of the Commission on Research Integrity, plagiarism is defined as "the presentation of the documented words or ideas of another as his or her own, without attribution appropriate for the medium of presentation." (*Integrity and Misconduct in Research: Report of the Commission on Research Integrity*, U.S. Department of Health and Human Services, Public Health Service, 1995.) This definition presents some problems. The civil-law definition of plagiarism covers the theft of expression, but the theft of ideas is quite different, and much more difficult to prove.

2. The address in question was given by Deane W. Malott; the striking resemblance of parts of the text was detected by both the Cornell student newspaper and the *New Yorker* (November 10, 1951, p. 102).

3. In one university, a professor was found to have made use of a graduate student's writing in a grant application without attribution or permission. No finding of scientific misconduct was reached, because evidence was presented showing that this was common practice in the professional school in which it occurred!

4. For an interesting account of several of these cases see T. Lieberman, "Plagiarize, Plagiarize, Plagiarize . . . Only Be Sure Always to Call It Research," *Columbia Journalism Review* (July-August, 1995).

5. Indeed, the notion that plagiarism is less serious has a respectable literary history. Edward Gibbon borrowed extensively from the works of predecessors in the fifteenth and sixteenth chapters of *History of the Decline and Fall of the Roman Empire*. When charged with plagiarism, he defended the practice, inviting readers to " . . . consider me not as a contemptible thief but as an honest and industrious manufacturer." See G. W. Bowersock, "Gibbon's Historical Imagination" (Stanford Humanities Center, 1987), 1–17.

6. There is a fascinating literary sequel to this story. Arthur Koestler devotes much of *The Case of the Midwife Toad* to an effort at post-mortem vindication of Kammerer. Lamarkian views became a state religion in the Soviet Union under the sponsorship of Lysenko; indeed, the inheritance of acquired characteristics has had an unexpectedly long life because of the Marxist desire for an alternative to "biological determinism." Koestler's argument is that the forgery was done by someone who wished to discredit Kammerer, and it depends heavily on villainization of William Bateson. In this effort Koestler gratefully acknowledges the help of the American anthropologist Gregory Bateson, the son of the geneticist. The book thus provides, in addition to an example of how political views can influence reason, a remarkable case of literary patricide.

7. R. A. Fisher, "Has Mendel's Work Been Rediscovered?" *Annals of Science* 1 (1936): 115–137.

8. G. Holton, "Subelectrons, Presuppositions, and the Millikan-Ehrenhoft Dispute," *Historical Studies in the Physical Sciences* 9 (1978): 166–224.

9. A careful account of the Moewus affair and its relationship to the history of biochemical genetics is to be found in J. Sapp, *Where the Truth Lies: Franz Moewus and the Origins of Molecular Biology* (Cambridge, England: Cambridge University Press, 1990).

10. W. Stewart and N. Feder, "The Integrity of the Scientific Literature," *Nature* 325 (1987): 207–214.

11. J. P. Swazey, M. S. Anderson, and K. S. Lewis, "Ethical Problems in Academic Research," *American Scientist* 81 (1993): 542–553. This study is a product of the Acadia Institute Project on Professional Values and Ethical Issues in the Graduate Education of Scientists and Engineers.

12. The *New York Times* articles appeared on November 12 (p. A-22), November 14 (p. E-2), and November 23 (p. C-3). For these citations, and for a more extended analysis of media coverage of the Swazey work than can be reported here, I am indebted to Dr. Sharoni Shamir.

13. Of course, the external (social) costs resulting from defaulted student loans are arguably less than the costs to research of faulty data. But the moral ground is equally shaky, and the direct cost is greater in the student loan case.

14. P. Woolf, "Deception in Scientific Research," *National Conference of Lawyers and Scientists Project on Scientific Fraud and Misconduct* (Washington, D.C.: American Association for the Advancement of Science, 1988–1989).

15. National Research Council, *Responsible Science: Ensuring the Integrity of the Research Process*, vols. 1 and 2 (Washington, D.C.: National Academy of Sciences Press, 1992).

16. Handbook on Ethical Conduct in Biomedical Research, University of Pennsylvania, September 1991. For further recommendations about the design of procedures, see the three workshop reports of the American Association for the Advancement of Science/American Bar Association, *Project on Scientific Fraud and Misconduct*.

17. The title was suggested in jest by Robert Charrow, who represented one of the first scientists charged. It is not known whether the NIH official who adopted it lacked a sense of humor or had an unusually good one.

18. The texts of these decisions are unpublished, but they are matters of public record. Interested readers should contact the Office of Research Integrity at the National Institutes of Health.

19. The Commission on Research Integrity, in reworking the definition of research misconduct, clearly recognized the importance of intent: "In order to qualify as research misconduct, an erroneous statement must be made with an intent to deceive" (*Report of the Commission on Research Integrity*, p. 12). But its definition is otherwise disappointingly vague, and was objected to strongly by (among many others) the council of the NAS.

20. Although the chairman declared himself to be the "sole signatory" to the document and announced that additional comments from the other members of the group might be forthcoming, none was received. It thus seems fair to view this as the equivalent of a group report.

21. This manuscript was eventually published four years later (W. Stewart and N. Feder, "Analysis of a Whistle-blowing," *Nature* 351 (1991): 687–691) under strange circumstances. The editor of *Nature* notes that the manuscript had been received in 1987 but objected to by referees, on the grounds that other data might have reversed the conclusions reached by the authors on the bases of the seventeen pages analyzed. The delayed publication "for completeness" was justified on the grounds that these unspecified supplementary data had been judged by the OSI report to have been fabricated. In fact, that report was a leaked draft, later to be reviewed and extended by the reformulated ORI.

22. Not so anonymous was the criticism aimed at Baltimore from a group of present and former Harvard molecular biologists, notably Walter Gilbert, Mark Ptashne, and James Watson. These three very distinguished scientists were relentless commentators. Gilbert, for example, told the reporter Philip Hilts, "Some of us are just aghast at David's behavior. Through his own doing, the case became a dramatic test of power between the Congress and the scientific establishment" (Philip Hilts, "The Science Mob," *New Republic,* May 18, 1992, p. 31).

23. One should not ignore the role played by a single newspaper, the *New York Times.* The reporter who covered the affair until 1996, Philip Hilts, wrote in the *New Republic* in 1992: "David Baltimore clearly failed as a scientist through his carelessness, his willful oversight, and his extraordinary attempts to protect his own reputation at the expense of a conscientious young colleague. In the end, Baltimore inadvertently revealed just how vulnerable the scientific profession is to abuse by those entrusted to protect it" ("The Science Mob," p. 31). Coverage of the appeals hearing and of future developments remained in Hilts's hands until 1996, when the ddenouement was covered by another reporter.

24. A thorough and highly readable summary of the process has been written by the historian of science Daniel Kevles. See D. Kevles, "The Assault on David Baltimore," *New Yorker,* May 27, 1996.

25. "The Baltimore Vindications," *Wall Street Journal,* July 2, 1992, p. A-14.

26. References to these reanalyses and a summary of the situation may be found in Committee on Measuring Lead in Critical Populations, Board on Environmental Studies and Toxicology, Commission on Life Sciences, National Research Council, *Measuring Lead Exposures in Infants, Children, and other Sensitive Populations* (Washington, D.C.: National Academy Press, 1993).

27. See, for example, *Chronicle of Higher Education,* December 14, 1994, p. A-26.

9. To Reach beyond the Walls

1. Faculty practice programs generally return some fee revenues to clinical departments, and many supply handsome salary bonuses to faculty practitioners depending on their level of clinical activity. Thus in most research universities, the highest-paid persons are the notably successful clinicians; the sculptor may own the revenues from his own work, but that doesn't mean he outearns the surgeon!

2. It is worth noting that there were numerous faculty textbook millionaires long before there were biotechnology and software millionaires. No one ever made much of a fuss about them.

3. A. Bartlett Giamatti, "The University, Industry, and Cooperative Research," *Science,* December 24, 1982.

4. H. Rosovsky, "Report of the Dean of the Faculty of Arts and Sciences."

5. Stanford University "Faculty Policy on Conflict of Commitment and Interest," adopted 1994, Stanford University Faculty Handbook.

6. Ibid.

7. One faculty member with a significant off-campus commitment of this kind said of himself, somewhat ruefully, "Once upon a time, when I woke up in the middle of the night, I thought about the next experiment. Now I find I'm worrying about money."

10. To Change

1. This seminal notion about organizational change comes from Herbert Simon; for a brief account of its origin and significance, see J. March, *Science* 202 (1978): 858–861.

2. See, for example, *Service Counts: Lessons from the Field of Service and Higher Education*, Campus Compact, Brown University, 1995.

3. This proposition, much as I believe it, is, unfortunately—in the words of my colleague Robert Rosenzweig—based on "rhetoric supported by anecdote."

4. *America's Academic Future: A Report of the Presidential Young Investigator Colloquium on U.S. Engineering, Mathematics and Science Education for the Year 2010 and Beyond* (Washington, D.C.: National Science Board, 1994).

5. National Academy of Sciences, *From Analysis to Action: Undergraduate Education in Science, Mathematics, Engineering and Technology* (Washington, D.C.: National Academy Press, 1996).

ACKNOWLEDGMENTS

I OWE A SPECIAL DEBT to the students in my seminar, with whom I discussed nearly all the issues covered in this book. They were the real inspiration behind my decision to write it. Chris Golde and Tim Dore became particularly close to the effort. This generation of students joins a parade of others whom I have known at Stanford during the years since 1960; they have provided a constant source of stimulation, challenge, and gratification.

At the beginning of this project, I had a critical year of support from the Echoing Green Foundation. More generally, my scholarly work since leaving the Stanford University presidency has been made possible by an endowment provided by one of Stanford's greatest friends, Dr. Peter Bing. It is a pleasure to acknowledge his help and his friendship.

I am also indebted to a number of those who served with me in the university's administration for providing important insight and critical judgments on some of the issues considered here. Al Hastorf, Bob Rosenzweig, Jerry Lieberman, Jim Lyons, John Schwartz, Norm Robinson, Michael Jackson, Rick Biedenweg, Valerie Veronin, Larry Horton, Catherine Gardner, Iris Brest, Michael Hudnall, Jennifer Westerlind, and Sally Cole were helpful in ways both direct and indirect. Walter Falcon, Roz Naylor, Larry Goulder, and all my colleagues in the Institute for International Studies were patient with an effort that was off the main course for our group, and they often provided important suggestions. Other colleagues—

Bliss Carnochan, Tom Ehrlich, David Kennedy, Roger Noll, Spyros Andreopolous, Michael Fayer, Carl Djerassi, Howard Bromberg, Irv Weissmann, Deborah Rhode, Pam Daener, and Karen Sawislak—helped with particular cases or provided valuable information. Among others who read and criticized parts of the manuscript, Pat Woolf, Jock Friedly, Joseph Onek, Michael Smith, and Peter Orszag deserve special thanks. President Emeritus William Bowen of Princeton, President Emeritus Frank Rhodes of Cornell, President Emeritus Richard Lyman of Stanford, and Professor (and former dean) Henry Rosovsky of Harvard undertook particularly valuable and thorough reviews. I am grateful for their criticisms and especially for their willingness to share a wealth of experience and knowledge about such issues as faculty supply and demand and the appointment and promotion process in higher education. Russell Edgerton of the American Association for Higher Education has given me years' worth of advice and editorial suggestion, and he has taught me a lot about change. I am also among the many who have benefited from the wise counsel of Professor John Gardner.

My assistant Joan Parker gave her usual generous, cheerful, and efficient help with every aspect of this project, from incubation to final production; her successor, Elissa Hirsh, followed without missing a beat. Jason Robison was my research assistant during the last part of the project, and he proved a determined and effective pursuer of difficult-to-find material. At Harvard University Press, I was lucky enough to find Joyce Seltzer, who understood what I was trying to do even when I wasn't entirely sure myself, and who helped me find my voice when I had lost it. Christine Thorsteinsson was a manuscript editor of unusual skill and extraordinary tact. Finally, my wife, Robin, encouraged me from the very beginning, supported me throughout, and provided wonderful editorial advice. Her participation was a source of inspiration as well as joy.

INDEX